Colonization, Commerce, and Entrepreneurship in Nigeria

Society and Politics in Africa

Yakubu Saaka
General Editor

Vol. 2

PETER LANG
New York • Washington, D.C./Baltimore
Bern • Frankfurt am Main • Berlin • Vienna • Paris

Adeline Apena

Colonization, Commerce, and Entrepreneurship in Nigeria

The Western Delta, 1914–1960

PETER LANG
New York • Washington, D.C./Baltimore
Bern • Frankfurt am Main • Berlin • Vienna • Paris

Library of Congress Cataloging-in-Publication Data

Apena, Adeline.
Colonization, commerce, and entrepreneurship in Nigeria:
the Western Delta, 1914–1960/ Adeline Apena
p. cm. — (Society and politics in Africa; vol. 2)
Includes bibliographical references and index.
1. Delta (Nigeria: State)—Economic policy. 2. Delta (Nigeria: State)—
Economic conditions. 3. Delta (Nigeria: State)—Commerce—History—20th
century. 4. Colonial companies—Nigeria—Delta (State)—
History—20th century. 5. Delta (Nigeria: State)—Colonial influence.
I. Title. II. Series.
HC1055.Z7D452 338.9669'36—dc20 96-19237
ISBN 0-8204-3131-1
ISSN 1083-3323

Die Deutsche Bibliothek-CIP-Einheitsaufnahme

Apena, Adeline.
Colonization, commerce, and entrepreneurship in Nigeria: the Western Delta,
1914–1960/ Adeline Apena. - New York; Washington, D.C./Baltimore; Bern;
Frankfurt am Main; Berlin; Vienna; Paris: Lang.
(Society and politics in Africa; vol. 2)
ISBN 0-8204-3131-1
NE: GT

Cover design by Wendy Lee.

Dedication

This book is dedicated to the Glory of God in Jesus' Precious Name, for His infinite Mercies and Love; the evergreen memory of my dear departed father, Venerable B. P. Apena and my mother Mary Afigo Apena whose unflinching love and prayers for me have kept me going in all circumstances.

Table of Contents

Acknowledgements

This book is a fulfillment of a life-long aspiration and challenge. For this, I thank God for his mercies. The opportunity to undertake this study would not have been possible without the study leave granted to me in 1984 by the authorities of the University of Benin in Nigeria. In this regard, I owe immense gratitude to Professors Philip Igbafe, Fred Omu, Steven Ogude, Tijani Serpos, Romanus Egudu, Adamu Baikie and his successor, Professor Grace Awani Alele-Williams.

At the University of Lagos, I am immensely grateful to my supervisors, Professors Babatunde Agiri and Jide Osuntokun. To Professor Babatunde Agiri, I owe special gratitude for his constant encouragement, guidance and suggestions, even in moments of despair. My sincere gratitude also goes to Professor Jide Osuntoku n for his constant moral support and diligent observation of my academic progress. I owe gratitude to Professor Tajudeen Gbadamosi who showed constant interest in my academic work.

I would also like to acknowledge the staffs of numerous institutions which I consulted. First, the secretarial staff of the History Department at the University of Lagos and the staff of the Ghandi Library who were never tired of my endless request for books and documents deserve my gratitude. I am grateful to the staff of the Africana Research Library of the University of Ibadan. My thanks go to Mrs. Patricia Uwakue and Mr. S. Unuigbe for their cooperation and goodwill, as well as the other staff of the Nigerian National Archives at Ibadan.

I wish to thank Reverend Father Christomanus, Reverend Sister Consolata and Reverend Sister Perpetual of the Pastoral Institute, Ibadan, for helping to minimize the financial burdens of accommodation in Ibadan. I thank the cheerful staff of the Public Relations Department of the United African Company (UAC) headquarters at the Niger House, Lagos and the Nigerian Ports Authority, Marina, Lagos, for granting me access to their library facility. The same goes to the library staff of the Institute of International Affairs, Victoria Island, Lagos and Nigerian Institute of Social and Economic Research, Ibadan. My special thanks go to the staff of the African Timber and Plywood (A.T. & P.), Sapele, Cowan Estate, Ajagbodudu and the Pamol Estate, Ogharefe, Sapele, for their assistance in data collection.

I am grateful for the assistance of the numerous informants who supplied vital oral information for this work. In this respect, I would like to thank Mr Guy Otobo for his patience and good sense of humanity and Chiefs Unokan, Omuvbie, Sokoh and Odibo. I must also not forget to thank Mrs. C. Agodo and Chief L. Agbaza.

I owe immense gratitude to my good friends and colleagues at the University of Lagos, Lagos. Nigeria, whose exchanges of pleasantries added color to the dull moments of the initial preparation of this work. Among these, I remember Dr.and Mrs. T. Ogunsanwo, Mr. J. Olowoyo, Mr. E. Meshe, Miss Toun Ilumoka, Miss Ayo Falusi, Mr. L. Dioka and Edward Tafah. I thank Mr. Jacob Odeghe of the Nigerian Institute of Advanced Legal Studies, Lagos, who typed the first draft of this work with skill and dedication. I remember the porters of the Great Amina Hall of the University of Lagos, Lagos, Nigeria, for their support during my stay at the Hall for the initial preparation of this manuscript.

I thank a dear and kind friend, Dr. Jeanne Dingome, for an unusual support and assistance with the final editing of this manuscript when it appeared almost impossible to complete. I, also, thank Professor Emiko Amoye for his sacrifice and patience in accepting to read the final copy of this manuscript.

Professor Steve Leibo deserves a special mention and gratitude from me for identifying the value of the manuscript and encouraging me to get it published. I am grateful to Professor Andor Skotneṡ, a colleague who has been consistently supportive of my academic goals and concerns. I thank Professor Falola for his academic advise on this work and Iris Berger for her constant encouragement in my academic and personal welfare. Prof. Lisa Aronson, a dear friend and colleague deserves my gratitude for her encouragement and support. She has always been keen on academic advancement. I also mention, Marcia Sutherland for her kind encouragement and hospitality in my first few days in Albany. She has always been keen on academic advancement. I thank Professor Joseph Sarfoh for his attention and concern for my professional upliftment. I am grateful to Bill Batt for taking pains to help out with the huge difficulties which confronted me with computing this work.

Finally, I acknowledge the support of my departed, loving father, Venerable B. P. for his love and relentless prayers for my wellbeing and success. Venerable Apena was a pioneer missionary, the first indigenous clergyman of Isokoland whose activities spanned from early this century up to 1988. He served as a major reference and a strong source of strength for me. My special thanks go to my mother for her prayers for my welfare. I thank my sisters and brothers, whose prayers for me constantly remind me of departed father whom I miss so much.

Foreword

Toylin Falola
Professor of History
University of Texas at Austin

The Niger Delta, the subject of this interesting study, has been well known for centuries. It used to be an integral part of the "slave basket", supplying forced labor to the trans-Atlantic slave trade. When the slave trade was abolished in the nineteenth century, the Niger Delta acquired more fame and attention as the world's largest producer of palm oil and palm kernel. Because of its natural resources, the region became embroiled in the local and international politics which ultimately ended in its inclusion with Nigeria, as part of the European scramble for Africa and the British gains in this competition.

During this century, the Niger Delta continued to supply palm produce and other commodities to the international market. After 1958, it became noted for yet another product: petroleum. This brought more complicated politics of establishing control over this lucrative resource. In the 1960s, the Biafran secession and the subsequent civil war saw Biafra and Nigeria in a bitter struggle to control the region, largely because of oil. Since the 1970s, the politics have been the control of the region by the majority groups in Nigeria. The protest for recognition of minority rights and environmental concerns continue, and most recently in the international uproar over the killing of Ken Saro Wiwa and the other Ogoni protesters.

Both the natural endowment of this region and the never ending politics to control it have made Dr. Adeline Apena's book both timely and relevant. It is timely because the Niger Delta is in the news, and will remain so for quite some time to come. The study is relevant because it provides the necessary historical background to understand and appreciate most of the current problems and politics. The study provides useful analytical description of the region and its peoples during the pre-colonial period, touching upon political institutions and indigenous economies.

The real concern of Dr. Apena is with the colonial period. She ably documents the gradual encroachment of British trading companies and consular authorities leading to the establishment of British rule. The African voice is privileged, as Dr. Apena sensitively talks of the African reactions to all these external issues. The system of the colonial administration receives serious consideration, as well as the economic changes of the period. Dr. Apena shows how the people of the Western Delta benefitted from the palm produce and rubber industries and, more importantly, how a group of local entrepreneurs emerged and grew wealthy. Other enterprising indigenes, according to her, turned their attention to lucrative merchandise and logging businesses. These entrepreneurs were able to contribute to the material and cultural upliftment of the region.

Dr. Apena uses her data to argue that British rule was neither synonymous with economic revolution nor with underdevelopment. Rather, it distorted certain aspects while it contributed positively to such others as trade, physical infrastructures, urbanization and food production.

This book accomplishes the objectives set forward by Dr. Apena. It offers useful information on the Niger Delta. The chapters on port authorities and indigenous entrepreneurs are both original and fascinating. Her conclusion reveals a non-ideological interpretation of British rule, striking a noticeable balance between pro- official liberal thinkers and the radical, dependency-oriented scholarship. Her choice of region to study is a wise one, enabling her to profit from established sources and adding a new body of materials, notably oral evidence.

Dr. Apena has written an important book, an essential reading to students of Nigerian History especially of the Delta region. She has provided a careful discussion of the development of local entrepreneurship and the role of the private sector in the development of the Niger Delta in a way that should merit a serious attention by policy makers and the economic historians of West Africa who are interested in significant changes and how to accomplish them.

Introduction

This is a socio-economic study of the people and society of the Western Niger Delta of Nigeria during the colonial period, 1914 to 1960. It is an in-depth study of the reactions and responses of the people of this region to the challenges of change initiated by the colonial authority in Nigeria, and the activities of expatriate commercial firms in the area. Specifically, it explains in what ways the economy and society of the Western Delta changed in response to the economic policies of the colonial administration and the actions of the expatriate commercial firms. Its objective is to assess whether the colonial economic policy and the operations of expatriate commercial firms, facilitated or retarded the advancement of the people and their society.

It examines the reactions of the people in a multi-dimensional approach within economic sectors and explains differences between one sector and another. In addition, the work emphasizes gender role in the dynamics and processes of change and their effects on the communities. Above all, it explains the impact of the people's reactions on the growth and development of the Western Delta communities.

Thus, it is the aim of this work to determine whether or not the economic policies and structures of the colonial administration helped to improve the society, economy and the welfare of the people of the Western Delta. This concern has influenced the writings of scholars like Claude Ake, Walter

Rodney, Bade Onimode, and Toyin Falola, with respect to the impact of colonialism on Nigeria and Africa.

This study would attempt to show if this concern applies to the Western Delta area of Nigeria.

Chapter one provides a theoretical framework, undertakes a review of existing literature on the the Western Delta and examines the main perspectives on colonization with special reference to Nigeria. In addition, it defines the major concepts used in this study.

Chapter two examines the precolonial society, in particular, myths of origin and socio-political organizations of the various groups which constitute the Western Delta.

Chapter three focuses on the precolonial economy. It examines the major economic activities of the people and trade with Europeans up to 1885. Also it explains the effects of the precolonial economy on inter-group relations.

Chapter four explores the methods of British conquest, the nature of African resistance, and the imposition of British rule. Further, it deals with British colonial administration and establishment of economic infrastructure up to 1929, with the introduction of a monetized economy.

Chapter five discusses government policy and programs regarding the palm produce industry. The problems of implementation of government policy, the contribution of the United African Company (UAC) and the reactions of the people toward the growth and development of the palm produce industry are also examined.

Governmental policy and programs regarding rubber is examined in chapter six. Problems of implementation and the reaction of the people, including the expatriate commercial firms, to the rubber industry is examined. The chapter ends with an examination of the major differences in both palm the and rubber industries.

Chapter seven focuses on the methods and extent of General Trade as well as the impact of import and export trade on primary production.

Chapter eight discusses the development of ports at Burutu, Warri, Sapele and Koko and analyzes the profile of labor in these ports. It also explains the role of port development in the growth of towns (urbanization) and processes of social integration.

Chapter nine focuses on the role of the UAC in the agro-allied industrialization of the area. It emphasizes the development of the timber industry including sawmill and plywood factories, the mechanization of the palm industry and the development of bulking. These developments are related to migration and urban growth in the region.

Chapter ten surveys the development of indigenous entrepreneurship in Nigeria examines indigenous entrepreneurs in palm produce trade.

Chapter eleven discusses entrepreneurial activities in rubber business, general merchandise and logging business while chapter twelve analyzes the contributions of the entrepreneurs to the socio-economic growth and modernization of the area.

The conclusion articulates the major findings of the earlier chapters and highlights the pattern of socio-economic growth and development in the area. Emphasis is placed on the contribution of both the public and private sectors. Thus, this book fits into the growing literature on the impact that colonialism had on socio-economic growth in Nigeria and Africa in general.

Sources

Apart from oral sources, most of the information used for this study is derived from the Warri Provincial Papers as well as those of the other townships and districts of the Western Delta located in the Nigerian National Archives, Ibadan. The Township records include those for Warri, Sapele, Burutu and Koko townships. The District records include those for Sobo (Urhobo), Jekri (Itsekiri), Kwale and Western Ijo districts. These archival materials provided information on agriculture, exports and the activities of the commercial firms in the Western Delta as well as indigenous reactions to operations of commercial firms.

Other official sources in the National Archives were also important. The Chief Secretary's office papers and those of the Western Region Ministry of Agriculture provided vital information on government policy on agriculture, especially palm produce, rubber and forestry. I did not have access to the official documents of the United African Company (UAC) except published articles in the *UAC Statistical and Economic Review,* which provided useful information on UAC activities, trade records and I classified these as anonymous secondary sources.

Only one of the indigenous entrepreneurs, Chief William Otobo, had private papers. Oral interviews, on the other hand, proved to be rich and invaluable sources of information. While some of the major entrepreneurs are deceased, their sons and daughters were able to provide information on the activities of their parents. As was expected, some informants were reluctant to discuss things they regarded as family secrets. Generally, informants could not supply statistical data of their (or their parents') activities. These imperfections however do not detract from the overall value and reliability of their evidence.

Methodology

The methodology of this study is to reexamine available documentary and oral data a priori and then reach conclusions thereon. Such an analysis, it is hoped, will enhance the understanding of the processes of historical change, both in its social and economic dimensions, and as they affected the lives of the people involved. It is therefore important at this stage to define the key terms "exploitation" and "development" used extensively in this book.

Exploitation

The word Exploitation connotes the optimization of efforts to ensure that resources are utilized for maximum benefit and profits. This does not necessarily imply unfair utilization of resources to the disadvantage of an area or people, colony or metropole. However, as the processes of maximization incur benefits, they bring disadvantages as well. Thus, the cost-benefit analysis of exploitation to both exploiters and to the exploited themselves must be carefully considered.

Development

As for the word Development, it can be defined as accumulation of changes which generate internal progress. The change can be internally and/or externally induced. The most important factor in gauging development is that it must be positively oriented, contributing to an improved standard of living for the majority of the people.

In general, the commercial firms engaged the services of African agents, who as part of the process, obtained some of the benefits. The main question to consider is what percentage of the benefits went to African agents and what percentage to the European firms. So far, there are no clear-cut or definitive studies which determine the ratio of the shares of profits enjoyed by each, primarily because of a general lack of adequate data to ascertain such figures. Thus, most studies tend to be qualitative and not quantitative.

List of Maps

List of Tables

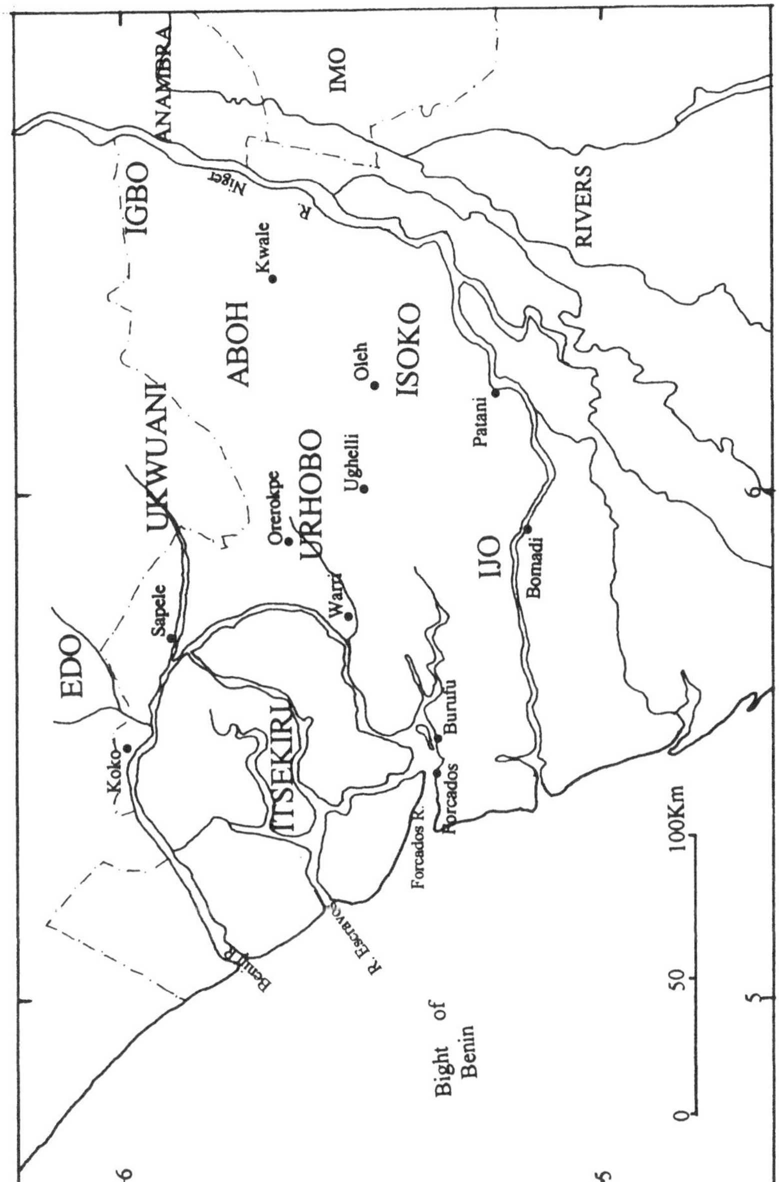

1. Western Delta Communities and their Neighbors

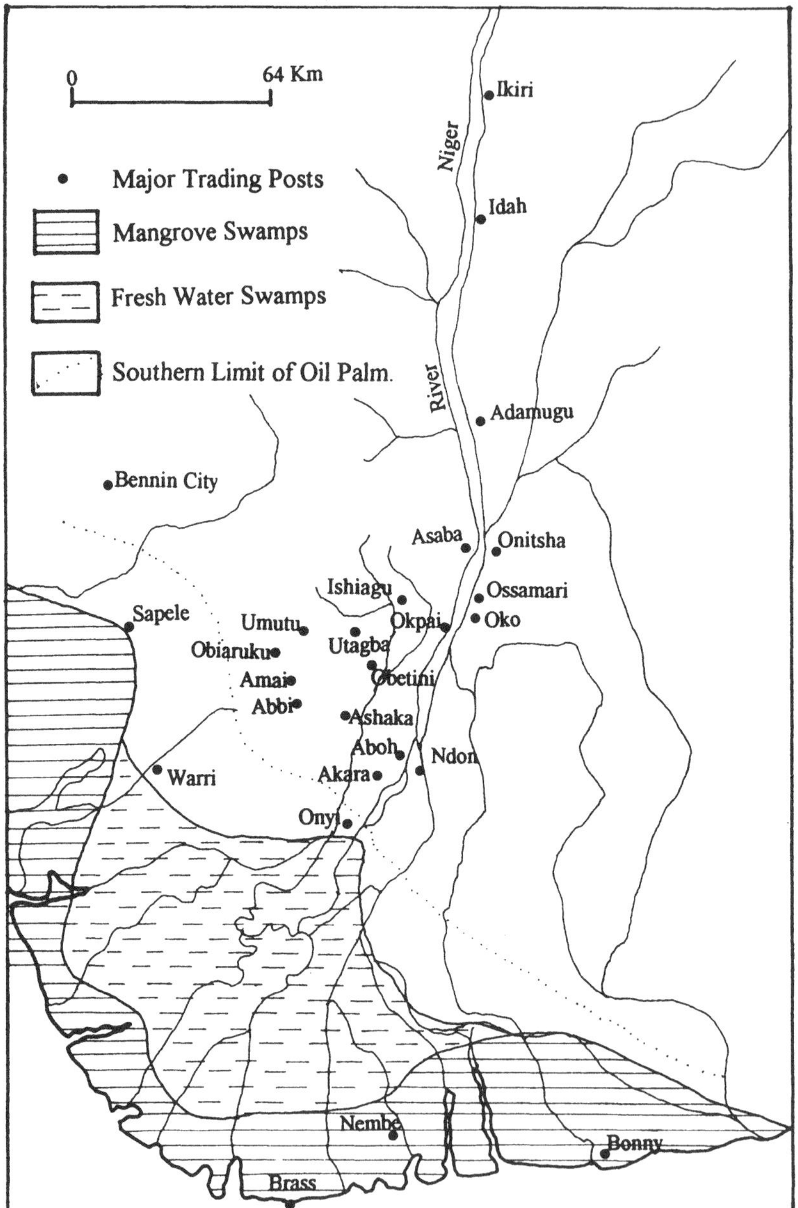

2. Vegetation of the Lower Niger and the Major Trading Posts during the first half of the nineteenth century.

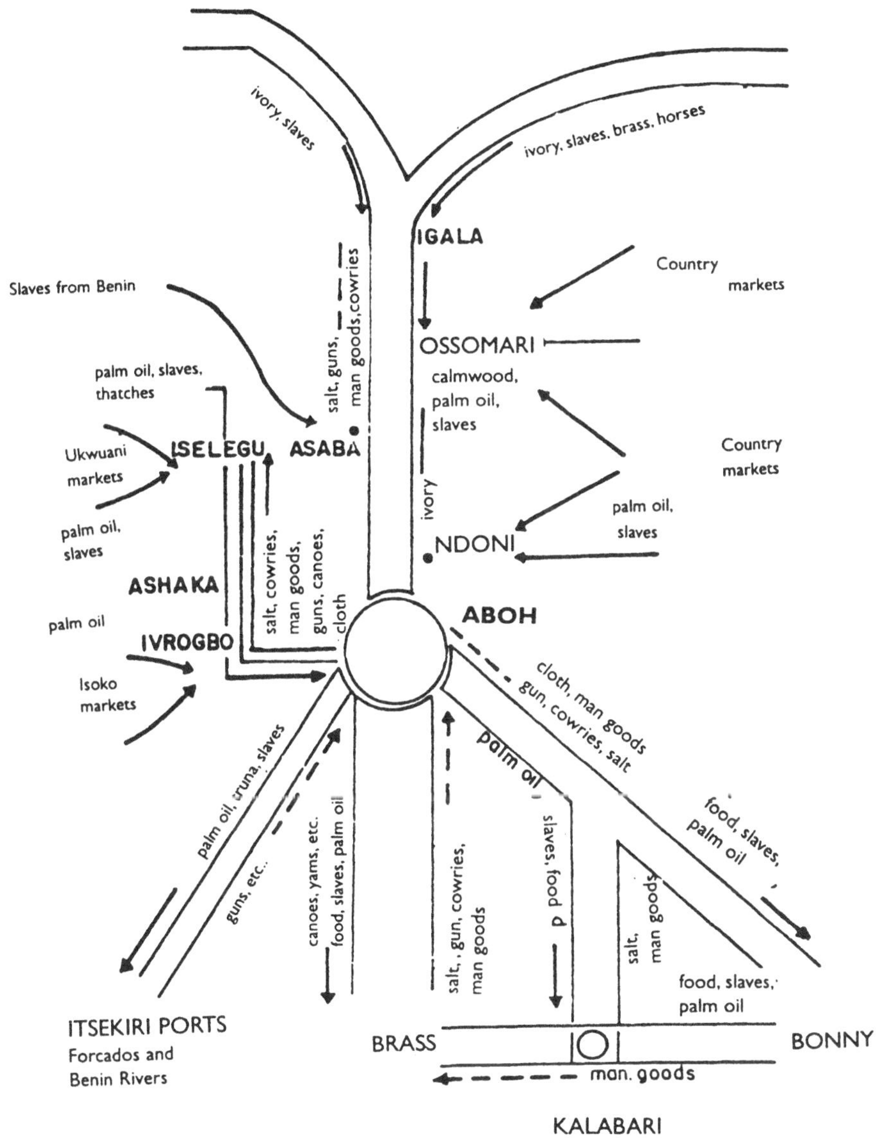

3. Trade Chart of the Lower Niger, 1650-1900.

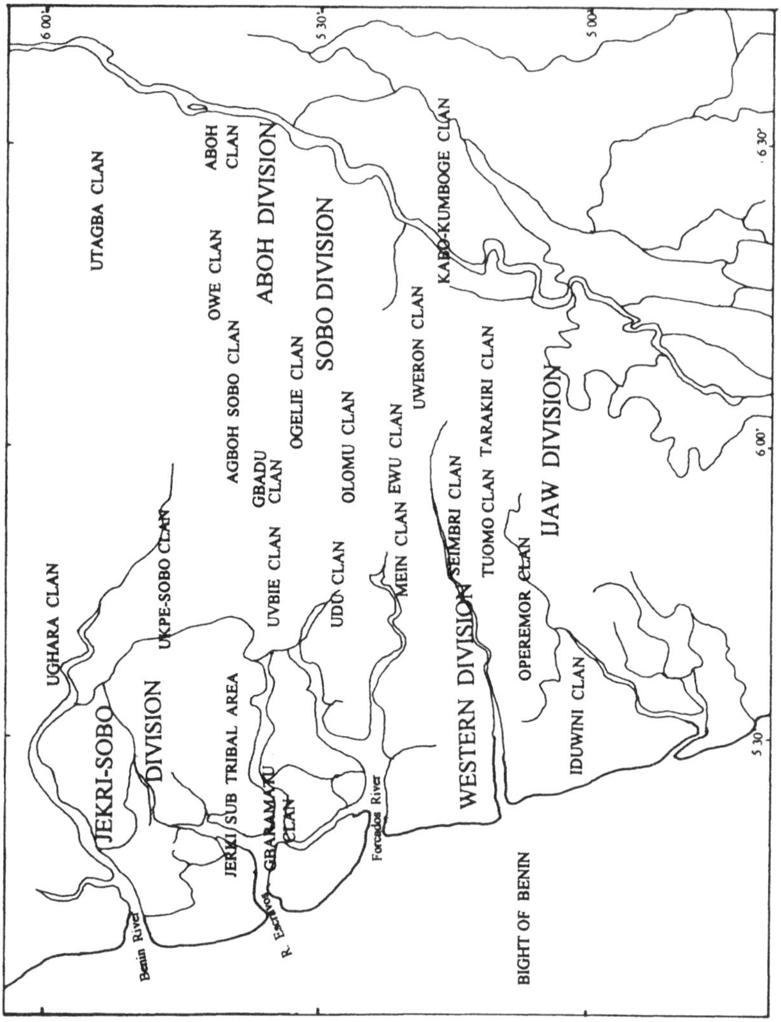

4. Political Divisions of Western Niger Delta.

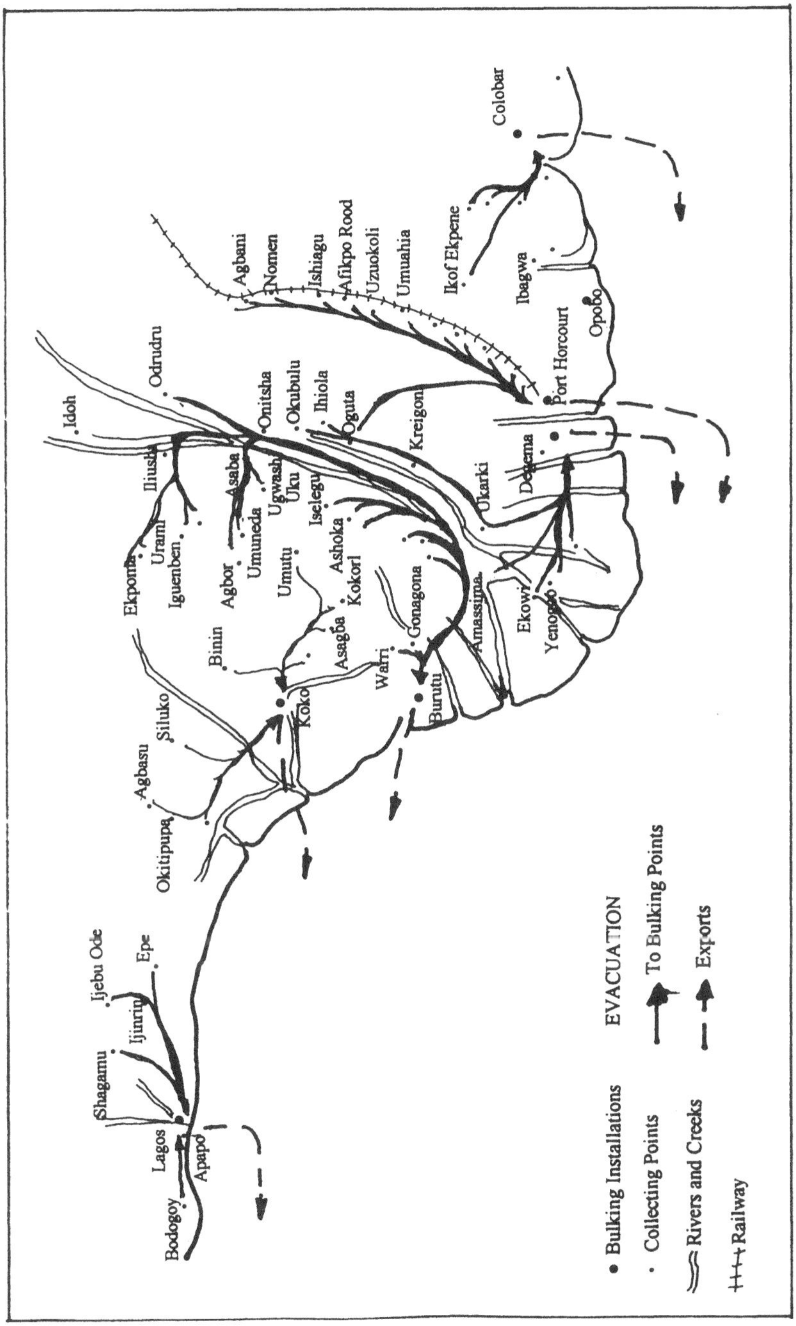

5. Palm Oil Production: Main Evacuation Routes to Bulking Installations.

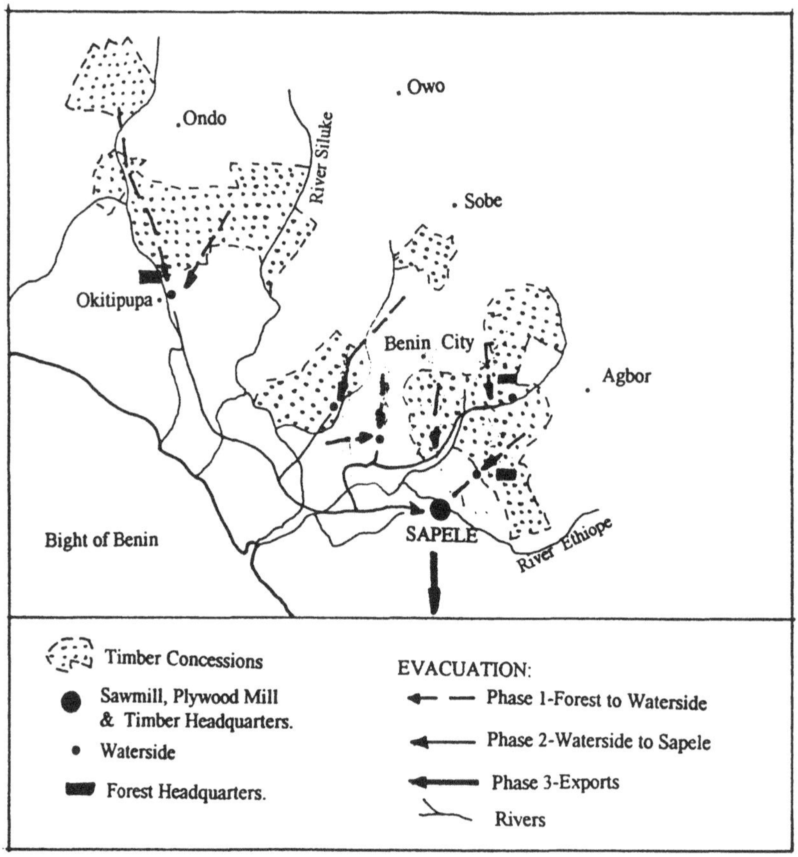

6. African Timber and Plywood Ltd. Concessions and Evacuation Routes.

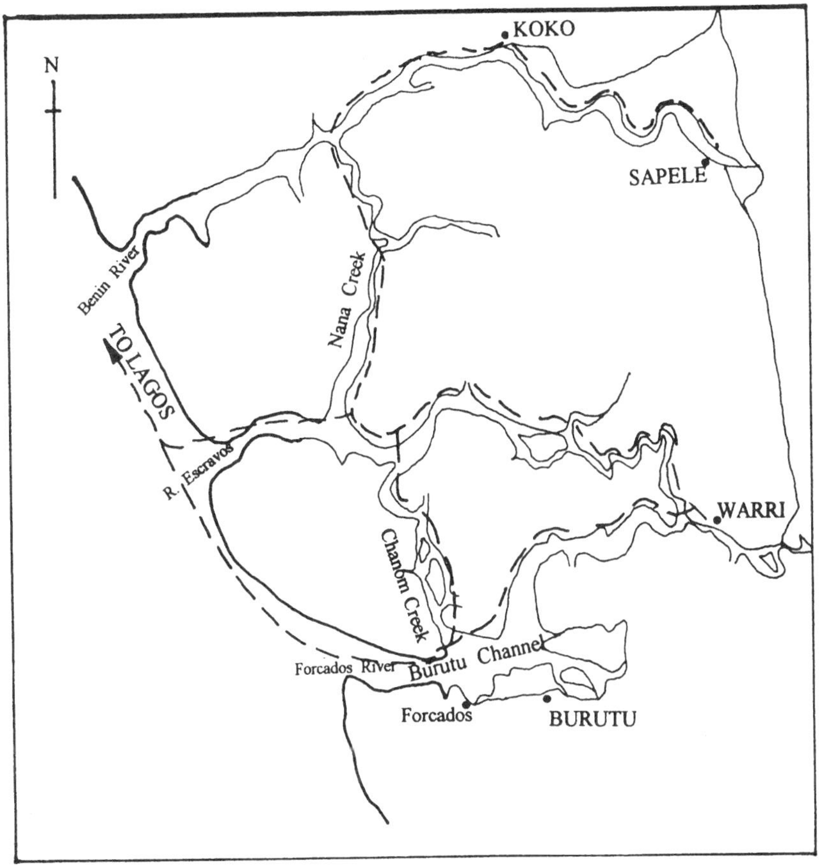

7. Western Niger Delta Ports.

Chapter 1

Literature Review on the Western Delta and Perspectives on Colonialism in Nigeria

Situated between longitudes 5 and 6 degrees E and latitudes 4 degrees 4 minutes and 6 degrees 10 minutes N, the Western Delta of Nigeria, lies in the equatorial climatic zone with regular high temperature, high humidity and heavy rains for most the part of the year. The area is bounded in the East by the lower Niger and its distributaries of the Eastern Delta; South and West by the Atlantic Ocean and a network of creeks and lagoons which stretch to Lagos and on the North by Edo and Igbo-speaking groups as well as the Ijo of the Eastern Delta.[1]

Six ethnic groups, the Urhobo, the Isoko, the Ijo, the Itsekiri, the Aboh and the Ukwuani, inhabit the Western Delta. A majority of these people belong to the Edo-speaking group of Nigeria. They were brought together under one administration known as Warri province following the amalgamation of the Northern and Southern Protectorates which culminated in the creation of the Nigerian colonial state by the British in 1914.

Warri province became part of the Western Region from 1946. Later, it formed part of the Midwest Region, created out of the Western Region in 1963. The Mid-West Region became Bendel state in 1976. And since 1991, the Western delta has been administered as part of the Delta State of Nigeria.

The Western Delta had connections with early European commercial activities from the late fifteenth century. As a result, the area felt the impact of the colonial economy, much more severely than most other parts of the country. More specifically, the Western Delta had been playing crucial roles in Nigeria's export economy since the early nineteenth century when it contributed significantly to the palm produce trade and later, rubber and timber exports. Today, it is second to the Eastern Delta in oil production, thus making it a sensitive area in the oil-based economy of Nigeria. The choice of the Western Delta for this study is based on the fact that it is one of the areas of Nigeria which has been seriously impacted by the processes of economic change but which has not been adequately researched especially with reference to the impact of the colonial economy.

Literature Review

The major scholarly works on the Western Delta are Obaro Ikime's *Merchant Prince of the Niger Delta: The Rise and Fall of Nana Olomu, the Last Governor of the Benin River (1968)* and *Niger Delta Rivalry: Itsekiri-Urhobo Relations and European Presence, 1884-1936* (1969).

The first of these books is an illustration of African resistance to European incursion into the interior of the coastal region, in their bid to expand trade through direct trading relations with producers and markets of the hinterland communities. The study claims that attempts at "opening up" the interior involved a clash of interests between European traders and African middlemen. It ascribes British conquest and the defeat of African resistance to the advantage of superior military machinery and Afro-European collaboration. This work also discusses the development of rivalry among major Itsekiri families.

The second book examines Urhobo-Itsekiri relations as well as British imperial conquest and imposition of colonial administration. Its particular focus is on the impact of colonial administration on Urhobo-Itsekiri relations up to 1936.

These two works provide valuable background information to this study. Both give a good description of the pre-colonial social, economic and political organizations of the Itsekiri and Urhobo and Isoko, early European commercial contact and activities as well as British imperial conquest and colonial government up to 1936. However, the focus is more on political developments. There is less attention on issues of social and economic change. In addition, they do not cover the entire period of the colonial experience up to 1960, the year of independence.

Other related works include E.J. Alagoa's *A History of the Niger Delta: An Historical Interpretation of Ijo Oral Tradition* (1972); K.O. Dike's *Trade and Politics in the Niger Delta, 1830-1885* (1966); and W.I. Ofonagoro's *Trade and Imperialism in Southern Nigeria, 1881-1929* (1969).

E.J. Alagoa's *History of the Niger Delta* discusses Ijo migrations and the growth of Ijo social, political and economic institutions. It provides useful information on the Ijo of the Western Delta and their relation with those of the Eastern Delta.

K.O. Dike's *Trade and Politics in the Niger Delta, 1830-1885* is an introductory study of the economic and political history of the Niger Delta from the period of the abolition of the Trans-Atlantic slave trade to the inauguration of the Oil Rivers Protectorate in 1885. It discusses the evolution of political, social and economic institutions of the Niger Delta and the gradual loss of effective power by African rulers as a result of the gunboat diplomacy of British Consular authorities. Its focus is the Eastern Delta with only occasional references to the Western Delta. It provides a fundamental background to an understanding of the economic and political developments in the Eastern Niger Delta up to 1885.

W.I. Ofonagoro's *Trade and Imperialism in Southern Nigeria, 1881-1929* examines the process of the imposition of imperial control in Southern Nigeria in response to the pressures of British traders. Also, it examines the economic institutions and infrastructures of the early colonial period in relation to the objectives of the expatriate commercial community. As in the previous work, the Western Delta does not receive adequate attention. Only peripheral references are made to it.

While the works of Ikime, Alagoa, Dike and Ofonagoro, cited above contribute background information to this study, they are neither concerned with the issues and questions which are addressed here, nor do the periods of their investigations coincide with that of this research. To the best of my knowledge, no major work exists on the period and subject covered in the current study.

It is the intention of this work, therefore, to cover the entire colonial period of the Western Delta in a consistent manner in order to fill in existing gaps and to focus on issues of social and economic change as it affects the area of study.

Also, by focusing on the people's reactions to change and emphasizing the growth and contribution of indigenous entrepreneurs to the advancement of their societies, this study deviates from previous discussions on the colonial impact which seem to concentrate on the role of the colonial administration in the development or exploitation and underdevelopment of colonial Nigeria.

Of direct relevance to the concepts used and examined in this work are the studies on colonialism by Claude Ake, Walter Rodney, Bade Onimode, Toyin Falola on one hand; Alan McPhee, L. H. Gann and P. Duignan, Hla Myint and G.K. Helleiner, on the other.[2]

This study reviews the perspectives contained in these works and evaluates the social and economic conditions in the Western Delta during the period under study in the light of these views.

Perspectives on Colonialism in Nigeria

There are two main perspectives on the colonial impact on Africa: the imperialist and the Marxist. The imperialist view, as purported by Mcphee, Gann and Duignan, Myint, and Helleiner, claims that colonialism was beneficial to the colonies where it promoted growth and development. As for the Marxist interpretation, represented by scholars like Rodney, Ake, Onimode and Falola, it argues that colonialism underdeveloped, distorted and retarded growth and development in the colonies.[3]

To the imperialists, colonialism activated the colonial societies, stimulated growth and generated considerable change. The colonial period is considered as a dynamic and expansionist period during which radical programs were launched to promote modernization, helping to uplift the people from backwardness, barbarism and ignorance to "civilization" and progress.

The imperialists argue that through the combined dynamics of both the "civilizing mission' and the "white man's burden," the colonies were rejuvenated by the transfer of material and spiritual benefits of the Industrial Revolution and European civilization. Further, it contends that the observable changes in the colonies resulted from contacts established by "much more advanced countries where attitudes and institutions had been adapted for centuries to a monetary economy."[4]

Mcphee argues that colonialism created an economic revolution in British West Africa. He states that,

> English capital has come in and built the railways and constructed the harbours and cleared the channels; it has built roads and towns and established markets; it has introduced banks and a convenient currency; it has exploited minerals . . . the English government has brought peace and security and abolished slavery. The result is an enormous expansion of trade, in which the natives performed their part and reaped their rewards.[5]

Gann and Duignan corroborate this view by stating that colonial administration generated revolutionary changes and provided the first impetus for rapid economic change, the innovation so generated transformed Africa from the stone age to the modern era.[6] They attribute this to the considerable transfer of resources from Europe to Africa . . . without the capital and skills and markets provided by Europe, development would have been greatly retarded.[7]

To Gann and Duignan, the colonies were a "burden" which drained the metropoles of resources and manpower. They state that by the standard of the times, British colonial expenditures remained high even in the palmiest days of laissez faire . . . every class in society was clamoring against what it regarded as the excessive weight of taxation.[8]

Inspite of this, these scholars argue that Africa did not return to its investors and traders what earlier imperialists and promoters had hoped for.[9] They contend that Britain owed none of its prosperity to colonial possession. The country derived infinitely more advantages from its intercourse with the United States.[10]

Gann and Duignan further posit that American trade had no drawbacks and that Britain was not obligated to purchase American commodities which it could obtain more cheaply elsewhere nor was it obliged to keep armament for the protection of extensive regions on the other side of the Atlantic.[11]

The concept that the colonial government and its agencies were primarily responsible for introducing and managing economic transformation is strenghtened by the claim that contact with the whiteman whether as merchant, mine owner, farmer or manufacturer also brought about economic changes of a more intangible kind.[12]

Hla Myint provides a good deal of background for this concept which he based on Adam Smith's view that external trade serves as a vent for surplus production. He argues that promoting export in the economies with limited domestic markets enhances productivity.[13] He points out that before colonial rule, land and labor were underemployed because of a lack of effective demand for its potential increase in output.[14] Colonialism created effective demand by linking the demands of the world market with the types of products that the peasants had locked in their subsistence economy.[15]

Myint argues that infrastructural development, the introduction of law and order, the encouragement that the colonial state gave to expatriate import-export businesses and the introduction of institutions which supported surplus extraction were part of the process of facilitating the development of unused resources for export production.[16]
Thus, he concludes that by stimulating new wants among the peasants, the expansion of imports was a major dynamic force which facilitated the expansion of exports.[17]

This approach also influenced G.K. Helleiner who claims that until the appearance of European trading firms, there was no culture, education, commerce, craft or any serious effort at agricultural progress in Nigeria.[18] This, he claims, became possible,

> with the appearance of European trading firms, missionaries sowing new ideas and bringing education and lately an externally imposed government. . . . Most significant of all was offering by traders of rewards for the sale of particular crops which were in demand abroad, principally palm oil and palm kernels and later cocoa, rubber and groundnuts.[19]

Helleiner and other theorists of "vent-for-surplus production"[20] conclude that,

> for the most parts . . . indigenous peoples of the underdeveloped countries took to export production on a voluntary basis and enjoyed a clear gain by being able to satisfy their developing wants for the new imported commodities.[21]

Marxist writers, on the other hand, bring a totally different perspective to bear on the colonial experience. They equate colonialism with underdevelopment and exploitation. They claim that the colonial economy was peripheralized and incorporated into the metropolitan capitalist system. The principal concern of the colonial mission, they argue, was to seek territorial outlets as solutions to the inherent and internal contradictions of the ever-expanding capitalist economies.

Since its motive was to facilitate expansion, consolidate and sustain capitalism, they find it difficult to associate colonialism with progress and development. Thus, to them, colonialism entailed a ruthless exploitation of land, labor, raw materials and markets of the colonies in favor of the metropoles. These scholars further contend that the only sufferers were the colonies whose progress was stifled and distorted, leaving them in stagnant backwaters.

Ake argues that,

> the colonial economy is a dependent one to the extent that its position in relation to the other economies in the international system and articulation of its internal structure makes it incapable of autocentric development.[22]

Of the monetary system, he asserts that,

> the monetary system of a colony was invariably an extension of that of the metropolis. . . . The lack of domestic capital resources on one

> hand and the pressure for investment of capital on the other made the African colonial economy highly dependent.[23]

On trade, he states that,

> colonial economies of Africa depended primarily on the metropolitan countries which colonized them for their external trade. . . . The structural integration was also a function of the coercive measures which the colonizing power used to gear the colonial economy to their interest.[24]

Concerning technology, Ake asserts that colonial Africa depended on the capitalist West for virtually all her technology. This put the colonial economy in a position analogous to that of a producer who has no instrument of labour.[25] Further, he argues that the colonial economy was characterized by disarticulation and lacked regional, sectoral linkages and complementarity.[26] These features are associated with the colonizer's efforts to maximize exploitation of resources. As Ake states,

> in some cases the extraction of the colony's resources entailed some investment in infrastructure development–roads, water resources, railways, electrical power and administrative structures. Following the Capitalist rationality of minimum input for maximum output they invested only what they had to and where they had to.[27]

He illustrates disarticulation through describing the transportation systems, especially the railways, the development of export commodities in response to the demand of capitalism, and the neglect of the manufacturing sector within the colonies.

Lastly, he claims that the colonial economy was characterized by monopoly of metropolitan commercial firms. This was an important element in the link between colonization and underdevelopment.[28] The monopoly of economic power arose from the political as well as the economic functions which the home government gave them.[29] Ake concludes that one of the functions which contributed to the creation and consolidation of monopoly status in the economy was power to take charge of economic development of the colony.[30]

Similar views are held by Onimode, Rodney and Falola. Falola's work appears highly influenced by the approach of Claude Ake. Supporting the concept of disarticulation, he opines that,

> whatever 'development' took place in the colonial period was very indirect or took place in the sectors limited almost exclusively to production for export, import trade and related collection and distribution of services. These sectors did not directly affect the bulk of the population . . . what economic growth did occur was directed to filling overseas market needs and providing markets for European manufactured goods. It took place within a framework which viewed metropolitan not colonial interest as dominant.[31]

Also Rodney supports Ake's claim of dependence by stating that African economies are integrated into the very structure of the capitalist economies in a manner that is unfavorable to Africa and ensures that Africa is dependent on the big capital countries.[32]

European trading firms, shipping companies, banks and the colonial state, as Rodney points out, were institutions and channels of economic exploitation and impoverishment of Africa.[33] The collaboration of these institutions contributed to intensification of exploitation within Africa. He contends that exploitation involved export of surplus in massive proportions. Africa fell within that part of the international capitalist economy from which surplus was drawn to feed the metropolitan sector.[34]

He adds that this amounted to consistent expatriation of surplus produced by African labour out of African resources.[35] In so doing, Africa made considerable contribution to the development of European capitalism, technology and military system. Rodney, therefore, concludes that colonialism gave capitalism an added lease of life and prolonged its existence in Western Europe.[36] Africa was undeveloped by the same process which helped to develop Europe.

Onimode subscribes to this contention by arguing that,

> the appropriation of surplus under the colonial system was monopolized by the British. Indeed, this British expropriation of the country

> was the fundamental raison d'être behind free trade imperialism in Nigeria; the central point of colonial relationship is to strengthen the capitalist mode of production in the imperialist country.[37]

He claims that surplus transfer and associated trade constituted the umbilical cord which linked the colonial economy to the international capitalist economy.

The free-enterprise policy of the colonial authorities enhanced the international division of labor, he asserts, in which the colonies were assigned the production of raw materials while the metropoles undertook the manufacture of goods. He concludes that not only did specialization in cash crop production entail wholesale integration of the colonial economy into the world capitalist system but it also tied African farmers to the land in abysmal ignorance, poverty and backwardness.[38]

Rodney disputes the claim that colonialism introduced the dynamic features of capitalism such as private property in land, private ownership of other means of production and money relations. To strengthen his view, he makes a distinction between capitalist elements and capitalism as a total system, contending that

> colonialism introduced some elements of capitalism into Africa. . ., colonialism did not transform Africa into a capitalist society comparable to the metropoles. Colonialism did not create a capitalist class among Africans. . . . In other words, capitalism in the form of colonialism failed to perform in Africa the tasks it had performed in Europe in changing social relations and liberating the forces of production.[40]

Falola and Rodney strongly refute the contention that colonialism involved exploitation and oppression on one hand and benefit and development on the other. As Falola states,

> colonialism had only one goal—to exploit, because given the domination of political and trading institutions, the power unilaterally to fix prices and determine which crops to produce . . . as well as to compel the indigenes to engage in activities through which they could earn money—mainly cash crop production—and finally the establishment of unviable political and administrative institution, colonial policies were hardly aimed at ensuring development.[41]

This view reinforces Rodney's assertion that colonialism had only one hand—it was a one-armed bandit that caused oppression and exploitation.[42]

The views of these authors provide the analytical tool for examining the period of colonial rule in the Western Delta and for assessing whether or not the area conforms to or deviates from these perspectives.

Notes

1 *See* Map I.

2 Claude Ake, Walter Rodney, Bade Onimode, Toyin Falola, Ibid.; Alan McPhee, *The Economic Revolution in British West Africa* (London: Frank Cass, 1971); L. H. Gann and P. Duignan, *Burden of Empire* (New York: Praeger, 1967); *Colonialism in Africa: 1870-1960*, Vols. 1-5 (Cambridge: Cambridge University Press, 1973); Hla Myint, "The 'Classical Theory' of International Trade and the Underdeveloped Countries," *Economic Journal*, 68, June 1958; and *The Economies of the Developing Countries* (London: Hutchinson, 1967); G. K. Helleiner, *Peasant Agriculture, Government and Economic Growth in Nigeria* (Homewood, IL: R. D. Irwin, 1966).

3 *Ibid.*

4 Gann and Duignan, *Burden of Empire*, p. 251.

5 McPhee, *The Economic Revolution*, p. 104.

6 Gann and Duignan, *Colonialism in Africa*, Vol. 5, p. 690.

7 See Gann and Duignan, op. cit., Vol. 4, *Economics of Colonialism, Economic Achievement of Colonizers: Assessment.*

8 Gann and Duignan, *Burden of Empire*, p. 13.

9 Lillian C. A. Knowles, *The Economic Development of British Overseas Empire* (London: Routledge and Keegan Paul, 1924), cited in Gann and Duignan, *Burden of Empire*, p. 13.

10 *Ibid.*

11 *Ibid.*

12 Gann and Duignan, *Burden of Empire*, p. 251.

13 Myint, "The Classical Theory."

14 Myint, *Economics*, p. 42.

15 *Ibid.*, p. 43.

16 Myint, "The Classical Theory," p. 129.

17 *Ibid.* pp. 40-44.

18 Helleiner, *Op. cit.*, p. 4.

19 *Ibid.*, p. 3.

20 For details on "Vent-for-Surplus production," see Hla Myint, "The 'Classical Theory' of International Trade and the Underdeveloped Countries," *Economic Journal*, 68, June 1958. See also R. E. Caves, "Vent for Surplus Models of Trade and Growth," in R. E. Caves and H. G. Johnson (eds), *Readings in International Economics* (Homewood, IL: R. D. Irwin, 1968).

21 Caves and Johnson, Readings; R. Szereszewski, *Structural Changes in the Economy of Ghana, 1891-1911* (London: Weidenfeld and Nicolson, 1965); G. K. Helleiner, "Typology in Development Theory: The Land Surplus Economy," *Food Research Institute Studies*, 6,2, 1966; R. Szereszewski and C. M. Elliot, G. K. Helleiner, "Agriculture and Economic Development

in Africa: Theory and Experience, 1880-1914," in E. L. Jones and S. J. Woolf (eds.), *Agrarian Change and Economic Development* (London: Methuen, 1969).

22 Ake, *Op. cit.*, pp. 55-56.

23 *Ibid.*, pp. 55-56.

24 *Ibid.*, p. 57.

25 *Ibid.*, pp. 57-58.

26 *Ibid.*, p. 43.

27 *Ibid.*

28 *Ibid.*, p. 46.

29 *Ibid.*, p. 48.

30 *Ibid.*

31 R. Green and A. Seidman, *Unity or Poverty: The Economics of Pan-Africanism* (Baltimore: Penguin Books, 1968), pp. 31-32, cited in Falola, *Op. cit.*, p. 8.

32 Rodney, *Op. cit.*, p. 25.

33 *Ibid.*, p. 25.

34 *Ibid.*, p. 149.

35 *Ibid.*

36 *Ibid.*, p. 137.

37 Onimode, *Op. cit.*, pp. 37, 38.

38 *Ibid.*, pp. 31-40.

38 Rodney, *Op. cit.*, p. 215.

40 *Ibid.*, pp. 215-216.

41 *Ibid.*

42 Rodney, *Op. cit.*, p. 205.

Chapter 2

Pre-colonial Society

Owing to its ethnic and linguistic diversity, as well as the lack of political centralization, the Western Delta is perceived as a highly fragmented region. Not only was there an absence of central authority in the region, with the exception of the kingdoms of the Aboh and the Itsekiri, but also, each of the other groups were further divided and organized into autonomous clans.

It is important, however, to note that the differences are overstated and the perspective a highly polarized one. For example, there exists a close linguistic and cultural affinity including common traditions of origin between the Aboh and Ukwuani on the one hand and between the Ijo, the Urhobo and Isoko on the other.

As will be demonstrated later, ecological variations stimulated commercial interaction and interdependence. This helped to forge social inter-relationships and integration among the various groups. Social and economic linkages effectively minimized the problems of the lack of central political authority. Broadly speaking, the Western Delta is divided into two major ecological zones, the Lower and Upper Delta.

The Lower Delta

The characteristic vegetation of the Lower Delta is the mangrove tree whose roots hang high above water level, as branches do from the trunk of a tree. An extensive system of meandering creeks and water channels cut through the thick vegetation. The area is honey-combed in such a manner that the land is converted into an interminable series of islands. The Itsekiri and Ijo live in this salt water mangrove ecological zone.

The Upper Delta

It is inhabited by the Urhobo, Isoko, Ukwuani and Aboh. The Upper Delta zone is marked by an imperceptible transition from fresh water swamp to the tropical rain forest. The luxuriant evergreen vegetation dominated by the profuse oil palm tree has an almost impenetrable undergrowth of other plant life. Another characteristic of this region is the intricate network of interlocking creeks and streams.[1] This network helps to create effective physical linkages among the various peoples and minimizes their "isolation." When other forms of communication and transportation were limited and difficult, this network proved invaluable for the people of the region.

Traditions of Origin

The Ijo

The Ijo of the Western Delta border the Ijo of the Eastern Delta to the east(now Rivers State), the Itsekiri on the west and the Isoko and Aboh to the north. It is significant that not all the Ijo groups live in the salt water mangrove swamps of the Lower Delta. Some clans migrated and settled in the fresh water and evergreen belts where they are neighbors to the Isoko, Aboh, and Urhobo.[2] Alagoa has identified thirteen main Ijo groups. Five of these claim Benin origin, six have traditions of origin relating to the Central and Eastern Delta while two groups have origins which place them in their present location, an indication that their origins date far back into the past.[3]

According to most of the Benin traditions, migrants settled at Aboh on the lower before moving to their present location. Alagoa concludes that reference to Benin does not necessarily amount to migration out of Benin city. He asserts that when a group collectively "forgets" its place of origin, it selects one that was powerful, old and distant enough that does not pose a threat to its autonomy.[4]

Alagoa also notes that the Ijo groups on the fringe of the Western Delta, right under the shadow of the Benin Kingdom, do not make claims of Benin origin, but rather lay claims to the Central and Eastern Delta.[5] The dominant pattern of migration he describes is one of outward migration in which ethnic groups of the Niger Delta move northwards and westward into the Edo, Yoruba and Igbo hinterlands.[6]

This view differs from that of Dike who claims that there was an influx of migration from the Igbo hinterland, and other parts of the mainland, to the Niger Delta.[7] The southward movement is likely to have been influenced by the search for more suitable land for settlement and the desire to engage in traditional economic activities in the Delta region. It is also possible to argue that the desire to participate in trans-delta trade and westward commerce to Lagos through the creeks and lagoon network provided an incentive for such a movement.

Alagoa claims that the traditions indicate political and commercial contacts with the Kingdoms of Benin, Aboh and Itsekiri. He argues that the Ijo had more intimate relations with the Isoko and Urhobo, whose women, the Ijo often took as wives.[8]

While the habitat may not be appealing today, Alagoa posits that it was much more attractive in the pre-colonial era because it provided protection from hostile neighbors. In addition, the area provided a more convenient form of transportation in the pre-colonial period, and economic activities like fishing, canoe building and salt making were profitable engagements. While it is possible that the Ijo are indigenous to the area, further research into the early history of the Ijo is necessary before conclusions can be reached on how the area was initially populated.

The Itsekiri

The Itsekiri live in the mangrove swamp of the Lower Delta and border the Ijo in the East. To the West, they are connected with the Ondo and Ijebu Yoruba communities through the network of creeks which connect the Delta to Lagos. In the North, the Itsekiri are separated from the Urhobo by an intricate system of streams which connect the Ramos, Escravos, Forcados and Benin Rivers.

The majority of the Itsekiri accept the tradition of Prince Iginuwa's migration from Benin, which Jacob Egharevba dates to about 1473 during the reign of Oba Olua.[9]
William Moore states that Prince Iginuwa was welcomed by some mythical beings called *Umale*, who were living in the area. These beings were highly impressed by the regalia and fame of Benin. Because of the awe which Benin inspired, they accepted the Benin Prince as their king. He claims that the word Itsekiri is derived from one of these beings.[10] Moore also argues that there were some Ijo and Urhobo elements in the area in the pre-Iginuwa period.

Obaro Ikime argues that there were a considerable number of Yoruba elements among the pre-Iginuwa period. Contacts with the Itsekiri were facilitated by the creek network which enabled the movement of goods, people, and ideas.[11]

The presence of Yoruba influence is demonstrated by the adoption of a language akin to Yoruba by the Itsekiri, says Ikime, though the court remained largely Edo. Benin kingship has been associated with Ife-Yoruba royal dynasty since the founding of the Eweka dynasty in the fourteenth century. It is likely that this influence could also be the basis for the adoption of a Yoruba-related language. Ikime concludes that even though the kingship of the Itsekiri clearly derived from Benin, the Itsekiri people that emerged in the post-Iginuwa period were a combination of Ijo, Urhobo, original Umale, Yoruba and Edo elements.

The Urhobo and Isoko

The term *Sobo* which translates as *Urhobo* was applied officially to both the Isoko and the Urhobo before 1963.[12] During the period of study, the Isoko were administered as part of the Sobo (Urhobo) division with headquarters at Ughelli. Since 1963 when the Isoko became a separate administrative division, the people have expressed a sense of separate identity and a collective pride which no longer identifies them as Sobos or Urhobos. But, the colonial experience provides the justification for grouping both groups as Urhobo in this work. It is not done with any sense of disregard for the pride and identity of the Isoko people, the author of this study being one.

Both the Urhobo and Isoko border the Benin to the North, the Itsekiri and Ijo to the West and the Ukwuani and Aboh to the East. The majority of Urhobo live on the edge of the evergreen forest, although the Southern and Eastern Urhobo and Isoko land is dominated by fresh water swamps.

The land is traversed by numerous water-ways, many of which did not provide access to the coast before the nineteenth century. Until the late nineteenth century, both groups remained an inland people almost entirely cut off from direct European contact which affected the Aboh and Itsekiri since the late fifteenth century. The Aboh and Itsekiri assumed the role of middlemen because their geographical position and centralized political organization enabled them to perform this role.

However, for the Urhobo people, although the waterways were not useful for direct coastal contacts, they were of great advantage in exchange and communication among the people. Isolation from the coast had a price in that the Urhobo depended on the Itsekiri and the Aboh to sell their products and in return buy overseas goods from them.

Among the Urhobo and Isoko, five clans claim origin from the Ijo, thirteen from Benin, four from Igboland, and two claim to be indigenous.[13] Exact migration dates are not available from the traditions. Fear of punishment for a misdemeanor or the hostility of the Oba or King of Benin are given as the reasons for migration.[14] The reasons also related to harsh economic exactions in the form of taxes and dues, military imposition, and severe social obligations.

It is also not clear if the migrations began from the Benin heartland around Benin City, or if they began in the peripheral areas of the kingdom.

The accounts of Ijo traditions claim disputes and inter-family strife as the main reason for migration.[15] It may be argued that these quarrels could have emanated from population pressure on land. As land became scarce for socio-economic purposes, people were forced to migrate in search of new land. The drier upland areas offered attractive fishing and farming environments for many migrants.

Claims of Igbo origin might have been part of the southward push or movement from Igbo land which Dike described as the "coastward moving Ibos."[16] The search for more lands, as the result of population pressure, is the most plausible explanation for such movements.

The claims of indigeneity which implies that they came from no where but have always been where they are, refer again to a group of great antiquity. It is plausible to contend that what emerged as the Urhobo and Isoko was a mixture of Edo, Igbo and Ijo elements in addition to the very original unknown inhabitants of the region. It is important to add that though the Urhobo and Isoko are more closely related to the Edo linguistically, they are more closely related to the Igbo in terms of social and political organizations.

J.W. Hubbard, using a king-list of some of the clans, places the date of migration and settlement near the end of the sixteenth century.[17] But, Jacob Egharevba claims that migrations from Benin started in the reign of Oba Eweka in 1370.[18] Duarte Pacheco Pereira, who visited the Forcados River at the beginning of the sixteenth century, spoke of the "Subou people to the hinterland."[19] Egharevba's position seems more accurate as Hubbard does not make clear how long it took for the settlements to form or adopt the institution of kingship.

The Aboh

K.O. Ogedengbe contends that the Aboh people and kingdom was founded as a result of a Benin incursion into the lower Niger valley.[20] He relates that before the Benin incursion, Igbo-speaking peoples lived in loosely-organized but independent communities. Edo migrants imposed an Edo-style political system on the Igbo-speakers, but the Igbo language survived as the language of the people. This indicates that Igbo cultural influence must have been significant and long-standing throughout the region.

Both Ogedengbe and Dike agree that the kingdom emerged in the seventeenth century. But, while Dike claims that it was founded by a third wave of migration from the Edo area to the delta, Ogedengbe asserts that Aboh was founded around 1650-

1680, from a migration wave from Ashaka, a local group also owing its origins to Benin.[21]

Despite this disagreement, both scholars contend that the primary motive for the founding of the kingdom was the need to participate and control the north-south Niger trade network, which had been monopolized by the city-states of the Niger until that point.[22] Therefore what emerged as Aboh society was a combination of Benin and Igbo. The idea of kingship was Benin while the language was Igbo.

The strategic location of Aboh on the Niger and the economic potentialities of its environment (rich in oil palm trees) constituted major advantages for its growth as a trading metropolis. In addition, such advantages made Aboh the center of the long-distance export trade, conducted between the hinterland and the upper stretches of the Niger and the Delta areas.

Similarly, Aboh was able to control the trade in imported and local goods between the Delta and the coastal area and the hinterland.

The Ukwuani

Most of the Ukwuani clans lay claim to Benin origin.[23] Okolugbo states that the migrations came in three waves, and agrees with Dike that the third led to the founding of Aboh.[24] He contends that there were Igbo settlements in the area before Benin incursion. But, unlike the Aboh, the Benin migrants failed to impose their political system on the Igbo-speakers.

The Ukwuani society which emerged, therefore, was a blend of Benin and Igbo people and influences, though the Igbo influence was the more dominant. It may be deduced that the number of Benin migrants was not considerable. Among the Ukwuani, the Igbo-speakers were of greater numerical strength and economics was not a large motivating force as was the case among the Aboh.

Issues and Questions of Benin Origin

A number of questions arise when examining the various claims to Benin origins among the people under investigation. There is need to exercise caution in their interpretation and acceptance. Until more research on the religion, art, culture and language of the people is undertaken, it will be difficult to make conclusive deductions. No doubt, such an exercise would help disentangle some of the complications in the traditions and lead to more meaningful conclusions on derivations and similarities.

There is credence in the views of Dike that the persistent and widespread claims to Benin origin is the evidence of the fame and powerful influence which the kingdom wielded over her neighbors.[25] Also, there is validity in Alagoa's thesis that where a group no longer remembers its place of origin, it chooses one that will confer prestige and legitimacy, especially when such claims pose no threat to their political sovereignty.[26]

Social and Political Organization

Two major categories of socio-political organizations are evident among the Western Delta peoples: the centralized kingdoms of Aboh and Itsekiri and the non-centralized political organizations of the Urhobo and Isoko, Ukwuani and Ijo.[27] In spite of this broad classification, some institutions, such as the age-grade system was common although the organization and their functions differed considerably in both cases.

The major socio-political organizations among the non-centralized peoples were the village and clan council, the age-grade system and titled societies. Clans, the largest political unit, were composed of villages which claim the same founding father, or ancestor.[28] The villages were made up of lineages which live in "quarters." The latter were made up of compounds consisting of members of extended families.

Each compound and lineage was headed by the eldest living male of the patriarchal descent group. This man performed religious functions by maintaining the shrines and offering sacrifices to the forefathers. In this capacity, he was also responsible for the welfare and discipline of the group.

At the level of the village, several lineage heads were selected to form the council of elders. The council was headed by the oldest living male. Membership of the council was not entirely limited to the elders (lineage heads), but often other village officials formed part of it, including the village spokesman, the war leader, village guards, messengers and members of titled societies.

With the exception of the Ukwuani, many clans had the institution of the priest-king.[29] Priest-kings performed priestly-religious functions as well as executive ones. They officiated at clan shrines, presided over annual festivals and offered sacrifices to the gods and ancestors for the welfare of their people.

The relationship of the priest-kings to the councils of elders varied from clan to clan. In nearly all cases the council of elders was distinct from the institution of the priest-king. Most of the time, priest-kings played roles complementary to the elders' council. They also had inter-related functions with the clan council.

The age-grade system was common to all groups, but their functions and organization differed among the different groups.[30] The role of the age-grade was less significant in the centralized polities than in the non-centralized one. Four classes of age-grade systems were evident in most societies. The first was composed of boys under fifteen, whose functions were limited to light communal activities such as the sweeping and clearing of village paths.

The second comprised of men between fifteen and forty years of age. This grade provided the labor and fighting force of the village. Men between the ages of forty and fifty-five, comprised the third age grade. This group shared some similar functions with the second. It also helped to maintain law and order and to settle minor disputes.

The fourth, and last, age-grade was formed of men over fifty-five. These men were considered as elders and were expected to possess great wisdom and have deep knowledge of the traditional laws and customs of the land.[31] As elders, they were the representatives of the people. They performed religious and administrative functions for the well- being and welfare of the people.

All of these ethnic groups had titled societies in which membership was associated with wealth and prestige. One of the qualification for entry was financial ability to pay prescribed fees and annual dues.[32] Young men aspired to membership in a titled society so that they could belong to the highest ruling council, the council elders or the council of the priest-king. In each titled society, they had their own councils which deliberated on matters affecting them and general matters affecting the welfare of the village.

Women were constituted into two main grades. The first grade performed similar functions as their male counterparts. The second grade constituted an important pressure, or lobbying, group which protected the welfare of the women. Their leader was the oldest woman. She controlled matters relating to land fertility, female fertility, prosperity and purity in the community.

In her official capacity, she often interacted with the elders and other village functionaries on matters relating to important community affairs. In all ways, she acted as the representative of the women and the mother of the entire society.

Despite the significance of age, the government of these communities cannot be described entirely as gerontocratic. Though age did confer certain rights and privileges, membership on the ruling council was based on other qualifications for the less-aged. For example, the spokesman of the community was selected for his eloquence, charm, and knowledge of the laws and customs of the land.

Some members of the titled societies were also represented on the councils because of their wealth and prosperity. The war leader, chosen for his valor and bravery sat on the council as well. Messengers and guards were often selected for their intellectual ability and physical prowess. All of these figures played important roles in the deliberation of the council. The spokesman served as both the solicitor and advocate when the council acted in its judicial capacity.

These governments were democracies in which the council of elders represented all the lineages and all other specialized constituents. The ruling council was the legislative and judicial bodies, while the younger age-set formed the executive arm. Each age-grade and titled society had its own council and passed their views on to the ruling council through their representatives.

It is important to emphasize that in crucial times such as natural disasters, wars or conclusion of peace, the entire community met in a forum to deliberate. A consensus was usually sought in the interest of the community. In such societies, talent and competition were recognized for social advancement, rather than circumstance of birth. Individual dynamism and hard work more than anything else, determined social mobility from lower social status to a higher one.

Centralized Political Organizations/Kingdoms

There were two centralized polities, the Itsekiri and Aboh kingdoms. The Olu was the king and head of the Itsekiri kingdom and society. He had a council of chiefs whom he appointed, although most of the positions represented hereditary positions.[33] The most important titles were that of the Ologbotsere, the Olu's chief advisor; the Iyasere, or war leader, and the Uwangue, the custodian of the Olu's regalia and the council chief spokesman.[34]

The king was both the religious as well as political head.[35] The chiefs had their own council and deliberations. The Olu was not bound to accept their advice. Oracles resolved conflicts between the council and the Olu. The Itsekiri had no priestly family, thus the Olu could not be undermined by any religious group. The priest of any oracle could be called upon to adjudicate in an Olu-council dispute.

The Olu and council constituted the supreme legislative, executive and judicial body among the Itsekiri. Age-sets with their stress on ability, played a less significant role in the Itsekiri socio-political system which was dominated by heredity. Individual villages were governed by the eldest male with the assistance of the village priest. Disputes were referred to the Olu and his council. The Olu was always a descendant of the original founding family of Prince Iginuwa.[36]

The Aboh kingdom was the most dominant political authority in the lower Niger valley. Its area of control extended on both sides of the Niger from Onitsha and Asaba in the North to Onyia in the South.[37] In addition, its influence spread from Igala in the Niger-Benue confluence to the city-states of the delta and inland over most of the Ukwuani, and some of the Isoko.[38] Control over trade of the lower Niger, together with its military and naval strength assured the Aboh of political dominance and continued allegiance to the Obi, the head of the Aboh state.[39]

Aboh town was a trading metropolis, divided into two major areas; the Umude section representing the descendants of the Benin migrants and the Ndiche section corresponding to the descendants of the Igbo migrants. The Igbo-speakers are claimed to be the earliest inhabitants of the region.[40]

The Obi selected his chiefs from both parts of the village. The most important advisor to the Obi was the Odua, who always came from the Umude section. The Odua's position had the highest power and status because its holder became the chief priest of the royal cult.[41] The next ranked officer, described as the prime minister, the Iyasele, had to be of Umude and Ndiche parentage.

The office of the Obi was not hereditary since any members of the Umude section could become king. There was no royal family or king-makers. The Obi and his council undertook the legislative, judicial and executive duties for the Aboh and its environs. In local matters, tributary villages were governed by a council of elders. The directives of the Obi were carried out through his agents, who were titled men, in most cases.[42]

It is important to note the differences in the two monarchies examined above. First, the Itsekiri monarchy was hereditary while the throne in Aboh was open to anyone of Benin descent. Itsekiri chieftaincies were often hereditary. But in Aboh, the need to maintain a balance between the two groups often resulted in appointive chieftaincies from both sections.

The Obi, unlike the Olu, was not necessarily the religious head of the Aboh, as religious roles were explicitly the function of the Odua. Itsekiri society did not retain its Yoruba, Benin and Umale divisions, as was evident in Aboh. The need for a delicate balance in politics and society was thus absent in this case. This chapter has demonstrated that the region was not as disparate as is conceived. People were united by language, traditions of origin and similar socio- political organization. But more significantly, trade forged crucial linkages among the various people who because of the challenges of their characteristic environment relied on each other for survival.

Notes

1 The most important waterways are the Forcados River, Ramos River, Escravos and Benin Rivers in the Lower Delta area, while for the Upper Delta, the Ase Creek, Ethiope and Jameson, Warri River, Kiagbodo and Kakpamre Creeks were the most important. Also see Map II.

2 E. J. Alagoa, *A History of the Niger Delta* (Ibadan: Ibadan University Press, 1972), p. 48; also E. J. Alagoa, "Ijo Origins and Migrations," *Nigeria Magazine*, 91, December 1966, pp. 279-88.

3 *Ibid.*

4 Alagoa, *History*, p. 187.

5 *Ibid.*

6 K.O. Dike, *Trade and Politics in the Niger Delta, 1830-1885* (Oxford: Clarendon Press, 1956), p. 21.

7 Alagoa, "Ijo Origins," pp. 279-88.

8 Alagoa, *History*, p. 84.

9 J. U. Egharevba, *A Short History of Benin* (Ibadan: Ibadan University Press, 1960), pp. 22-23.

10 W. Moore, *History of Itsekiri* (London: Frank Cass, 1970), Chapter Two.

11 Obaro Ikime, *Niger Delta Rivalry: Itsekiri-Urhobo Relations and European Presence, 1884-1936* (London: Longmans, 1969), pp. 32-33.

12 *Ibid.*, p. 1.

13 *Ibid.*, pp. 6-10.

14 Obaro Ikime, "People and Kingdoms of the Niger Delta," in O. Ikime (ed), *Groundwork of Nigerian History* (Ibadan: Heinemann, 1980), p. 93.

15 *Ibid.*

16 Dike, *Op. cit.*, p. 28.

17 J. W. Hubbard, *Sobo of the Niger Delta* (Zaria: Gaskiya, 1948), p. 152.

18 Egharevba, *Op. cit.*, p. 21.

19 H. T. Kimble's translation of Esmeraldo De Situ Orbis by D. P. Pacheo, London, 1937, p. 129, cited in Obaro Ikime, "The People and Kingdoms of the Niger Delta," *Op. cit.*, p. 187.

20 For details about Aboh migrations, see K. O. Ogedengbe, *Op. cit.*, Chapter Two.

21 *Ibid.*

22 Dike, *Op. cit.*, p. 22.

23 E. O. Okolugbo, "Christianity and Ukwuani Traditional Region: A Study in Religious Encounter," (Ph.D. Thesis), University of Ibadan, 1972, Chapter 1.

24 *Ibid.*

25 Dike, *Op. cit.*, p. 21.

26 Alagoa, "Ijo Origins," p. 21.

27 Discussion of socio-political institutions would be in the past tense as some of them have become non-existent and others have changed significantly.

28 Ikime, *Niger Delta Rivalry*, p. 19.
29 *Ibid.*, p. 18.
30 For details on age grades and generally on socio-political organizations of the Aboh, see Ogedengbe, *Op. cit.*, Chapter 3. For Ukwuani, see Okolugbo, *Op. cit.*, Chapter 1; For Isoko and Urhobo, see Ikime, *Op. cit.*, Chapter 1; For Ijo, see Alagoa, "Ijo Origins," *Op. cit.*
31 *Ibid.*
32 Ikime, "Peoples and Kingdoms," p. 18.
33 *Ibid.*
34 *Ibid.*
35 *Ibid.*, p. 98.
36 Ogedengbe, *Op. cit.*, p. 270.
37 *Ibid.*, pp. 270-274.
38 *Ibid.*, p. 269.
39 For details, *see Ibid.*, Chapter 4.
40 *Ibid.*
41 *Ibid.*, pp. 269-270.
42 O. Ikime, *The Isoko People: A Historical Survey* (Ibadan: Ibadan University Press, 1972), pp. xviii-xxi.

Chapter 3

Pre-colonial Economy

It is a truism that environmental factors influence the modes of behavior and cultural patterns of people. But, it is even truer that they determine economic activities, modes of production and the nature of interaction among different people. Ecological variations were responsible not only for the varying economic activities and occupational engagements, but also for the growth of commercial exchanges and interdependence among the peoples of the Western Delta.

Writers like Helleiner and Myint claim that pre-colonial societies were static and that their resources were necessarily underdeveloped because of an adequate lack of demand.[1] The major economic activity among the Ukwuani, Isoko and Urhobo was agriculture. For the Itsekiri, it was fishing, pottery and salt-making; while among the Ijo, canoe building, salt-making and fishing were the dominant economic engagements. Riverine activities like fishing and canoe building were not limited to the Ijo and Itsekiri, as some Isoko, Urhobo and Ukwuani of riverine areas engaged in similar activities.

However, it appears that the main occupation of the Itsekiri and Aboh was trade. Their strategic locations on the coast (Itsekiri) and on the lower Niger (Aboh), in addition to their rich hinterland, made them prosperous middlemen both before and after European contact.

Agriculture

As already noted the main agricultural areas are among the Ukwuani, Urhobo and Isoko of the Upper Delta. The Ukwuani enjoy better agricultural lands because of their closeness to the more fertile land of the Benin area, which lies in higher, drier grounds.

Among the Southern and Southeastern Ukwuani whose area was liable to flooding, yams were cultivated for consumption and sale to neighboring peoples(Isoko, Urhobo, Itsekiri and Ijo). Oil palm trees were leased to Isoko and Urhobo collectors who processed fruits for local consumption and sale to their with neighbors especially those of the lower Delta.

In the drier and higher land of the Northern and Western Ukwuani, intensive agriculture was undertaken. Common products grown in these parts included yams, beans, cassava, melon, corn, plantains, groundnuts, and coconuts which served subsistence and trade purposes.[2] Gari, a popular staple food all over the Western Delta processed from cassava, formed one of the major trade items between the Ukwuani and their neighbors. The production of palm produce was undertaken, but it was largely for local consumption and not necessarily for trade.

But most of the Isoko and Eastern Urhobo areas lie in the fresh water swamp, which is not so well suited for agriculture. The Isoko, in particular, suffer from the lack of suitable agricultural land because their land is part of the great deltaic swamp. Here, oil palm groves abound, thus making palm collecting and production the major occupation.

However among the northern and Western Urhobo agriculture was intensive because flooding constituted less threat. Cassava, plantains, yams, corn and pepper were the main food crops here. In the Eastern part which includes the Isoko, fishing was also a major occupation, and the people were almost as skilled in fishing as the Ijo and Itsekiri.[3] It is interesting to note that the people of Ikpide of the Isoko of the Niger were also experts at canoe manufacturing.

As Ikime notes, among the different groups, the varying occupational activities was a basic factor in the development of economic interdependence and more intensive socio-economic relations.[4] Also, this phenomenon led to the growth of markets at strategic locations within and among these groups.

For the Urhobo and Isoko, the palm tree was the center of social and economic life. It constituted the primary factor in their well-being and advancement. The palm tree is indigenous to this area where it grows luxuriantly, and provides the basis for people's occupations.

The oil palm produced materials for making essential products required by the people. These include palm oil, soap, pomade and lotion, palm wine and gin, medicinal products, lighting, fuel, baskets, brooms, fishing traps and numerous other items. These were both basic and specialized items which provided important articles of trade between the Urhobo-Isoko and their neighbors, especially the Ijo and the Itsekiri. For example palm oil was an important food item among all the groups.

The palm produce industry was a family business. The men undertook the more strenuous task of climbing the tree and cutting down the bunches of palm fruit, as well as making palm oil. Women controlled the processing of palm nuts into palm kernels and related activities like the making of soap and pomade.[5]

The dependence of the people of the Lower Delta on the agricultural products of the upper Delta was crucial because of the unsuitability of their land own for intensive agriculture and production of food. Commercial relations among the people of the two ecological zones were crucial for the survival and sustenance.

Salt Industry

Salt making was a general occupation in the salt water mangrove region. But among the Itsekiri, it was a major occupation. Salt was a vital food item. The peoples of the Upper Delta depended on their Lower Delta neighbors for their salt requirement; in the same way that the Lower Delta depended on the Upper Delta for food items.[6] Not only was salt important in the upper and lower delta trade, it was also a significant trade item in the east-west long distance trade network through the creeks which linked the Western Delta to Lagos.[7]

Salt, also, featured prominently in the north-south Niger trade network. Captain John Adams, who visited the area between 1786 and 1800, noted the "neptune or large brass basins used for the salt making and remarked that a great trade is carried on in this article with the interior."[8] Consul H.H. Johnson remarked in 1888 that "the Itsekiri salt industry is of old standing and it continues."[9] This industry was controlled by women.

Pottery Industry

Pottery was a specialty of Itsekiri land where suitable clay for making pottery products could be found in great quantity. Pottery industry among the Itsekiri was dominated by women similar to the way that palm kernel industry was a women's engagement among the Ukwuani and Urhobo-Isoko. A variety of pots were produced for a number of different purposes including water jars and various household utensils.

As Captain John Adams noted, earthen-ware constituted a considerable article of trade for the Itsekiri and Ijo. Pottery was traded to the upper delta neighbors, as well as to the Brass, Bonny and New Calabar peoples, who came to Warri in large canoes from the Eastern Delta.[10] The Aboh and other peoples along the Niger, and the Ondo and Ijebu Yoruba participated in the pottery trade.

Canoe Industry

Canoe building was a was a major occupation of the Ijo. At present, two stories exist about the Ijo and canoe production.[11] The first story states that four types of canoes were produced. The first type was manned by a paddler. It was for strictly for pleasure.

The second manned by two paddlers was for fishing. Six paddlers manned the third type which was used for agricultural gathering and small-scale trade. The fourth type was capable of carrying twenty four paddlers and was used for long distance trade, regattas, ceremonies, festivals, naval formations and military operations.

According to the second story, the Ijo built five types of canoes. The first with three fathoms, and the second with four fathoms was used essentially for fishing and they plied the inlets and small channels. The third, of six fathoms, was used for food transportation. The eight fathom type, or fourth type, was used for trade. The fifth, and largest type, of ten to twelve fathoms, were used for war.[12]

The canoe industry was highly significant in the socio-economic system of the people of the Delta. In particular, it was a necessity for the coastal and riverine people who depended on canoes for transportation and communication. Canoes provided the most economical form of transportation between the coast and the hinterland. The Ijo, especially the Apoi group, traded canoes to as far west as Lagos and as far north as the Niger-Benue confluence.

Trade and Commerce up to 1830

Before the beginning of European trade, intensive trade and extensive commercial activities were already in operation in the area. Trade linked the Lower and Upper Delta, the Eastern and Western Delta, the Western Delta and Yoruba areas and the Western Delta and the Niger-Benue confluence region. The trans-Niger trade which linked the lower Niger to the delta was a vast and complex trading network with interdependent markets positioned at strategic locations. Specialized and non-specialized products were traded from one area to another through complex trade connections. Trade which directly related to surplus production was regulated at every stage within the network. Therefore, it becomes difficult to accept the claim of Helleiner and Myint that pre-colonial economies were static and were not stimulated until the appearance of missionaries, European commercial firms and colonial administration.

As already alluded to, the Aboh and Itsekiri were the leading trading communities and middlemen traders because of their strategic location for such roles. The Aboh kingdom will be discussed first because of its dominance of pre-colonial trade in the Western Delta. The trading activities of the Aboh were intensive and extensive and its dependence on her trading partners was crucial for her trade. Trade expanded because there was surplus production of agricultural and other industrial products. This indicates that the local economy was vibrant.

Aboh's Trade and Commerce before 1830

Before the Niger valley became open to European trading activity in the 1830's as a result of "discovery of the mouth" of the river Niger by Lander Brothers, Aboh was one of the leading commercial centers of the lower Niger valley. With her position at the apex of the delta, Aboh had greater advantages to become a greater trade center than its rivals, Onitsha, Ndoni, Asaba and Idah located further north.

Aboh's trade had three main dimensions: export, import and local trade.[13] Import trade consisted of European manufactured goods, the most common of which were salt, cloth, rum, muskets, gun powder, glasses, beads, hats, snuff boxes and hooks. Exports consisted of slaves, and after the abolition of the slave trade in the nineteenth century, primarily of palm oil. Local trade consisted of exchanges of such items as yams, beans, rice, poultry, canoes, thatches, ivory, horses, horsetails and livestock.[14]

A great deal of capital investment was required for long distance trade. The security of trade compelled the formation of alliances among many leading states in the Lower Niger valley. For instance, the Aboh had an alliance with the Attah (King of) Igala and the King of Brass.

Such arrangements led to the emergence of spheres of influences among the trading partners.[15] As a result, the Attah Igala controlled the trade between the confluence of the Niger and the Benue as far as Onitsha. The Obi of Aboh dominated the section between Onitsha and Aboh, while the King of Brass controlled the trade from Aboh to the coast.[16] This division was to ensure that there were no conflicts among trading partners and that relationships of mutual interdependence were promoted.

Aboh markets were frequented by the Itsekiri and Ijo who traded salt and fish for food, livestock and other items of from the north. They were also connected with the Urhobo-Isoko markets through the important Isoko market town of Ivrogbo and with the Ukwuani through the market towns of Iselegu, Utagba and Ashaka on the Ase Creek.[17]

Aboh was a major slave trade center which was attended by traders from the coast. Some of the slaves were obtained from the Isoko, Urhobo and Ukwuani through the established markets. There is some evidence to support the view that the Aboh did undertake some raiding expeditions to obtain slaves.[18] But, the bulk of the slaves sold at Aboh were obtained from the Igala area northward in the Niger-Benue valley.

The slave trade continued in the nineteenth century despite its abolition in 1807. But, the subsequent activities of British naval squadrons caused Aboh to divert her trade in slaves from the Bonny and Brass markets through the Benin region, to Lagos and Wydah.[19] By diverting the trade westward, Aboh was able to avoid harassment from the British Royal Navy. Export of slaves continued until 1864, when the overseas market was finally cut off.

Palm Oil Trade

With the abolition of the slave trade, a gradual switch to the export of palm oil developed. Palm oil had always been produced for local consumption and trade. This permitted easy transition to export production. The bulk of the palm oil was produced by Isoko migrant farmers who leased rich oil palm lands from the Aboh.[20]

The Urhobo were also major producers, while the Ukwuani also made significant contributions. Aboh's location ensured that most of the oil produced in the area passed through its hands. In 1854, Consul Hutchinson noted the value of the Aboh in the oil trade of the Itsekiri and Brass.[21]

In 1830, John and Richard Lander noted that most of the oil purchased by Englishmen at Bonny and adjacent trade centers was brought from Aboh, while Brass was entirely supplied by Aboh.[22] The primacy of Aboh in the palm oil trade was openly acknowledged by King Boy of Brass who held the Obi in deep reverence and remarked to Laird during the 1832 Niger expedition that "King Obie too much oil, King Boy too little."[23]

Despite Aboh's primacy in palm oil trade, Aboh economy was not self sufficient. It depended on northern markets, especially Igala, the Ukwuani and the Urhobo and Isoko for slaves and palm oil, the Ijo and Itsekiri for fish, salt and canoes and the city states, especially Brass, for European goods and gun powder.

Aboh's dependence on trade and trade connections was significant for her military and naval strength and consequently for her political authority. Her military and naval power was dependent on the wealth that was derived from trade. The situation changed drastically and Aboh's fortunes were greatly affected after 1830 when British traders attempted to establish trade directly with inland markets. This move cut Aboh off from her markets and minimized her middleman position on which she depended for her prosperity and defense.

European Commercial Intervention and the Fall of Aboh, 1830-1886

By 1820, Aboh had maximized the advantages of her position in the palm oil belt and Niger trade network. Her control of the Lower Niger trade was nearly complete. Dike claims that in the nineteenth century, Aboh exercised a monopoly of trade up and down the Niger valley and that the entire region could be held up at her will by her war canoes armed with brass and canon.[24]

With this might, she was also able to control the trade of the Ukwuani and most of the Isoko areas. By 1885, Aboh was to become involved in a death struggle with the British to save her position as the major trading center and middleman of the Lower Niger.

Until the European discovery of the mouth of the Niger in 1830, European merchants were content to remain on the coast and to procure commodities through the coastal middlemen who organized trading expeditions to purchase commodities for sale to European traders. The Ijo city states were strategically located on the coast to prevent any unwelcome interference in the interior. They exploited the advantage of their located to the best of their abilities since their economic well-being depended on this position.

The notoriety assigned to the resources of the Niger valley, and the subsequent British expeditions designed to exploit the trade of the area through a direct trade contacts, radically upset this situation. British attempts at achieving direct trade were strongly opposed by the coastal middlemen.

The first British expedition in 1832 was a dismal failure. The Obi of Aboh was eager to establish friendship and trade with the Europeans for a number of reasons. First, he perceived that direct trade would ensure him a regular supply of much needed arms and ammunition and expand Aboh trade. Secondly, Aboh would no longer be subject to the whims, exploitations and caprices of the coastal middlemen.

More importantly, he hoped that direct trade with the Europeans would divest most of the Igala trade southward, thereby increase trade revenues. Finally, the prestige associated with British friendship would consolidate and institutionalize Aboh's position as the middleman and the "power" of the Lower Niger.

But, the Obi did not have a full understanding of the impact which the British presence would have on his trade and sovereignty. The British wanted to promote trade by establishing contact with numerous inland trading centers, not only with the Aboh. The ambition of both Aboh and the British to control trade in their own interest led to a number of British-Aboh conflicts with the end result being Aboh loss of trade, loss of sovereignty and the eventual collapse of the kingdom.

Although the first expedition was a failure, its strategy became the policy of subsequent British traders and expeditions. During the 1841 expedition, the British signed an anti-slave trade treaty with Aboh. Conscious of the increase in the activities of the British Royal Navy squadron, the Obi concluded that the slave trade would soon collapse.

Consequently, he requested that British ships buy oil from Aboh in return for arms and ammunition.[25] But, until his death in 1844, no British ship visited Aboh. In order to avoid a decline in trade, Aboh was forced to resume direct trade with Brass in 1851. It was not until 1857 that the first British trading post was established at Aboh.

Aboh opposed the establishment of similar stations up the Niger at Onitsha, Asaba, Ndoni, Idah and Lokoja because it detracted from their role as middlemen and deprived them of monopoly trade with the British. British strategy was to eliminate Aboh's middleman role just as it had done to the coastal traders. This tension strained Aboh-British relation, which was aggravated by the irregular supply of provisions to the British factory at Aboh.[26] Aboh-British conflict culminated in the bombardment of Aboh in 1862 by the British navy.

From 1850, with the establishment of consular rule, British traders enjoyed the support of British gunboats. From that point on, the balance of power was heavily in favor of the British, who could use the threat of bombardment to dictate terms to local rulers and traders.

The threat to Aboh's economic primacy and hegemony escalated with the activities of Tubman Goldie and his United African Company (UAC). This company, and a French firm, Compagnie Francaise de l'Afrique Occidentale (CFAO), established stations at Aboh in 1880. The Aboh resented Goldie's efforts to push the French firm out and establish a monopoly. The crisis that developed between the two resulted in another bombardment in 1886. By this, Aboh lost her independence in trade and witnessed the erosion of her political authority.

Aboh's conflict with British traders and consular authority resulted in the escalation of internal weaknesses and in the assertion of independence by tributary people such as the Ukwuani. This situation disturbed the trading arrangements between Aboh and her trading allies. As a result, the Nupe fought Aboh in 1851. The Annam Igbo fought Aboh from 1870-80 in order to prevent the Aboh from reaching the Igala markets. Thus, the penetration of the interior markets by European traders led to loss of markets and a decline in trade for the Aboh. Ultimately, it culminated in the loss of territories and political authority.

Itsekiri and European Trade, 1830-1885

By the beginning of the nineteenth century, there was a decline of trade in the Itsekiri area. This was principally due to the difficulty experienced by ships crossing the Forcados bars and later by the activities of the British naval squadrons. There was a general shift of trade during this period to the Benin River which had better and more accessible harbors.

The movement of trade from the Forcados and the relocation of Itsekiri trading settlements on the Benin River, created problems for the Olu. This caused the loss of trade and decline in trade revenue weakened the monarchy. By 1848, when Olu Akengbuwa died, the Itsekiri monarchy was facing the imminent danger of total collapse.[27] The succession disputes and the civil strife that followed the death of Akengbuwa resulted in an interregnum which lasted until 1936.[28]

The establishment of consular rule marked an important stage in the gradual loss of political and economic independence for the Itsekiri. By the 1840's, British firms including Miller Brothers, James Pinnock and Douglas Stewart arrived in the area with the goal of reviving trade. However, the problems of the Trust system created conflicts between the traders and the firms. The conflict resulted in bombardment by the British. In reaction to the bombardment, a number of traders stopped doing business with the British only to be threatened with further bombardment if they did not resume trade.[29] In 1868 and 1879, Itsekiri merchant princes, Idiare and Isanomi, who were governors, ceased trade because of low prices for palm oil. In 1886, Governor Nana also stopped trade, but under threat of force was compelled to rescind his decision.

Thus, as was the case with Aboh, direct European control of trade led to the Itsekiri loss of trade and the collapse of monarchical authority. But, unlike the Aboh, her central political authority was transferred from the hereditary monarchy to elected merchant princes. Despite this, by 1885, the power of the merchant princes was highly threatened and undermined by the consular system whose activities considerably reduced the independence of the Itsekiri people.

On the whole, indigenous economic activities, both production and trade, served to integrate communities in the area. The area was not after all as disparate as it has been described. There were effective linkages through the Niger river, lagoons and creeks. More importantly, the volume, diversity and complexity of commercial activities on the Niger and through the delta does not give credence to the contention that the pre-colonial economy was static. Specific needs in the different sections were met through intensive production and complex trading system. The effect of European commercial activities was the loss of control of trade by indeginous authorities, disruption of the pre-European trading pattern and alliance arrangements as well as destruction of indigenous commercial hegemonies. But what appears more disruptive was the loss of sovereignty by the traditional local authority as demonstrated in the cases of the Aboh and Itsekiri kingdoms.

Notes

1 Okolugbo, E.O. " Christianity and Ukwuani Traditional Religion: A Study in Religious Encounter". Ph.D., Dissertation, University of Ibadan. Nigeria. 1972. pp. 3-4.
2 Ikime, *Niger Delta Rivalry*, 1969. p.5.
3 *Ibid.*
4 *ibid.*
5 For more information on the activities as well as the role of men and women in the industry, especially as it relates to other areas, the Igbo in particular, see B. N. Ukegbu, "Production in the Nigerian Oil Palm Industry 1900-1954," (Ph.D. Thesis) University of London, 1974; Mba, N. E. *Nigerian Women Mobilised: Women Political Activities in Southern Nigeria, 1900-1965* (Berkeley: University of California Institute of International Studies, 1982), pp. 105-114.
6 E. J. Alagoa, "Long Distance Trade and States in the Niger Delta," *Journal of African History*, Vol. XI, No. 3, 1970.
7 Captain John Adams, Sketches Taken During Ten Voyages to Africa Between the Years, 1786-1800 (London: 1823), p. 35, cited in Ikime, *Niger Delta Rivalry*, p. 31.
8 F. O. 84/1882, "Memorandum on British Protectorate of Oil Rivers," cited in Dike, *Op. cit.* 52., p. 22.
9 Adams, *Sketches*, in Ikime, *Op. cit.*, p. 31.
10 Interview with Mr. N. Obaro at Bomadi, December 1986.
11 Interview with Chief S. O. Ojobo at Burutu, December 1986.
12 Interview with T.N Tamuno, Lagos. June 1986.
13 Ogedengbe, K.O. " The Aboh Kingdom of the Lower Niger, 1650- 1900". Ph.D Dissertation. University of Wisconsin, 1971. Also see Map 111
14 *Ibid.*
15 *Ibid.*
16 *Ibid.*, p. 314.
17 *Ibid.*, p. 297.
18 *Ibid.*, pp. 306-309.
19 *Ibid.*
20 *Ibid.*
21 *Ibid.*
22 *Ibid.*, p. 250.
23 Dike, *Op. cit.*, p. 26.
24 Okolugbo, *Op. cit.*, pp. 178-180.
25 Ogedengbe, *Op. cit.*,P. 251
26 *Ibid.*

27 Ikime, O." The Western Delta and the Hinterland in the Nineteenth Century" in Ikime, O. *ed.* Groundwork of Nigerian History. 1980. p. 264.

28 Ikime, op. cit. P. 269

29 *Ibid.*

Chapter 4

British Conquest, Colonial Administration, and Economy up to 1929

Consular Period, 1850-1885

Although the principle of effective occupation did not become internationally recognized by the colonizing powers until the Berlin Conference of 1884-85, West African territories, particularly those under study, had witnessed a systematic erosion of political authority since the 1850's with the appointment of John Beecroft as the first British Consul for the Bights of Benin and Biafra.[1]

The primary objective of the consular authority was to ensure the protection of British trading interests, lives and property on the coast, in addition to promoting the growth of legitimate trade. The operation of the consular system was backed by the use of British gunboats and Courts of Equity. The latter, which amounted to "imperium in imperio" (meaning an *order* within an *order*) considerably undermined African sovereignty, particularly as the court's decisions were backed by force through the use of gunboats. The use of gunboats involved the shelling of African towns, the destruction of African lives and property. These operations were aimed at intimidating African rulers and traders into submitting to the dictates of European merchants.

In the Western Delta, the impact of consular authority was felt largely in the main trading communities of the Itsekiri and Aboh. As illustrated among the Aboh, most conflicts developed out of the British strategy to establish direct commercial relations with interior markets.[2] The determination of Aboh to maintain its middleman role led to deterioration of relationships between them and European traders. This problem was further complicated by the Aboh refusal to accept the monopolization of her trade by British merchants like Tubman Goldie, and the subsequent bombardment of Aboh capital in 1862 and 1886.

Among the Itsekiri, disputes largely emanated from the operation of the trust system and imposition of prices by European traders and conflicts led to the shelling of Bobi, an important trading center in the Itsekiri state in 1851[3].

British gunboats forced the reopening of trade in 1868, 1879 and 1886 after Itsekiri princes declined to trade. Therefore, by the time of the inception of the Oil Rivers Protectorate in 1885, African authority and sovereignty had declined significantly, and the balance of power was overwhelmingly in favor of the British authorities and agents, the merchant firms.

Oil Rivers Protectorate, 1885-1890

The fierce competition that accompanied late nineteenth century imperialism witnessed serious rivalries among European powers (Britain, France, Germany). Their merchants vied for control of markets in the interior. In the Western Delta, the British were challenged by French and German trading firms backed by their home governments.

Competition forced the British to adopt an effective policy and ultimately declare sovereignty over the areas where British interests were dominant. This concern compelled Consul Hewett and the National African Company under Tubman Goldie to make treaties. These treaties gave Britain the legal authority to lay claim to the Delta and the Niger Valley at the Berlin Conference of 1884-85.[4]

In 1884, Consul Hewett signed treaties with the Itsekiri[5] This was followed by similar treaties with the Ijo.[6] A great deal has been written on whether the Africans understood what they were signing.[7] Governor Nana of the Itsekiri refused to sign the clauses that allowed free missionary enterprise and the right of Europeans to trade freely anywhere in the area. He reckoned that such a right would deprive him and his people of the benefits of their religious beliefs and the middleman position on which they depended for survival and prosperity. However, these treaties formed the basis for the declaration of the Oil Rivers Protectorate in 1885, which included parts of the Western Delta.

The National African Company, which had become the Royal African Company with the grant of a royal charter in 1886, similarly intensified and extended its activities in the area, particularly along the Niger. In 1883, an attack by the Aboh on Goldie's factory led to the bombardment of the town and the establishment of a monopoly over Aboh's trade and markets.

This was followed by the imposition of a treaty on Obi Imegwu in October 1884.[8] In return, he was to receive an annual subsidy of £32.3.2d. The treaty ceded the whole of Aboh and its territories to the company which assumed the right to settle and to exclude foreigners from the kingdom.

The political consequences were decisive as Aboh now became dependent on the company's agents at all levels. The final loss of sovereignty occurred with the treaty of 1896 in which Aboh was incorporated into the Niger Coast Protectorate administered by a British consul.

Niger Coast Protectorate, 1891-1899

In general, the Oil Rivers Protectorate lacked effective and consistent administration. Debates existed as to the type of administration to adopt. The recommendations of Consuls Hewett and Johnston for a formal and effective administration were not adopted.[9] The Royal Niger Company operation and rule involved harsh taxes on trade. This provoked protests among the people and created complications for the consular administration.

The Foreign Office was then compelled to send the Macdonald Mission to study the situation and make recommendations for a more effective administration. The result of the Mission led to the establishment and inauguration of the Niger Coast Protectorate in 1891, with Sir Claude Macdonald as Commissioner and Consul-General.

Two vice consulates were established in the region, at Warri and Benin River. From these centers, consular officers toured the interior to explain the major aspects and implications of the new administration to the people. The chiefs were to continue to govern the people, but under the supervision of the High Commissioner who was also to take charge of inter-ethnic and foreign relations for the traditional authorities.[10] The administration was supposed to encourage direct trade with the interior in order to expand trade and impose import duties to raise revenue for administrative expenses.

The issues which led to the overthrow of Governor Nana of Benin River, ostensibly the most important middleman trader in the area, had to do with the strategy of the administration and its European merchant allies to promote direct trade with the interior.[11] To achieve this, the merchants pressured their home government to establish effective political control in the area and help create a politico-economic hegemony that would facilitate the exploitation of resources.

The British saw the powerful and influential Nana as the major obstacle to this goal in the Western Delta because he had created an "economic empire" himself. He was accused of blockading trade, inhibiting commercial developments and dealing in slaves. The British allied with some of Nana's rivals, led by his competitor, Dogho of Emaye House, in an effort to bring him down.[12]

In the disagreements that ensued between Nana and the authorities of the protectorate, Nana suffered a joint military and naval defeat in 1894. His expulsion marked the end of Itsekiri independence and the establishment of British political domination over Itsekiriland.

The conquest of Nana was a vivid demonstration of the policy of effective occupation, which was designed to remove all obstacles from the path of effective resource exploitation in the interior. The administration thought that if the protectorate was going to be financially self-sustaining through trade and custom duties, the interior must be penetrated and opened to trade. Trade would have to be encouraged and the people stimulated to produce more.

But, the British merchants and administration misjudged the situation because, as they would soon discover, the conquest of Nana and the incorporation of the Itsekiri into the protectorate did not imply subjugation of the entire area. It required special efforts to bring this area and some other parts of the Western Delta under effective British control.

The first British penetration into Urhoboland in 1891, by H.L. Gallaway was mutually greeted with enthusiasm by the Urhobo people. Its aim was to,

> Establish law and order, select suitable sites for vice-consulate, barracks and constabulary posts, impress on the native the great advantages to be gained by the cultivation of such crops as coffee, cocoa and enquire into the reasons for the slackness of trade in Sobo districts.[14]

The enthusiastic response of the Urhobo could be explained largely by the deprivation and disadvantages which they had suffered in relation to their Itsekiri neighbors. The latter had utilized their middleman position to dictate the prices of palm oil and imported goods. For the most part, the Itsekiri bought palm oil at low prices from the Urhobo while imposing high prices for imported goods.

The Urhobo and others reckoned that the penetration of their area by European merchants would bring them closer to the export/import trade and help eliminate the exploitation of the Itsekiri. But the enthusiasm of the Urhobo did not last long and soon changed to cold indifference, and in some cases, to hostility.

An important effect of the mission was the establishment of a vice-consulate at Sapele and the consequent closure of the one at Benin River.[15] There is little doubt that the establishment of Sapele, nearer to the palm oil producing Urhobo area, stimulated much more palm oil production than Benin River.

Treaty Making

The period of 1891-1893 was one of intensive treaty making in Urhoboland. In spite of the boundary fixed by Macdonald in 1891 between the spheres of influence of the Niger company and the protectorate, there were conflicts between the two authorities over treaties made with the same people in the area. This lead to claims and counter-claims.[16]

The British government's attitude to the conflicting claims was not decisive as it did not take steps to end the on-going conflicts. The reaction of the government was based on the conviction that it could use any of the treaties as a legal guarantee for territorial claims in the international situations. It was also reasoned that no matter how conflicting such claims may be, they were sufficient to ward off the French and German competitors.

There was a lull in the conclusion of treaties between 1897 and 1899. It was only after Niger Company lost its charter and its territories were handed over to the Niger Coast Protectorate that systematic moves were again resumed to bring the entire area under British protection. The protectorate of Southern Nigeria was inaugurated in 1900.[17] Most parts of the Western Delta were placed in either its Western or Central Province.

However, the British realized that treaty making alone was not sufficient enough to establish Pax Britannica meaning the Peace of Britain. Thus, when the second phase of signing treaties began in 1900, it was accompanied by a greater concern to make the British presence more effectively felt in the area more. This involved the establishment of "native" courts, visits by administrative officers, military patrols and expeditions to enforce treaty regulations. The courts were designed to perform judicial functions, act as the executive arm of the government in ensuring the maintenance of law and order. In addition, they were to guarantee that the laws were carried out in ways that the British defined as ethically proper.[18]

The use of patrols and expeditions was a means of achieving pacification and anglicization of the region with the overarching goal of exterminating all inhibitors of trade and securing trade routes for the free movement of goods and people.[19] Although the primary goal was to promote trade, it was thought that the installation of British institutions would help to destroy anti-progressive old values and put in their place new ones conducive to economic advancement. Faced with superior military power, the people had no choice but to submit and accept the dictates of a new dispensation. In general, pacification took place from 1900-1911, although in Ukwuaniland, it lasted until 1919 with the storming of Abbi.[20]

The turning point in the process of bringing the Urhobo and Isoko under British rule came with the abolition of the *Eni Ordeal* in 1903.[21] Eni, an oracle with judicial powers in the Isoko area, developed as the highest judicial institution for the people of the Western Delta cross the ethnic groups. Its verdict in all disputes was considered as final. The British considered the Eni as disruptive since adhering to its judgments meant continued adherence to traditional beliefs. Its abolition, therefore, culminated in the people's surrender to British rule. However, the recurrence of military expeditions and patrols shows that acceptance of British rule and dictates was often called to question.

Contrary to the expectations of the British administration, the pacification of the hinterland did not induce firms to move into the interior. It was anticipated by the British authorities that trading firms would flood the interior markets to expand trade and help consolidate British rule. This move was to occur at a much slower pace than had been in high quarters.

Between 1906 and 1907, the John Holt Company, began the drive for the interior markets.[22] The firm established a station at Okpare on Okpare creek and succeeded in persuading some producers to bring their produce to the company's factories at Warri, Sapele and Ganagana.

The Isoko were encouraged to channel their produce to Patani, where the company had established a factory.[23] The Niger Company, based at Ase, expanded its activities to establish a station at Patani and compete with John Holt. Its first factory in the Isoko mainland territory was established at the market town of Ivrogbo on Ase creek in 1908.[24] At the same time, it moved into the Ukwuani-Aboh area and founded trading stations at Ashaka, Iselegu and Isala.[25]

The colonial authorities used missionary enterprises to facilitate the establishment of a Pax Britanica (British hegenomy).[26] The first missionary stations were located in the commercial centers established by the trading companies or in the administrative centers. More than the other Western

Delta groups, the Ukwuani were staunchly resistant to missionary penetration, and not until 1930 did Christian activity begin in their land.[27] Where the administration failed to pacify the population, the missionaries succeeded through persistent indoctrination in Christian philosophy and ideas.

Perhaps a more conspicuous and enduring aspect of missionary work was the introduction of Western education to the people. There was a great demand for education from the beginning because of the practical use to which its achievements could be put. To this extent, this study supports the missionaries claim that "their religious instruction is tolerated and accepted because it is a means of acquiring English, the language of the trade, the law courts and governing administration".[28] The significance of missionary education becomes evident when one considers the fact that the government did not establish schools in the interior until the 1930s, a decade after the missions had begun to establish schools.[29]

The Establishment of Colonial Administration

"Native Courts"

The establishment of British rule was accompanied by the creation of "native" courts, the icons of British authority. These courts functioned not only as tribunals or judicial courts, but also as the executive arm of the government. By 1891, native courts were established at the Vice-Consulates of Warri and Sapele. The latter were transferred to Benin Rivers a year later.

There were two types of courts, the Native Council and the Native Court. Created by the Native Court Proclamations of 1900 and 1901, the Native Council was presided over by the District Commissioner and was higher than the native courts whose members were selected on a three-month rotational basis from among traditional rulers.[30]

The councils adjudicated on various matters including land, debt and damage while the courts administered only those laws sanctioned according to natural morality and humanity as the British administration deemed fit. The Native council heard appeals from the Native court. Another amendment of the Native Court proclamation in 1903 made the District Commissioner a member of the Native Court under his jurisdiction. In 1906, another modification of the Native Courts Proclamation empowered the High Commissioner to appoint any member of the native court as its president.

Reactions of the People to the Native Courts System

Up to 1914, most of the courts in the province were not seriously patronized. In the pre-colonial days, the village councils catered to the judicial and legislative needs of the people. They did not need to travel outside their villages to attend a court.

Under British rule, court attendance more often than not involved undertaking tedious journeys over long distances. Thus, the people did not share any feeling of belonging to the institution. The people's sense of alienation was all the more compounded by the fact that they were arbitrarily grouped together in a judicial unit without their approval. The administration claimed it was not possible to establish courts in every clan because of shortage of British supervisory staff.

The selection of the court members also created discontent. Membership was limited to the appointment of few warrant chiefs from each clan.[32] This was a markedly different system from pre-colonial times when the courts included the whole village council, and at times of crisis, the whole village. Though the warrant chiefs were considered to be men of worth and merit, the people were still contemptuous of the new courts system and continued to use their pre existing judicial institutions.[33] This tenacity provoked a number of military expeditions before 1914.[34]

The British were sensitive to administrative convenience and efficiency, but showed little concern for the welfare of the people. It should also be stressed that the warrant chiefs were appointed by the High Commissioner who was the only one who could remove them from office. As agents of the central and provincial government, they were not accountable to the people. Often they were overbearing and constituted themselves as sole overlords in their communities. Resentment against the new system was directed against them. The practice of appointing chiefs who were not responsible to the people they ruled was a strategy of divide and rule aimed at making the area more governable.

The laws which were administered in these courts were not derived from preexisting traditions and customs. But they were laws, compatible with the principles of morality and humanity with which the British saw fit to achieve their social, economic and political goals. Some of the salient aspects of traditions which held society together were disregarded in favor of what the British defined as right and moralistic behavior. The supervision of the courts by British officials subjugated the African legal system and values to the British legal system.

The courts undertook more than strictly judicial functions. They were involved in a whole range of issues from maintenance of law and order, agricultural regulations, trade control and the development of health programs. Such a concentration of executive, legislative and judicial roles was hitherto unknown in the society.

Furthermore, the arbitrary attitude and extortionate activities of the court clerks and messengers made the courts even more reprehensible to the people. But, on the whole, the courts can be described as effective instruments for consolidating British political control and bringing the area more effectively under the influence of the British.

In many parts, the British used force through military patrols and punitive expeditions to compel the people to attend the courts. If the system can be said to have had some measure of success among the Ukwuani, Urhobo and Itsekiri, the same cannot be said for the Ijo. Enforcement was difficult in Ijoland whose creeks and rivers were inaccessible to government officials. The Ijo traditional political system did not support the type of cohesion that the British system demanded. They ignored the courts and any British attempts to enforce attendance was met with hostility. To the British authorities, this was interpreted as a deliberate refusal to accept the introduction of their rule.

Administrative Reorganization after 1914

After the amalgamation of Northern and Southern Protectorates and the formation of the Nigerian state in 1914, Lord

Lugard introduced Northern-style native courts which he regarded as ideal.[35] He was impressed by the emirate-type of paramount chief and the tax system that developed within it. As a result, he enacted the Native Court Ordinance of 1914 which empowered the resident to establish two types of "native" courts in the area under his jurisdiction.

The first type consisted of a paramount chief, with or without minor chiefs, while the second had chiefs and other members of the communities serving in various capacities. In addition, the Resident was empowered to declare the court of a paramount chief a judicial council and as the court of appeal for all the native courts in the province.[36] The new ordinance contained some important innovations. British administrative officers ceased to be presidents of native courts. This enabled the courts to have a considerable degree of independence and responsibility, a thing which was difficult to attain if the British officials had remained court presidents.

However, the idea of a paramount chief created problems where more than one ethnic group was compulsorily subjected to the same court and to the same appointed British made paramount chief. In this sense, the court of appeal worked differently here than it did in Britain. The courts handled cases from people who did not have the same laws. It was inappropriate to compel people with varying legal traditions to attend the same court of appeal. Nevertheless, the Native Court Ordinance (1914) was strengthened by the Native Authority Ordinance of 1916 by which the resident appointed any chief as native authority.[37]

In Warri Province, Chief Dogho was appointed as the Native Authority for Warri Division in 1916. As paramount chief of the region, his judicial court also became the court of appeal.[38] By this, all native courts in the area were arbitrarily subordinated to him. Lugard was anxious to develop the Northern-style paramount chief and did not pay much attention to the ethnic differences and sensitivity of the people

In this arrangement, only the Native Court of Sapele and the Court of Appeal for Kwale Division were independent of the Court of Chief Dogho at Warri. The system generated dissatisfaction and agitation among the Urhobo and Isoko clans who protested against being subjected to a paramount chief from a different ethnic group. Consequently, the Isoko were constituted into a subdistrict with headquarters as Aseh on the Niger, which also became the Isoko Court of Appeal. In the same year, all Urhobo courts became native authorities with jurisdiction over their respective native court areas.[39] Through this, they became independent of the jurisdiction of Chief Dogho.

It was decided in 1927 that taxation be introduced in Warri Province in order to obtain funds for the development of the area and implement government policies. It was hoped that such an introduction would bring the Western Delta up to the level of the rest of Nigeria, especially the Northern and Western parts where taxation had been part of the local administration.

The imposition of taxation proved unacceptable to the people, and the compilation of a census provoked them further. This period also coincided with an era of low prices for palm produce.[40] Incomes were reduced, and there was general dissatisfaction with the new system. Thus, the people agitated not only against the introduction of taxation, but also against the unpopular native courts system and low prices.

A major administrative reorganization took place in the next two years after the anti-tax riots and the implementation of taxation in 1928.[41] The reorganization provided for the establishment of village and clan councils as local authorities among the Urhobo and the Isoko, the creation of a central council and village-group council for the Itsekiri, and finally, the reorganization of the entire province into administrative divisions to coincide with the various ethnic groups.[42]

The only exception to this was Jekri-Sobo Division which incorporated all Itsekiri and five neighboring Urhobo clans, because it was deemed that the Itsekiri were not populous enough for a separate administrative unit. The new divisions: Aboh, Jekri-Sobo, Sobo and Western Ijo were officially inaugurated in 1934.

Village and clan councils were recognized as native authorities and were constituted into native courts of various levels. The village councils were given powers of grades D and C, while clan councils were awarded grades B and C, depending on their size and financial capability.[43] One of the primary assignments of these new authorities was the collection of taxes, underscoring the importance of taxation to the administration.

By 1929, the major infrastructures had been initiated for the establishment of the colonial economy. Earlier, by the Roads and Creek Proclamation of 1903, some roads were built in the area to link major commercial centers and administrative headquarters.[44] The Warri-Sapele road had been constructed much earlier in 1896. Minor roads were also built to link other centers of activities. Some, such as the Gbogidi-Okpare road, were built in 1904.[45]

Another major road was built to link Kwale to Sapele and another, Sapele to Agbor.[46] Okpara road was built to connect Kwale District to Warri District, while within Agbon clan efforts were made to create inter-connecting roads between the mainland and the waterside by building a road through Kokori.[47] At the same time, the Sapele-Agbor road was extended to Asaba.

Similar developments took place in the Isoko area, but heavy flooding tended to hamper road construction there. Developments eluded the Ijo and Itsekiri whose environmental condition was not suited to road construction. By the end of 1929, the area was adequately connected by road with Benin and Onitsha provinces through Asaba.

The land proclamation had little impact on the Ijo, although the activities of trading firms began to increase land value in many Ijo villages. It is also important to note the Public Lands Proclamation of 1903 put a new emphasis and value on land and land use.[48]

Between 1902 and 1930, the colonial administration attempted to monetize the economy by introducing a common currency in place of the multi-currency and barter systems. The story of monetary and currency evolution has been vividly discussed in earlier works.[49] The colonial administration reckoned that the monetization of local economies would be an advantageous drive for promotion of trade.

Executing the new tax system necessitated the introduction of a new and common currency. The changing labor requirements of the colonial economy and administration increasingly required a new wage system which demanded the use of a common currency. Thus, though the introduction of a new currency controlled by the metropole demonstrated the extent of British financial responsibility towards her protected people, it did contribute toward laying the foundation of the colonial economy by 1929.

The growth of commercial organizations and the formation of commercial conglomerations were also important. The most significant of these was the emergence of the United African Company (UAC) in 1929. It was an amalgamation of all British commercial interests in Africa, with the exception of the John Holt.

The emergence of this huge conglomerate eliminated commercial competition. As the UAC began to wield irresistible influence on policy, the barriers which it imposed on producers became almost impenetrable especially as they were reinforced by governmental controls.[50]

By 1930, the British were entrenched administratively and the growth of a monetized economy and roads had great promise of entrenching them economically.

Notes

1 K.O. Dike, *Trade and Politics in the Niger Delta, 1830-1885* (Oxford.Clarendon Press 1956) p. 93.
2 For details of Aboh relations with British traders, *see* Chapter 2 of this work.
3 *Ibid.*
4 For details on the Berlin Conference see S. E. Crowe, *The Berlin West African Conference 1884-1885,* (Westport, Connecticut, Negro University Press, 1840).
5 O. Ikime, *The Merchant Prince of the Niger Delta: The Rise and Fall of Nana Olomu, the Last Governor of Benin River* (London: Heinemann, 1968), Chapter 3.
6 O. Ikime, "The Western Ijo, 1500-1950: A Preliminary Historical Survey", *Journal of the Historical Society of Nigeria,* 4:1 (December, 1967).
7 O. Ikime, "The Western Delta and the Hinterland in the Nineteenth Centuries", in O. Ikime, ed., *Groundwork of Nigerian History,* (Ibadan: Heinemann, 1980), p. 276.
8 K. O. Ogedengbe, "The Aboh Kingdom of the Lower Niger 1650-1900", (Ph.D. Dissertation, Wisconsin, 1971), p. 379.
9 J. E. Flint, *Sir George Goldie and the Making of Nigeria,* (London: Oxford University Press, 1960), Chapter 7.
10 FO84/2110, FO to Macdonald Draft No. 2, 18 April 1891 cited in O. Ikime, *Niger Delta Rivalry,* (New York: Humanities Press, 1969), p. 97.
11 For details on Nana-British Conflict, see O. Ikime, *The Merchant Prince,* op. cit, Chapter 4.
12 *Ibid.*
13 O. Ikime, *Niger Delta Rivalry,* Chapter 4.
14 FO84/2111, Callaway's Report on his Visit–Enclosure in Macdonald to FO No. 30, 12 December 1891 cited in O. Ikime, *Niger Delta Rivalry,* p. 128.
15 Ikime, *Op. cit.,* Chapter 6.
16 FO84/2111, Macdonald to FO 13 June, 1891 cited in O. Ikime, *Niger Delta Rivalry,* p. 134.
17 J. C. Anene, *Southern Nigeria in Transition, 1885-1906,* (Cambridge: Cambridge University Press, 1966), p. 213.
18 O. Ikime, "Chief Dogho: The Lugardian System in Warri, 1917-1932", *Journal of the Historical Society of Nigeria,* 3:2 (December, 1965).
19 *Ibid.*
20 E. O. Okolugbo, "Ukwuani Religion and Christianity: A Study in Religious Encounter", (Ph.D. Dissertation, University of Ibadan, 1972), p. 202.
21 Interview with Venerable B. P. Apena, age 95, first Anglican Priest and Archdeacon in the Isoko area at Irri, December 1986. For details on

the Eni ordeal, see O. Ikime, *The Isoko People: A Historical Survey*, (Ibadan: Ibadan University Press, 1972), pp. 46-48.

22 Interview with Chief O. Mazoje–age 90, one of the first produce dealers in the Isoko area, December 1986 at Oyede (Isoko Local Government Area).

23 *Ibid.*

24 *Ibid.*

25 Interview with Chief Enuesike (former employee of John Holt), age 86, at Isselegu, November, 1986.

26 Interview with Venerable B. P. Apena, op. cit. Apena was highly involved in the spread of Christianity in Ukwuani, Aboh, Isoko and Urhobo areas. He was very knowledgeable in Christian activities in the area under study.

27 For details on the growth of Christianity in Ukwuani, see E. O. Okolugbo, op. cit., p. 202. Okolugbo is an authority on the growth of Christianity in Ukwuani. He is used as the major reference for such studies.

28 Proceedings of the C. M. S. 1914-15, cited in Ikime, *Niger Delta Rivalry*, p. 163.

29 Interview with Archdeacon Apena, op. cit.

30 Calabar Province, Cal. Prof. 10/2, Vol. I, Native Courts Proclamation 1900 (No. 9 of 1900, C.O. 588/1, The Native Courts Proclamation 1901 No. 25 of 1901 cited in Ikime, *Niger Delta Rivalry*, p. 168.

31 Southern Nigerian Government Gazette No. 8, March 30, 1905, pp. 192-95, National Archives Ibadan, hereinafter referred to as NAI.

32 For details on Warrant Chief system, see A. E. Afigbo, "The Warrant Chief System in Eastern Nigeria: Direct or Indirect Rule", *Journal of the Historical Society of Nigeria*, , 3:4, (June, 1967).

33 O. Ikime, *The Isoko People: A Historical Survey*, (Ibadan: Ibadan University Press, 1972), p. 51.

34 O. Ikime, *Nigeria Delta Rivalry*, Chapter 5.

35 F.D. Lugard, *Notes for Political Officers*, Lagos, 1914, Para. 2.

36 *Ibid.*

37 CSO 656/2. The Native Authority Ordinance 1916, (No. XIV of 1916).

38 For details on the career of Chief Dogho, see O. Ikime, "Chief Dogho", *op. cit.*

39 N.A.I., Nigerian Gazette, 13:35 (1926), Notice No. 79.

40 See Chapter 4 of this work for economic explanation of the anti-tax riots.

41 For details on the spread and development of anti-tax riots, see Obaro Ikime, "The Anti-Tax Riots in Warri Province," *Journal of the Historical Society of Nigeria*, 3:3, (December, 1967).

42 N.A.I., Annual Report, Warri Province 1930, File 11857, Vol. VIII. Also see Map IV.

43 N.A.I., Warri Province, War. Prof. 3"15, File 48/1932, Quarterly Reports, Warri Division March 1932. There was no Grade A Courts in

Warri Province. This category was reserved only for the Alkali Courts of Northern Nigeria.

44 C.O. 588/1 Proclamation No. 15 of 1903, cited in Ikime, *Niger Delta Rivalry*, p. 157.

45 Government Gazette, No. 10, June 1904, Quarterly Report, Warri District, January-March, 1904.

46 N.A.I., C.S.O. 1/19, Vol. IV, Annual Report Central Province 1906.

47 Supplement to Southern Nigerian Government Gazette, 30 September 1908, pp. IV-IX; Annual Report on Roads Construction in Central Provinces, 1907.

48 *Ibid.*

49 W. I. Ofonagoro, *Trade and Imperialism in Southern Nigeria, 1881-1929* (New York: NOK Publishers, 1979).

50 See Chapter Six of this work for details on commercial firms.

Chapter 5

Growth and Development of the Palm Produce Industry 1929-1960

As already noted in the last two chapters, palm produce was the most vital export from Nigeria since the abolition of the trans-Atlantic slave trade. Rodney claims that Britain was,

> forced by the internal logic of their competitive system to seek abroad in less developed countries opportunities to control raw materials supplies, to find markets and to find profitable fields of investment."[1]

He adds that,

> Africa's greatest value to Europe at the beginning of the imperialist era was as a source of raw materials such as palm products, groundnuts, cotton and rubber. The need for these materials arose out of Europe's expanded capacity, its new and larger machines and its increasing wage-earning population in towns.

Onimode corroborates this by suggesting that the creation of the colonial economy was associated with the crucial economic requirements of the industrial revolution, which made Britain the "workshop" of the world. This created a serious demand for raw materials and a need to sell manufactures world wide.[3]

This view is strengthened by Falola and Ihonvbere who claim that the principal objective of imposing direct control after the 1884 Berlin Conference included the need to win strategic advantages over the other imperialist nations. This qualified the need to obtain a cheap and constant supply of raw materials, secure markets, obtain outlets for investment and finally, provide employment for British surplus labor.[4]

This contention underlines Ake's argument that colonization was the vehicle for capitalist penetration which involved the creation of sources of cheap raw materials for manufactured goods.[5] These contentions are explicit in the claims of Lord Lugard, one of the principal "dramatis personae" of colonization, that the "Partition of Africa was due primarily to the economic necessity of increasing the supplies of raw materials and food to meet the needs of industrialist Europe."[6]

As already discussed in Chapter 1, some writers believe that colonialism did not exploit but rather expanded agricultural production and introduced incentives which increased peasant productivity.[7] Myint confirmed this contention that colonization helped to maximize African land and labor, which had hitherto been underutilized because of a lack of effective demand for potential increase in output.[8]

The subsistence economy, he posits, did not create enough opportunity for maximum utilization of resources, and consequently, exchange and trade were not optimally developed. Colonialism unleashed "effective demand" by linking the surplus products of the peasants to the world demand, which until that point had been locked up in the subsistence economy.[9] Further, he states that the activities of European firms were advantageous to the peasant, because they provided them with imported goods, encouraging them to produce more.

Helleiner corroborates this view that the appearance of European administration encouraged the sale of cash crops which led to expansion in production.[10] Similarly, McPhee argues that colonization introduced a revolution which culminated in the expansion of trade, in which Africans performed their own part and reaped rewards.[11] He ascribes this to the development of modern transportation system, the establishment of banking and the maintenance of peace and security. These arguments undermine the contribution of internal factors in the development of cash crop production.

General Background and The Growth of the Palm Produce Trade

Evidence abounds that the oil palm is indigenous to tropical West Africa.[12] It grows wildly in the Southern areas (including the Western Delta Nigeria) over a total area of 70,000 square miles.[13] Before palm produce became an important export crop in the nineteenth century, palm oil was a vital food source in the domestic diet. In particular, it provided cooking fat, a staple item in food preparation and processing. Both palm oil and the palm kernel oil were used for medicinal purposes, for lighting and fuel. They were also used for producing soap and lotion.

The palm tree also produces palm wine. From the wine, gin was produced. Both the wine and gin, were of considerable value in rituals and ceremonies like marriages, naming ceremonies, funerals and religious observances. The gin, in particular, being the principal alcoholic drink of the region, was of considerable significance in the social life of the people.

In an agrarian area with low level of technology, the palm tree provided products for construction and industry. Palm kernel shells were used as material for road and home construction. They served as concrete for raising the banks of rivers and streams in low-lying areas.

The ribs of the stalks of the palm trees were used in making fishing equipment, like traps, nets and baskets. The trunk of the tree produces a delicate food item referred to as *edo*, which together with tapiocca is considered a delicacy among the people.

Palm fronds were used for ornamentation during festivals. In particular, young boys and men adorned their bodies with palm fronts in dance performances. In addition, the branches produced poles for buildings and pulling up canoes. The tree was a necessity in the lives of people, obviously, occupying a central position in their socio-cultural and economic system.[14] Trading its products was an important source of wealth. It formed the basis of wealth and economic well-being, occupying the same position for the people as the cow is to the Fulani in the North.

The search for fertile palm groves prompted migratory movement outside of the Delta region. Thus, whether in Yorubaland, Calabarland or even in present day Ghana, the Urhobo/Isoko were always in search of the oil palm tree with which they had become identified. The tree had become synonymous with their economic survival, their lives and activities became tied intrinsically to the oil palm industry.

This development accounts for the fairly large concentration of Urhobo/Isoko in Ife, Ondo, Ekiti and Ijebu Yoruba areas where they have maintained a separate identity despite long periods of interaction with neighboring ethnic groups. In the lower Niger region, it was also a cause for migration from one zone to another. The presence of a large number of Isoko villages in the Aboh and Ijo areas is closely related to late-nineteenth and early-twentieth centuries migrations from the Isoko mainland for economic reasons, the most important of which was the search for new and fertile oil palm areas.[15]

The products of the palm tree formed important items of a viable trade among the peoples of the upper and lower Delta, and between them and others through the trade network along the creeks and rivers. Palm oil became more important in the African-European trade that developed in the nineteenth century in which the Itsekiri and Aboh became middlemen.[16]

Export Trade

Palm produce refers to both palm oil and palm kernel. Of all of Nigeria's principal exports, palm oil has the longest history. It was one of the earliest commodities to be exported from the area now known as Nigeria. It became important in the first half of the nineteenth century with the abolition of the trans-Atlantic slave trade and the inauguration of "legitimate commerce," It formed the basis of the legitimate commerce or new trade and consequently, it became the most important item in British-Nigerian trade.[17]

The increase in the significance and demand of palm oil relates to the demands of the industrial revolution, industrial population and the development of railways. Industrial machinery required lubricants for effective functioning. Palm oil was used for making lubricants in the age when petroleum had not yet been discovered.

Palm oil was also a basic ingredient in the soap making. Soap was a necessity in industries and factories. Also, it became a vital requirement for the growing industrial population of Britain and the rest of Western Europe. Similarly, palm oil was also used in the making of candles and cooking fats.[18]

Palm kernel oil was significant in the manufacture of soap and pharmaceutical products, while the residue was fed to livestock. The significance of palm kernel was further enhanced with the discovery of its use for making margarine in 1870. This significance assured it greater importance than palm oil itself.[19]

From the above, it is needless to emphasize how the industrial revolution tied the resources of the Western Delta to the basic requirements of industrial societies in Britain and the rest of Europe. This explains why procurement of palm oil was so sensitive to British firms and why it was the basis of the European-African trade during the industrial revolution. The Delta region contributed significantly to the palm oil trade which brought Britain and other European powers increasingly into greater contacts with producing areas in present day Nigeria.

Between 1865 and 1910, the export of palm produce from West Africa more than doubled, with Nigeria taking the lead.[20] By 1834, Nigeria was already supplying 14,000 tons of palm oil.[21] This increased to 45,000 tons by the turn of the century. By 1900, palm produce constituted eighty to ninety percent of Nigeria's total exports.[22]

But the value of palm produce in Nigeria's total export began to decline with the export of other products like rubber, cocoa and groundnut after 1900. The volume of palm kernel oil and palm oil exports remained relatively constant from 1900 to 1950, with 450,000 and 200,000 tons for palm oil and palm kernel, respectively. But the total value of palm produce exports declined to twenty-five percent in the same period.[23] This fall in value was due to deteriorating prices after the first World War, a decline which encouraged the farmers of the Western Delta to switch to the production of rubber and food items.

Enlistment in the army also became increasingly attractive to the people because it was financially rewarding in addition to its social advantages. Population growth increased the local demand for palm oil and the price of oil in local markets increased. Therefore, throughout the depression years between the two world wars, the producers sold to the local markets instead of exporting. Improvements in the internal transportation systems also provided a boost to market activities.

Problems of the Palm Produce Trade

After World War I, the primacy of Nigeria in palm produce export was threatened by the growth of scientifically managed plantations in Sumatra, Malaysia and the Belgian Congo, which increasingly began to export higher grades of palm produce.[24] The threat of competition and the challenge of possible displacement raised important and urgent questions in the relative advantages of plantation production.

Although planting in Southeast Asia did not begin until the first decade of the twentieth century, and export not until after World War I, the volume of exports reached 26,246 tons in 1924-8 and grew to 202,161 tons in 1936. This represented 42.2 percent of the world's total exports.[25] In 1937, while exports from West Africa dropped by 20,000 tons, oil exports from Java and Sumatra increased by 15% and by 45% in Malaysia. Another threat was also raised in the Belgian Congo plantations started in 1912 by Sir William Lever.[26]

Plantation trees were hybrids which produced fruits with 30% oil content.[27] Harvesting usually began in five or six years after planting. The methods of production involved minimum waste, ensuring a production of high quality oil with 5% or less of free fatty acid, a higher grade preferred by the industrialists in Europe.

In Nigeria, the production was largely on a small scale by different oil palm collectors who gathered the fruits from wild palms in scattered groves over considerable distances. Harvesting here was tedious. Men climbed the trees which were on the average thirty feet tall, followed by cutting off bunches of palm fruits. Damage was done to fruits as the bunches fell to the ground, making them to ferment more quickly.

Two types of oil, the hard and the soft, were extracted by the traditional method.[28] Production of Soft oil required more labor. It is obtained by boiling and pounding of the palm fruits and then allowing the oil to flow out of the mash. Hard oil is produced through processes which involve fermenting of fruits followed by foot-pounding by men to produce a mash which is mixed with water out of which oil is drained.

Fifty-five percent of hard oil contained a free fatty acid content of upwards of 30%.[29] In the case of soft oil, about 50% of the oil content was extracted with a relatively lower free fatty acid level of between 10 and 25%. By these methods, 100 tons of fruit produced 11 tons of oil, while the plantation method produced 28 tons of oil out of 100 tons of fruit.[30] It is clear that the plantation system was much more effective than the traditional method.

The production of hard oil was popular in the Warri and Benin areas, while soft oil was more common in the Eastern region. In the Western Delta, both types were used interchangeably. The soft oil was used more for lighting and medicinal purposes while the hard oil was preferred for cooking. European firms preferred to purchase the higher quality soft oil.

It should be noted that the plantation production of Southeast Asia and the Belgian Congo was primarily for export, while the Nigerian production was first for local consumption and then for export. The traditional methods and quality of oil they yielded was satisfactory to the people and met local requirements. As overseas demand increased, traditional the methods and quality of oil became inadequate because industrialists preferred the higher quality grades of oil in greater quantities.

It became obvious that if Nigeria was to retain her position in palm produce in the international market, the traditional methods of production had to be modernized. This concern became urgent in the face of the growing challenge from Southeast Asian and Congolese plantations. Therefore, in spite of the growing internal market for oil, the modernized processing of export oil became imperative.[31]

The colonial administration and the expatriate firms heavily depended on palm produce exports (50% of Nigeria's exports) as an important source of revenue.[32] It was in their best interest that the modes of production be advanced in ways that were similar to those of the plantations. It was also feared that a decline in exports might lead to a fall in productivity.[33] The colonial government needed the palm produce export to fund administrative expenses. The commercial firms also had vital stakes in the palm oil trade which had been the basis of international trade, in which they had considerable investments. To industrialists in Britain, sustaining the palm produce trade was important for obtaining vital raw materials. It was, also, important that the level of income and the standard of living of the people did not fall in order to sustain the import trade. A reasonable amount of purchasing power was necessary if the people were to be able to afford some of the imported items which had become necessities, in addition to payment of taxes and other necessary expenditure. Fall in incomes was, therefore, dangerous for all concerned, especially, the industrialists, firms and colonial administration.

But more specifically, in the interest of both internal and external trade, it was proposed that improved methods of production be adopted along the lines of the Southeast Asian and Congolese models. These concerns seriously influenced both government and business circles and they were committed to finding an acceptable solution. Modernization of the industry became the only option as change became imperative in the interest of all concerned. But it must be emphasized that the change that was to take place was more in response to external demands and interests than internal ones.

Government Policy Toward Palm Produce

The initiative for modernizing the Nigerian palm produce trade came from Sir William Lever of Lever Brothers who suggested that concessions be granted to commercial firms to establish plantations. But the introduction of the plantation system in Nigeria was opposed by the British Government, the UAC, John Holt, as well as British public opinion led by E.D. Morel.[34]

They argued that it would disrupt the traditional communal land tenure system which could lead to violent outbursts and protests by the Africans whose land would be alienated. For the government, such an atmosphere would prevent efficient administration and increase costs. But, the main reason why the plantation system was not adopted in Nigeria was its failure in Sierra Leone.[35]

In the face of mounting pressure from the joint West African Committees of Chambers of Commerce of Liverpool, London and Manchester, the Secretary of State for the Colonies set up a committee in 1923 to study the Nigerian palm produce industry and make recommendations for its improvement.[36] The committee urgently made two recommendations: a mechanized system of extraction to enhance quality and minimize waste and, secondly, improvement of the palm groves.

As a result, after 1924, the government experimented with mechanization of the extraction process. The Culley Hand Press was adopted in 1929 and the Duchscher Hand Press in 1932.[37] The first had a capacity for producing five gallons of oil and sold at £15-£35. The second had a capacity for twenty-two gallons and sold between £9 and £13. The latter was German-made, with lower cost and higher capacity, it was preferred to the English made one.[38]

The hand press had a 10% higher extraction rate in comparison with the traditional method. It extracted 65% of the oil content from the fruit, with a free fatty acid rate of 1.5%, or even less.[39] But the adoption of handpresses for processing was slow in spite of their advantages, because the majority of Africans could not afford to buy them.

A more advanced system in mechanized production was attained by the use of the Pioneer Oil Mill. Pioneer Oil Mill was introduced by the United African Company and was adopted by the Department of Agriculture.[40] The Pioneer Oil Mill could extract as much as 85% of the oil content with a free fatty acid rate of less than 5%.[41] But, the cost was higher, ranging from £1,500-£2,000. This made it out of the financial reach of the producers. Thus, it remained a white elephant project until the Department of Agriculture began to install it in strategic locations for the use of producers.

Improvement in Palm Groves

Grove improvement involved the cultivation of improved seedlings in a scientific manner to replace the wild palms in scattered groves. It was expected that the new types of palms would replace the old types. It was to be accomplished by a gradual process of interplanting existing groves with the new seedlings.

It was expected that the scheme would change the people's perception of the oil palm tree and the entire palm produce industry. They were to be educated to consider the oil palm tree as a crop which could be cultivated and tended rather than as just a wild forest tree. It was hoped that through this experience, individual plantations would be encouraged.

Though grove replacement was accepted, it was different from the proposition of Sir William Lever. It did not involve large- scale alienation of land to foreigners nor did it turn peasant farmers to wage earners on white owned plantations, as was the case in the Belgian Congo. Grove replacement was a gradual process which ensured that the land would continue to yield profits while the young palms were reaching maturity.

Plantations Initiative of the United African Company

The first major step toward establishing oil palm plantations on a large-scale was pioneered by the UAC. The UAC, being the biggest trading concern in Nigeria was highly enthused with the idea of boosting palm produce exports. Though the colonial government steadily refused to grant land concessions to firms to establish plantations, it did make one exception by granting plantation concessions to the UAC.

The UAC established plantations at Ajagbodudu (Cowan Estate) in the Western Delta, Ikotombo in Calabar and Ndian in Cameroon.[42] It was expected that the plantations would serve and encourage farmers to establish new palm plots. The UAC plantations were expected to work closely with the Department of Agriculture in the supply of improved seedlings and fertilizers to the people in the grove replacement exercise.

Cowan Estate

Cowan Estate is located on the Benin River between Koko and Ajagbodudu. Work started in 1935, and by 1941, a total of 6869 acres of oil palms had been planted.[43] Apart from 400 acres of thick shelled deli palms, the entire estate was planted with selected seeds of the thin-shelled lisombe variety.[44] Soil fertility was encouraged by planting a mixture of leguminous covers.

Experiments with manure were also carried out to help discover the most economical and efficient method of maintaining soil fertility and high crop yields. The Department of Agriculture cooperated in all these and participated actively in these experiments with a view to extending benefits to the farmers and government nurseries.

The estate also agreed to undertake a program of propaganda in conjunction with the Department of Agriculture. It encouraged its workers and the neighboring people to take to palm plot development on their own. It was hoped that the introduction of selected seedlings, scientifically cultivated under the guidance of the estate's officials and the Department of Agriculture would gradually spread into adjoining communities.

In addition, the services of its Pioneer Oil Mill were to be made available to producers to enhance the production of high quality oil.[45] The company was the only source of supply of improved seedlings to the Department of Agriculture and to local producers. This estate was the only source of supply of improved seedlings in the Western Delta and throughout the palm-producing area. Through this the UAC played a crucial role in the new scheme and in the gradual disappearance of wild palm in the Western Delta and throughout the palm producing areas.

The response of the people around the estate was low because of the difficulty of obtaining land for individual plot development. The absence of statistical data makes it impossible to relate the level of output of the mills. The estate began production in 1941, and because of the efficiency of the Pioneer Oil Mill, it installed two more mills to enhance high quality oil production.[46]

By 1951, the mills employed about 894 laborers and artisans, most of who came from various parts of the Western Delta and other parts of Southern Nigeria, largely from the Igbo and Benin areas.[47] Apart from exposing these workers to the mechanized plantation system, the estate provided improved living conditions for them with such modern facilities like pipe-borne water, electricity, school, hospital, market, play ground and a church.[48] Further an anti-mosquito program was launched to rid the estate of mosquitoes while flush toilets were also provided.

Compared to the surrounding community, the Cowan housing scheme with its advanced facilities was a much more improved housing system. These provisions were aimed at creating a "contented" labor force which would ensure that workers maximized their output. The neighboring people were allowed to use some of the services of the estate (school, church, market, roads) at no cost. Thus, the company did for the people what the government should have done.

It has been asserted that the establishment of the estate created a distortion within the larger community by juxtaposing modern housing conditions within a rural social environment hardly touched by modern influences.

Others have contended that the creation of this modern community was necessary to maximize production and resource utilization. Therefore, the benefits which accrued to the workers are considered as indirect benefits rather than direct ones. The UAC acted in its self-interest to maximize production and enhance profits.

In spite of the lack of statistical evidence to substantiate the actual number of seedlings supplied to the Department of Agriculture and the people, it can be argued that the Cowan estate was at the center of the palm-produce modernization program in the Western Delta, and that it contributed significantly to the overall production of better quality oil in the region, especially after 1947.[49]

Reactions of the People To Innovations

The reactions of people are illustrated by responses to plot development and the adoption of the Pioneer Oil Mill.

Plot Development

The people regarded plot development with suspicion and distrust. The oil palm tree had an important position in the socio-cultural and economic systems of the people. The tree was regarded as an inheritance to be passed from one generation to the another.

Initially, the people were unwilling to accept the notion of the tree as a crop to be cultivated on individual plots. This explains why the development of individual plots did not begin until 1934, six years after it was officially introduced by the Department of Agriculture. The people feared that adoption of the plantation system would interfere with their traditional economic and cultural values and would have serious adverse effects on their well-being.

The implications of the plantation system on land tenure was bound to be profound. Land was based on collective ownership, and held in trust for the people by the elders. Oil palm trees grew wildly on community lands and did not belong to particular individuals. Rather it belonged to the whole community.

Plot development stressed individualization of land over collective ownership. Therefore, the introduction of individual plots was a radical departure from the existing system. Change posed difficulties for potential plot owners.

The elders, as custodians of tradition, were more resistant to change because they perceived that individualization of land would deprive them of control over land matters and would weaken their authority in the community, especially among the youth. Thus their fear of erosion of authority made them adopt a stiff resistance to granting land to people to develop plots.

This attitude appears more rigid among the Urhobo/Isoko where land was scarce and there was substantial pressure on land. Population pressure on land had been responsible for numerous inter-clan disputes.[50] In Aboh division, especially among the Ukwuani, pressure on land was less severe and they were less resistant to the innovation of plot development.

There were many stages that potential plot owners had to go through before the development of plots began. The first stage began with seeking allocation of land from the village elders. The next stage was acceptance of approval by the District Officer who alone could authorize the Department of Agriculture to supply improved seedlings and give required advice and directives for laying out and maintaining young palms.

This stage was important for the success of the program. An unauthorized planter would not have the benefit of obtaining seedlings or visitations by Agricultural Assistants. The final stage involved the permission of the Divisional Officer if he was pleased with the report of the District Officer and the Agricultural Department.

This complex bureaucratic process caused delays and uncertainties. It appears that obtaining the approval of the village council was a fundamental stage of the process. Planting was also complicated by a shortage of seedlings.

The UAC had a monopoly on the supply of seedlings through the Department of Agriculture. Shortages caused delays and created distortions in the plots as some planters resorted to planting wild palms, as was the case in 1937.[51] In Urhobo Division, the ratio of wild plots to that of selected seedlings was 1:3 while in Aboh Division it was 1:2.[52]

Tables I and II show the progress of planting improved seedlings in both Aboh and Urhobo Divisions. The figures demonstrate growth in the cultivation of improved oil palm trees. It suggests that the response of the people to the program became increasingly favorable.

Even though planting began one year earlier in Aboh Division, Urhobo Division had larger acreage under cultivation with fewer planters, by 1937.[53] Urhobo/Isoko clans had higher

Table I: Progress of Planting Oil Palm Trees in Urhobo/Isokoland, 1932-37

Year	Number of Planters	Number of Extensions	Acreage
1932	4	–	19.2
1933	3	3	16.4
1934	–	1	0.2
1935	6	2	21.0
1936	2	4	9.0
1937	8	1	12.7
Total	23	11	78.5

Source: Ughelli Dist. I, File No. 391, Annual Report, 1937.

Table II: Progress of Planting Oil Palm Trees in Aboh Division, 1931-37

Year	Number of Planters	Number of Extensions	Acreage
1931*	1	–	2.2
1932	1	1	3.0
1933	–	1	1.3
1934	7	1	6.2
1935	9	3	12.1
1936	6	11	18.0
1937	15	5	32.7
Total	39	22	73.5

*Planting started one year earlier in Aboh Division
Source: Kwale District, Kwale District 2, File No. KNA 143.

stakes in oil production than the Ukwuani-Aboh. As already noted, the oil palm industry was the major preoccupation of the Urhobo/Isoko whereas food production and trade were more activities of the Aboh-Ukwuani.

It was easier for the Urhobo/Isoko groups to adapt to the changes in oil palm cultivation. The tables show that between 1935-37 there was an increase in planting. This may be attributed to the partial recovery in the price of palm oil after the Great Depression, as illustrated in Table III.

Table III: Palm Oil: Produce Price £/Ton

Year	£/Ton	Year	£/Ton	Year	£/Ton	Year	£/Ton
1911	24.0	1934	5.0	1944	10.1	1954	65.0
1915	18.3	1935	11.4	1945	12.3	1955	58.0
1919	43.9	1936	10.6	1946	13.1	1956	50.0
1923	23.6	1937	13.4	1947	15.3	1957	50.0
1927	22.5	1938	6.4	1948	35.25	1958	50.0
1929	23.7	1939	5.8	1949	42.75	1959	47.75
1930	16.0	1940	5.9	1950	42.75	1960	47.75
1931	6.3	1941	6.0	1951	55.0	1961	47.75
1932	9.6	1942	6.2	1952	61.0	1962	40.0
1933	7.0	1943	9.4	1953	75.7	1963	40.0

Source: G. K. Helleiner, *Peasant Agriculture, Tovernment and Economic Growth*, (Homewood, Illinois: R. D. Irwin, 1966).

The acreage under cultivation continued to grow and by 1946 there were over 101 acres of plots in Urhobo Division and 99 in Aboh Division. It is difficult to entirely attribute this to rising prices, however. A plausible explanation lay in the dynamism and enterprise of the people who required cash earned from sale of produce to meet their social and economic obligations. It was people's responses to challenges of the new society like the payment of taxes, school fees for children and the need to purchase essential items such as kerosene. These needs motivated people to increase acreage and productivity. Also during this period, palm produce economy lost labor to the more lucrative undertakings of rubber and food production. Losses were also sustained by rural-rural migration for better economic opportunity.

People were drawn to other more profitable oil palm tree belts, rubber estates, logging, sawmilling, and the timber industry at Sapele. Others were attracted to urban areas for trade, port activities, and to other aspects of the economy.[54] What these movements signify is expansion of economic opportunities and less reliance on land as the only means of livelihood.

Reaction to Mechanized Extraction (Pioneer Oil Mill)

The adoption of the hand presses was not popular in the area because many producers could not afford to purchase them. It was not until introduction of the Pioneer Oil Mills by the government that the people were reasonably exposed to the mechanized system of extraction.[55] In the Western Delta, the response of the people was affected by the nature of mill operations and the basic characteristics of the traditional pattern of palm production.

Initially, people's reactions to the mills included general resentment, irregular patronage and boycott, especially in the Urhobo/Isoko areas. Installation of the mill involved compensation for land and crops. In most cases, the capacity of the mill could not cope with the volume of palm nuts. Consequently, the people began to boycott the mills. This action was prominent among the Isoko around the Ivrogbo Mill established in 1952. It resulted in the total inactivity of the mill and its eventual closure in 1954.

The problem of the inability of the mills to cope with the volume of fruit was a general one, but was more acute in areas which had denser palm groves.[56] The capacity of the mill was limited to extracting sixteen tons of fruit per day. Associated with this was resentment over rejection of fruits which were deficient because they were already fermenting.

It has been stated that wild palms normally grow 30-35 feet high and stand scattered in groves often at some distance from the villages. The process of harvesting involved climbing the tree and hacking the bunches off. As the bunches fell to the ground, damage resulted to the fruit which then soon began to spoil and ferment. The difficulty of the use of headportage for conveying the fruits increased fermentation which was further intensified by the hot weather. In a period when many people could not afford bicycles, and road transport was little developed, the fruit did not arrive at the mills in conditions of optimal freshness.

Often, the mill officials rejected the fruits, prompting resentment against the mill and its officials. This situation had serious implications when one understands how important palm produce income was to the people. This was in addition to the painful waste of energy. Compensation for economies destroyed in the face of installation of new mills created difficulties for both the mills and the people. As in the case of the Ukan Mill, the first to be established in 1949, payment of compensation caused delays in the signing of leases with community leaders.[57]

There was a more uneven distribution of Pioneer Oil Mills in the Urhobo/Isoko region than in the Ukwuani-Aboh area. This can be explained by the fact that the Urhobo/Isoko produced mainly hard oil. Pioneer Oil Mills were installed to minimize the production of hard oil, not to mention the fact that the Urhobo/Isoko region was the center of the oil palm belt.

The operation of the Pioneer mill involved the loss of palm kernel in oil production. Women suffered loss of activity and income. Traditionally, the men produced the oil and the women processed the kernels for sale. The income derived from the sales provided clothing, for the children and husband, and for themselves. Thus, loss of this income undermined family incomes and reduced the financial power of women.

Locating mills also contributed to intra-clan land disputes. The compensation paid to landowners was attractive enough for villages within clans to vie for the location of mills. For example, among the Udu clan, there was a dispute between Obodo and Omia, both of the Udu clan, over the location of a Pioneer Oil Mill.[58] Such disputes caused delays in signing of leases, and therefore production was delayed as well. But there were instances where land owners did not seek compensation. This was the case with Ekakpamre (Urhobo Division) mill established in 1953.

The installation of Pioneer Oil Mills in the Aboh area created fewer problems as the people looked upon them more favorably and resentment there was minimized. The first mill in Aboh Division was built at Iselegu on Ase creek in 1952.[59] This occurred three years after the first was built in Urhobo Division. By 1953, mills were constructed at Ashaka and Asaba Assey on Ase creek. By the end of the period under investigation, there were eight mills in the Urhobo area and three in Aboh Division.

Often mills were located at strategic centers of trade and many were also trading stations of European firms. Pioneer oil mills enhanced the significance of commercial centers. Ivrogbo (Isoko) had been an important center of trade and was a UAC station. Its market served the Isoko, Aboh and Ijo areas. Similarly Ekakpamre (Urhobo) attracted traders from Isoko, Ijo and Urhobo areas while Iselegu (Aboh) served the Ukwuani, Aboh and some of the Isoko clans.

From 1950s to 1960, Pioneer Oil Mills became increasingly popular and there was an upsurge in applications to the authorities of Western Nigerian Development Board for establishment of mills. Most of these requests did not include compensation request.[60] Increasing popularity of mills can be attributed to the growing awareness of the need to produce higher quality grades of palm oil.

Mills became associated with progress and modernity, enhancing the status of the towns in which they were located. The presence of government officials and visits by supervising staff of the Department of Agriculture further brought new attractions to the locations of the mills.

There was a contradiction between operations of the mills and the realities of palm production by farmers. This contradiction created a lack of understanding between the two. The problem of collecting fruits from wild palm trees was not adequately addressed before the installation of Pioneer mills. This would have minimized rejection of fruits. Also, the program failed to adapt the new program to the socio-economic system of the people. Such adaptations would have minimized the difficulties connected with loss of palm kernels and income. Some of the problems related to the lack of trained local personnel to man the operations or the mills.

Although focus has been on two areas, it should be noted that some planting did take place among the Itsekiri, who had planted some 35 acres by 1938. But, by 1960, the trees had died off. The Itsekiri did not appear to pay sufficient attention to palm trees. Their attention and interest turned on other commercial activities.

The Urhobo continued to increase acreage, in spite of poor prices until 1946, because they were used to producing palm oil and kernel. The push for greater activity was dictated by the need to satisfy vital socio-economic needs in addition to tradition. This increase in acreage was largely due to internal factors, with the external ones playing less significant role.

In the Western Delta it is not possible to ascribe the increase in productivity to the impact of missionary enterprise or modernized transportation as has been claimed by Helleiner (1966). The area was not seriously touched by developments in transportation, especially railways and major roads. Only feeder roads constructed by the communities provided transportation for the evacuation of produce. It can be asserted that though the government adopted a consistently progressive attitude toward the palm industry, some aspects of the program were inadequately and inappropriately implemented, as demonstrated from the examples of the installations of the Pioneer Oil Mills. The Department of Agriculture could not satisfy all the demand for mills, even when the people involved were willing to contribute meaningfully to the construction of access roads, as demonstrated in the cases of Igbide and Olomoro in Isokoland and Mereje in Western Urhoboland.[61] To this extent, it is difficult to support the claim that the colonial government consistently provided the necessary incentives for increased and improved production.

In conclusion, it may be argued that the modernization programs in palm produce were initiated in the interest of the government and commercial firms, especially the UAC. Such a policy was crucial to maintaining Nigeria's exports in the international market. Modernization program engendered considerable changes. More significant among them was a new awareness and sensitivity to the palm tree as a crop which could be cultivated. Mechanization of production did not fundamentally affect the people, especially as the prices of extraction equipment was beyond their financial capability. For the majority, change to mechanization was an imposition which did not take the traditional systems into consideration.

Women were hard hit by loss of kernels to the mills. They did not have a share in the money which accrued to their spouses from sale of palm oil. The British administrators seemed to have confused the British family system with the African–Nigerian family values. Therefore, those who imposed the mechanized system of pioneer oil mill did not take the nature of families and welfare of the people into account. What mattered to the British was production of high grades in greater quantities. In promoting mechanization, the UAC did what the government was expected to have done. But, in view of the nature of the relationship between government and the firms, what was good for one was good for the other.

Notes

1 W. Rodney *How Europe Underdeveloped Africa*.(Washington.D.C. Howard University Press 1982). p. 136.
2 *Ibid.*
3 Bade Onimode *Imperialism and Underdevelopment in Nigria.* The Dialectics of Mass Poverty.(London. Zed.1983) p.131.
4 Ihonvbere and Falola," Colonialism and Exploitation" in Falola, T. *ed. Britain and Nigeria:Development or Exploitation.*(London.Zed, 1978) p. 26
5 C. Ake, *A Political Economy of Africa.* (London. Longman 1981) pp. 17-20.
6 F. J. D. Lugard, *The Dual Mandate* (London: Frank Cass, 1965), p. 613.
7 *See* Chapter 1 of this book.
8 Myint, "The "Classical Theory" of International Trade and Underdeveloped Countries," *Economic Journal,* 68, June 1958
9 Hla Myint, The *Economics of the Developing Countries.* (London: Hutchinson,1967) pp. 42-43.
10 G. K. Helleiner, *Peasant Agriculture, Government and Economic Growth in Nigeria* (Homewood, IL: R. D. Irwin, 1966), p. 3.
11 Alan McPhee, *The Economic Revolution in British West Africa* (London: Routledge and Sons, 1926), pp. 104-105.
12 Helleiner, op. cit., p. 91.
13 *UAC Statistical and Economic Review,* No. 7, 1949.
14 It produced the thatches for roofs, poles for raising the roof of houses, brooms for home use, baskets for domestic and farming use, trays for use for drying, containers for storage and foot mats, soaps, lotion and fuel.
15 A. I. Apena, "Isoko of the Niger: Some References to Tradition of Origin," *Nigerian Magazine,* Vol. 53, No. 4, October-December 1985. pp. 25-30.
16 *See* Chapter 2 of this book.
17 K.O. Dike, *Trade and Politics in the Niger Delta, 1830-1855: An Introduction to the Economic and Political History of Nigeria* (London: O.U.P., 1956), Chapter 3.
18 K. O. Dike, *op. cit,* pp. 49-51.
19 Helleiner, *op. cit.*, p. 97.
20 N. H. Stilliard, "The Rise and Development of Legitimate Trade in Palm Oil in West Africa," (M.A. Thesis, History) University of Birmingham, October 1938, p. 158.
21 Dike, *op. cit.*, pp. 49-51.
22 Helleiner, *op. cit.*, p. 97.
23 *Ibid.*

24 Stilliard, *op. cit.*, p. 160.
25 D. Forde, "The Native Economics of Nigeria", in M. Perham, ed., *The Economics of a Tropical Dependency,* (London: Faber and Faber, 1941), Vol. I, p. 225.
26 *Ibid.*
27 Forde, *op. cit.*, p. 229.
28 Interview with Chief Omena Oyibo at Oleh (Isoko), August, 1986.
29 *UAC Statistical and Economic Review*, No. 7, March, 1951.
30 *Ibid.*
31 Forde, *op. cit.*, p. 231.
32 *Ibid.*
33 Stilliard, *op. cit.*, p. 161.
34 L. R. Buell, *The Native Problem in Africa*, Vol. I, (New York: Macmillan, 1928), p. 770.
35 Stilliard, p. 162.
36 Forde, *op. cit.*, p. 232.
37 *UAC Statistical and Economic Review*, No. 7, March, 1951.
38 See Chapter 7 below for detailed discussion on hand presses.
39 *UAC Statistical and Economic Review*, No. 7.
40 *Ibid.*
41 *See* Chapter 7 below for details on comparison of hand press and pioneer oil mill.
42 *UAC Statistical and Economic Review*, No. 9, March, 1952.
43 Warri Province, War Prof. I, *Annual Report*, File 11857, Vol. XV.
44 *Ibid.*
45 *Ibid.*
46 *UAC Statistical and Economic Review* 7 (March, 1951).
47 Sapele Dist. 1/1/306.
48 *Ibid.*
49 *UAC Statistical and Economic Review* 7 (1952).
50 Obaro Ikime, *The Niger Delta Rivalry* (New York: Humanities Press, 1969), pp. 1-43.
51 *Ibid.*
52 Ughelli Dist. I File 391, *op. cit.*
53 *Ibid.*
54 N.A.I., Warri Province, War. Prof. I File WP 235, Vol. III, Palm Planting.
55 See Chapters 6 and 7 of this book.
56 See chapter seven below for detailed discussion.
57 N.A.I.: File 1315, Urhobo Division, Ughelli District Ivrogbo Pioneer Oil Mill.
58 N.A.I., Warri Province, War. Prof. I File 1309, Asagba Western Urhobo Pioneer Oil Mill, Plantation and Nursery.
59 N.A.I.: Kwale Dist. I File 1308, Ukan Pioneer Oil Mill.

60 N.A.I.: File 1315, Urhobo Division, Ughelli District Ivrogbo Pioneer Oil Mill; also N.A.I. Kwale Dist. 1 File 1316, Proposed Pioneer Oil Mill, Plantation and Nursery for Omia.

61 N.A.I., Warri Province, War. Prof. I File 1309, Asagba Western Urhobo Pioneer Oil Mill, Plantation and Nursery; also Kwale Dist., 1 File 1316, *op. cit.*

62 N.A.I.: War. Prof. I File 1308, Ukan Pioneer Oil Mill.

63 N.A.I., Kwale Dist. I File 1316, Proposed Pioneer Oil Mill, Plantation and Nursery for Omia.

64 N.A.I., Kwale Dist. I File 1316, Aboh Division Pioneer Oil Mills Iselegu.

Chapter 6

The Growth and Development of the Rubber Industry, 1929-1960

Origin of the Rubber Industry

The expansion of the rubber industry is one of the most phenomenal developments in industrial history. Until the invention of railways in 1825, and the discovery of the vulcanizing process in 1840, the world market demand for natural rubber was almost negligible.[1] Rubber was used predominantly for the manufacture of footwear, toys and floor mats.

But, within the first half of the nineteenth century, its value increased substantially in industrial Europe and North America. Natural rubber was used not only in making springs for increased comfort on trains, but also to make conveyor belts, medical and surgical appliances as well as the insulation of electrical cables and wires.

The industrial demand for rubber increased in the 1880's with the invention of pneumatic tires by John Boyd Dunlop, followed by Michelin in 1895.[2] To meet the rising demand, merchants and industrialists turned to tropical territories in search of supplies. Before the nineteenth century, Brazil was the first major supplier of natural rubber. Her supplies were exhausted within a short time owing to crude and reckless tapping method described as slaughter tapping.

From the 1860's, attention turned to Madagascar, Mozambique, Angola and the Congo. West Africa joined the rubber trade in the 1870's and 1880's. By 1875, Sierra Leone assumed a leading position in West African rubber export, followed by Ghana. By the 1890's, Lagos Colony had emerged as the world's third largest producer of rubber.[3]

The increase in the demand for rubber in the 1880's coincided with depression in the palm produce trade of West Africa. Therefore, the rubber trade became important to both traders and the colonial administrators. To the latter it became a profitable source of earning revenue for colonial administration, and therefore offsetting losses sustained from palm produce sales. Apart from guaranteeing stable finances for development, it promoted the diversification of the economy and reduced dependence on a single export cash crop such as palm produce. Thus, rubber was seen in both government and business circles as a useful alternative or complement to palm produce.

Using the vent for surplus production theory, writers like Mcphee, Myint and Helleiner claim that the expansion in rubber production and export was due to external trade, stressing also that colonialism did ctreate effective demand by linking up the world market for the type of things which the peasants could produce with the surplus capacity, had locked up in the subsistence economy. In this perspective, the role of the people is neglected while local and internal dynamics are de-emphasized.

It may be argued that the efforts of the colonial authority under governor Moloney would not have been sufficient to guarantee sustained production without the enthusiasm and interest of the people. It is infact, the combination of three factors, the pressure of external demand, the efforts of the colonial administration and commercial firms as well as the commitment of the people which sustained increased production and exports.

Early History of the Rubber Industry in Nigeria

Until the introduction of higher rubber yielding trees from Brazil in 1895, rubber-bearing trees and wild vines which grew wildly provided the first source of rubber exports. The first major Nigerian exports of rubber came from the colony of Lagos and its hinterland. Exports rose from 634 lbs. in 1885 to 6,484,365 lbs. in 1896.[4] But production declined within a short time. By 1899, seventy-five percent of the rubber trees had died and exports had fallen to 1,780,000 lbs.[5] The decline was due to reckless tapping methods.

But there was an increase in production in the Niger Coast Protectorate from 520,000 lbs in 1897 to lbs. to 880,000 lbs. in 1899.[6] This increase took place after the British conquest of Benin and expulsion of the Oba of Benin in 1897. The Royal Niger Company and Sir Ralph Moor, the High Commissioner of the Protectorate, encouraged the cultivation and production of rubber on all available communal land.

A. and F. Swanzy, an expatriate commercial firm, received a monopoly concession from the Lagos colonial administration to exploit and promote rubber trade in the Ibadan-Ijebu forest region. This monopoly deprived indigenous tappers of active participation in rubber production in the area. They were forced to migrate southeastward to the forest areas of Benin, the Anambra River valley and the upper Cross River in search of rubber trees to tap. These regions were rich in rubber resources which were virtually unexploited up to this time. In 1899, while Lagos colony exported £160,000 of rubber, the rest of Southern Nigeria exported £1,500.[7] This could be attributed to the intensive exploitation of rubber by A and F. Swanzy.

The policy of promoting the cultivation of higher yielding (Funtumia Elastica) rubber trees on communal land was part of a general colonial policy on Forest Preservation of 1905.[8] The Benin area responded positively to the policy of planting rubber trees. C. Cuberth reports that every village in Benin had its own communal plantation.[9] E.D. Morel also claims that about 700 villages in Benin had planted 100,000 trees. By 1913, the export of rubber from the area exceeded 100,000 lbs.[10] The highest export volumes were recorded in 1906 and 1914.

The colonial office favored the granting of concessions to commercial firms for exploitation of forest resources. This was opposed by Sir Ralph Moor who contended that such an imposition would lead to dissatisfaction among the people and create difficulties for the administration. He stated that, the natives should be taught to exploit the vegetable products of their country.[11]

In the Benin region, the exploitation of rubber was regulated by a policy described as the Benin Conditions. According to this, tappers were required to obtain a license for ten shillings, pay an annual fee of ten shillings on all rubber collected and pay a royalty fee of thirty shillings. Owners of rubber trees were to use half of the revenue collected to replant rubber trees.

By 1902, the amount of royalty fees in the area amounted to £702. The policy imposed a lot of constraints on local producers especially as they could not market their products without a license. It is not surprising that many could not afford to pay the cost of the license.

Government Policy Towards Rubber Production

Neither the home government nor the colonial administration had a coherent policy towards rubber production in Nigeria. Both attitudes and policies vacillated. Their responses were determined by international interests and market conditions which were not sensitive to local interests and the concerns of the people. Such attitude helped to create distortions in the local economy and confusion in the minds of the people who were frequently disturbed by these vacillations in official policy.

Up to 1921, the colonial government supported the cultivation of rubber. It supplied improved seedlings as well as technical advice to planters and tappers. The Department of Forestry and Agriculture established demonstration plots for the supply of improved seedlings in Southern Nigeria. By 1916, the Department had distributed about 149,000 seedlings. This practice enabled the replacement of wild rubber species.

But the government reversed its policy between 1921 and 1935, and became indifferent to producers' interests and efforts. It adopted the Stevenson Scheme of 1921 aimed at regulating the volume of rubber production and export to the British and other international markets.[12] According to this scheme, each rubber producing region in the world was allocated a proportion of total requirement of rubber by Britain and other industrial nations with a view to harmonizing demand with supply. This policy demonstrated the high dependence of the colonial economy on that of the metropole. It confirmed the weakness of the colonial economy and the helplessness of the producers. Although the government became indifferent to the rubber industry in Nigeria, expansion of acreage and production continued. Better world prices for rubber in comparison with the depressed prices of palm produce seemed to have provided some incentive for expansion and consequent defiance of government directives.[13]

In 1928, over 2,000 tons were exported. People were motivated to expand in order to earn cash to meet the growing needs and demands of the changing society. In this case, external factors, did not necessarily promote the expansion of efforts and production. [14]

With the approach of the Second World War, and the rise in the importance of natural rubber, the government changed its policy and began to encourage the cultivation and production of rubber. The effect of the second world war on the rubber industry will be discussed later in this chapter. But it will suffice to state here that Japanese occupation of Malaysia and other Southeast Asian rubber producing territories in 1942 and, consequently, the shortage of rubber supplies from this attractive source prompted a renewed interest in Nigerian rubber production.

Thus, in Nigeria, production was only encouraged when South East Asian supplies were cut off. As the war came to a close, and the supplies from South east Asia became assured again, Nigerian rubber was shunned again. The demand for natural rubber during the Korean war led to another show of interest in rubber production in Nigeria. This momentum continued until 1960 as shown in Table IV.[15]
The decision to encourage Nigerian rubber even at this time was essentially in the interest of the colonizing power and its allies. It was without regard to the effects of such policy on economy and people of the Western Delta.

The response and reactions of the people to Rubber cultivation and production can be examined at two levels. The first

Table IV: Rubber Export from Nigeria, 1900-1960

Year	Volume in Tons	Value ( )	Price per Ton
1900	1,271.27	185,528	145.95
1901	863.59	121,674	140.89
1902	454.04	56,217	123.82
1904	1,193.93	181,952	152.40
1905	1,390.12	249,635	178.14
1906	1,533.16	307,076	200.29
1908	545.63	98,529	180.58
1909	619.65	109,075	176.03
1910	1,175.90	311,691	265.09
1911	966.20	179,353	185.63
1912	705.00	125,021	177.33
1913	510.75	89,995	176.21
1914	166.47	38,854	233.21
1915	248.20	38,112	153.42
1916	395.68	34,192	86.41
1917	392.09	32,350	82.51
1918	157.38	19,667	124.97
1919	398.25	43,903	110.24
1920	491.91	57,044	15.96
1921	85.19	10,248	120.67
1922	124.25	14,377	115.71
1923	214.58	21,221	99.26
1924	522.11	52,437	100.43
1925	950.21	108,234	113.91
1926	1,594.19	203,143	127.43
1927	1,997.12	236,020	128.19
1928	2,294.21	255,771	111.49
1929	1,974.05	163,864	82.93
1930	2,177.31	150,326	69.04
1931	1,821.36	71,319	39.16
1932	845.41	31,362	37.10
1933	1,007.29	33,089	32.25
1934	1,612.76	44,488	27.35
1935	2,058.89	61,522	29.91
1936	2,172.72	90,137	41.40
1946	11,488.00	1,404,000	122.21
1947	7,445.00	677,000	90.93
1948	8,019.00	719,000	89.68
1949	6,858.00	391,000	86.18
1950	13,652.00	2,834,000	207.59

Table IV: Continued

Year	Volume in Tons	Value ( )	Price per Ton
1951	20,856.00	7,483,000	358.79
1952	18,331.00	4,138,746	255.78
1953	21,260.00	3,286,522	154.59
1954	20,397.00	28,448,933	139.67
1955	30,329.00	5,566,859	183.55
1956	38,032.00	6,382,422	187.82
1957	39,946.00	7,012,201	175.54
1958	41,130.00	7,617,019	183.19
1959	53,352.00	11,602.00	217.47
1960	57,167.00	14,241,223	249.12

Source: K.R. Anschell, "Economic Aspects of Rubber Production in Mid-West Nigeria," (Michigan State University, Ph.D. Thesis, 1965).

is the plantation experience of expatriate commercial firms, and the second is the efforts of indigenous people at plantation and the small-scale levels.

Expatriate Rubber Plantations

Pamol Estate

Pamol started as Sapele Rubber Estate and Jamieson River Estate founded by the firm of Miller Brothers in 1895. Located in the Sapele area, it was the first expatriate rubber estate in the Western Delta.[16] By 1925, 2,500 acres of rubber plantation had been established and production began in 1910 and 1925, respectively.[17]

These plantations introduced major changes in the rubber industry, not only in the Western Delta, but also in the entire country. They demonstrated the advantages of high yielding rubber trees, the Funtumia elastica.[18] Also, they introduced improved methods of production, especially, mechanized methods of processing while utilizing organized forms of labor. But their output was not sufficient to make Nigeria a serious threat to Southeast Asian rubber where production was based on the plantation system. Inspite of this, production from the Sapele estates was a major contribution to the increase in Nigerian rubber exports in the 1920's.

In 1936, the Sapele and Jamieson estates became known as Pamol Rubber Estate, after their acquisition in the same year by Pamol, a subsidiary of Unilever.[19]

Production process was intensive and required a large labor force for tapping, grading, sorting and packing. This attracted migrations from other parts of Southern Nigeria, in particular, from Calabar, Igbo, Ishan and the Benin area.

The estate was declared a health labor area in accordance with Section Two of the Labor Ordinance of 1929 which provided housing and basic human facilities for a labor force. From the 1920s, Labor camps were established within the estates to accommodate the workers.

In 1938, Pamol constructed homes of concrete blocks, provided social amenities like playing fields, dispensary, school, market and church, for the workers.[20] These facilities were aimed at making the workers more comfortable and contented, and, consequently, more productive. The interaction of migrants workers of different ethnic groups served as an integrative mechanism in inter-ethnic relations.

Some of the facilities, school, road and market were used by members of the larger community outside of the estate. As noted in the previous chapter, the firm was criticized for creating social division within the society by creating "modern" sector separate from the traditional community.[21] However, this study notes that provision of amenities was the firms best way of maximizing productivity among its labor force.

They fulfilled their obligation towards the communities by paying rent for use of the land of the estate. The extension of the estates facilities could be considered as some of the mutual benefits of the presence of the commercial firms.[22] These provisions increased the welfare of the people. The plantations and the estate community vitalized the area by stimulating other social and economic activities. More significantly, the Pamol estate became a model in the rubber industry.

The period between the two world wars also witnessed the influx of rubber purchasing firms to Sapele.[23] In particular, the Bata Shoe Company and the UAC sought to purchase and lease mature rubber trees for tapping.[24] In addition, a few indigenous people established large estates.

Indigenous Plantations

Having worked with the firm of Miller Brothers early in the century, J.A. Thomas, an Itsekiri, established his own rubber estate near Sapele in 1916. The estate began production in the first half of the 1920's.[25] I. T. Palmer, and J. Asaboro, established similar plantations in the Sapele area during the same period.[26] These estates made contributions to the increase in exports during the 1930's.

Small-Scale Indigenous Rubber Plantations

The people of the Western Delta responded favorably to the attractive rubber production. Initially they obtained seedlings and technical advice from the Department of Agriculture. But faced with shortage of improved seedlings after 1921, when the government discouraged further distribution, they reverted to planting the wild species. It could be argued here, that this colonial policy had a distorting effect on the local economy and people.

The first indigenous small scale-rubber cultivations took place in Agbarha in the Urhobo, and Ukwuani areas where dry and high lands suitable for rubber trees were available. As a general rule, however, the people were confronted with problems of land insufficiency, lack of capital to establish required infrastructure and conflicting government policies.

The colonial administration was committed to maintaining the traditional land tenure system, not wanting to interfere with it in order to avoid conflicts among the people and between the people and the administration. It was believed that large-scale land alienation for the purpose of cultivation could disrupt the social, economic and cultural systems of the people.

To the people, land alienation to foreigners would mean a loss of invaluable property, the only security they had in their predominantly agrarian society. Such a radical departure would upset the traditional balance of power held by the elders and clan heads on whom the administration depended for support in the execution of its programs. There was fear that such loss of power could be detrimental to the implementation of government programs.

Government's restriction orders on continued expansion of rubber acreage provoked resentment first among the Ukwuani. Prohibition orders forbidding rubber planting in certain zones in order to make more land available for food production were instituted.[27] Although the people who undertook illegal planting were prosecuted, fined or imprisoned, they claimed that they had an inalienable right to freely use their land in whatever way they saw fit so long as they did not break their own customs and laws. But, the people did not realize that their system was no longer autonomous and that their economic decisions now depended on external interests deemed paramount.

Continued defiance of the prohibition orders was blamed by the government on the collaboration of Agricultural Assistants and incitement of the educated members of the community, the inefficiency and complicity of the courts and councils. The participation of all segments of the community in rubber production rendered the prohibition orders ineffective.

The authorities' argument that continued cultivation was impeding food production did not even convince the people. But, this argument was unsustainable because food shortage and rise in food prices were related to the broad socio-economic changes of the period. To isolate rubber production as the primary cause of food shortage was a simplistic explanation amounting to misjudgment on the part of the colonial authorities.

Food was scarce and expensive because of population growth and migration to other parts of the region. As shown in the previous chapter, there were migrations from rural to rural areas, from rural to urban centers and for enlistments into the army. But obviously, the issue of food shortage was used as an excuse by the colonial authorities to discourage the planting of more rubber trees which enabled the people to earn cash. They failed to realize that land, unsuitable for food production, could be suitable for rubber production. For example, the low-lying swamp land of Utagba-Uno, the black land of Akoku, the red land of Umutu and the white sandy areas of Amai unsuitable for food production, were suitable for rubber.[28]

Also, the colonial administration failed to take into consideration the fact that rubber production does not necessarily have to pull labor away from food production. In an integrated rural economy such as that of the Western Delta, the same people were engaged in both rubber and food production. There was no effective specialization of labor. It is, therefore, obvious that the real reason for the prohibiting orders lay in the fall in the demand for Nigerian rubber.

To confront the people's defiance, the government transferred the prohibition orders from the jurisdiction of Native Law and Customs to the District Officer and Native authority. These orders which involved serious penalties became known as the Native Authority Order of 1943 for the Kwale and Aboh Native Authorities. The fear of the District Officers bred compliance in the people and the village councils who now cooperated in enforcing the orders. As a result, planting of rubber declined noticeably. In 1944, for example, only 307 acres were planted compared to 960 in 1943, prior to the orders.[29]

It should be noted that the government had a double standard in implementing the restrictions regulations. On the one hand, it turned a blind eye to offending expatriate plantation owners while on the other hand, it was quick to arrest and even imprison alleged local offenders.

The highest proportion of the planted acreage was around the Abraka-Obiaruku area up to Umutu and Utagba-Uno in Ukwuani.[30] In these districts, Ede and Ogboru of Abraka established large planted areas. An explanation for this concentration was advantage of proximity to the highly interactive Benin rubber belt. High concentration of rubber plantations later influenced establishment of a latex processing factory in Umutu.[31]

Ukwuani Native Authority witnessed a proliferation of court cases related to rubber.[32] Disputes arose from land agreements between the owners and foreign lessees, in particular the native foreigners. Another bone of contention concerned the expansion of plantations and defining land boundaries.

The Ukwuani communities also had problems with a group of people described as "native foreigners." These were dynamic and enterprising indigenous people who sought to lease or purchase rubber plantations outside their own native communities. At times, they required land for cultivation and this created difficulties within their host communities. Often conflicts arose between the council of elders and the youth.

The elders were amenable and prepared to sign leases on behalf of the community. But, the youth protested against such alienation and challenged the legal right of the councils of elders to alienate land, their only guaranteed source of livelihood. Such tensions tended to divide the communities into progressive and traditional groups. What has just been described appears contradictory, as the elders were supposed to be the custodians of custom and traditional values including protecting land and using land. A plausible explanation is that the "native foreigners" who had substantial financial power and influence persuaded the elders and their councils with gifts.

In Urhobo and Isokoland, the situation was radically different where the Native Authority prohibition order was not seriously discussed until 1945. For the most part, planting went on unrestricted as village councils and paramount rulers opposed the prohibition orders.[33] They argued that the people would be able to bear the losses and difficulties of the postwar period if the prices of rubber fell. The result was that people undertook more planting here than in any other area of the Western Delta. Between 1958 and 1960, the number of small holders in the province was as follows:

Table V: Small Holders of Rubber Plots, 1958-60

Urhobo	130,000
Aboh	3,000
Western Ijo (Ezon)	850
Warri	500

Also between 1958-1960 there were about 207 acres of land cultivated with rubber in Aboh, 25 acres in the Warri and Ijo areas and 960 acres in Urhobo and Isokoland.[34] The average acreage per person was about two to three acres. Great expansion took place during the boom period of the Korean War and the succeeding years though planting among the Ijo and Itsekiri was minimal because of shortage of dry land in these areas.

One of the problems faced by tappers in these areas was that of low productivity due to poor production methods. The use of the share-cropping method led to overtapping which reduced the tree life span and the quality of their latex. The search of quick returns also led to the overproduction of rubber lumps rather than higher quality rubber sheets. Since the Department of Agriculture did not play an important role in the rubber industry after 1921, the late comers did not receive official education on rubber cultivation and processing. It was only after 1957, with the launching of the Rubber Improvement Campaign that a formal effort was made to teach better tapping methods to producers.

Many of the producers lacked the necessary capital to purchase tapping, processing and drying equipment. They often purchased and used available equipment cooperatively. Such collective use caused delays and difficulties, especially during boom periods.

Inspite of the expansion of acreage, the rubber industry continued to be largely a small-scale peasant production characterized by a low level technology. This supports the views of Helleiner that beyond offering the peasant farmers a vent for their potential surplus, the foreigner did next to nothing to alter the technological background of the economy.

The major beneficiaries of this industry were the exporting firms and their indigenous agents/dealers, as will be discussed in greater detail in Chapter Ten. The dealers, referred to as buying agents, gave credit to their middlemen, who in turn bought from other middlemen who bought directly from producers. The credit was intended to guarantee a regular supply of rubber. The middlemen did not appear to have made much profit. They had to travel by bicycle to remote areas to purchase rubber. At times they exploited the ignorance of the producers and paid them very low prices in order to increase their own profit.

Most of the dealers owned stores in urban centers, or other strategic location, where collected rubber underwent further processing to enhance its quality before sale to the firms. The agents made enough profit to rent stores in towns and purchase their own vehicles and rollers. In addition, they were able to build standard ovens for the proper drying of rubber sheets and crepe.

Second World War and Colonial Rubber Policy

The rubber policy of the colonial government was determined by the demands of the metropolitan economy. In Nigeria, the rubber policy took a new turn after Japan occupied Malaysia and other rubber producing territories of Southeast Asia in 1942. This event created a crisis in rubber supply to the British and her allies. Rubber was a necessary material for the war effort.

For example, rubber was most highly needed for the tires of military vehicles and for the manufacture of weapons, and other military hardware. As the allied powers faced a threat of a shortage of rubber, a new attitude was assumed by British colonial authorities toward rubber production. To guarantee adequate supplies, a new policy was necessary, hence the despatching of a rubber mission to Nigeria in 1942 from Britain.

The mission recommended a new grading and price differentiation system for plantation and wild rubber similar to that of Malaysia. Such a measure was aimed at inducing farmers to produce high quality grades of rubber.[35] The mission recommended that the native authorities be encouraged to expand production in their areas of authority. They were to organize mobile buying units to purchase rubber in areas where buying facilities were inadequate. Four outlying areas were to receive vehicles at regular intervals to purchase all available rubber.

The authorities were also supposed to establish better tapping and processing systems in strategic locations. Tapping knives, wooden rollers and climbing ropes were to be offered at reduced prices. Apart from expanding production, these measures were also designed to protect producers in remote areas from the exploitation of the middlemen. It was to ensure that the government was able to monitor prices, ensuring that the same prices were upheld in all areas.

Gunpowder served as an incentive for guaranteeing increased production in both rubber and palm produce.[36] For the people, gun powder had socio-cultural and economic significance. It was used in rituals especially funerals and for hunting. Rubber producers received gunpowder directly from the native authority, whereas palm producers received supplies through their village and clan councils in lesser quantities. Before the mission's recommendation and its application in 1943, there was a rise in the prices of food items, a situation intensified by an increase in population. The new rubber recommendation also aimed at stemming the tide of rural migration.

The British Board of Trade was organized as the central buying agency in 1943. It bought all available rubber and guaranteed minimum prices for producers. Although this measure did encourage higher production, it did not necessarily guarantee higher quality production. It is also important to note that there was a major contradiction in the government's war time rubber program. On the one hand, it advocated greater production, and on the other, it restricted further cultivation and expansion in plantations.

This created problems for the people who regarded further planting to be part of the campaign for increased production. The government argued that further cultivation was unnecessary in anticipation of falling prices as the Second World War drew to a close.[37] This attitude became more evident following the liberation of Asian rubber producing territories. It has been noted earlier that European industrialists preferred higher quality rubber of East Asian plantations.[38] This seems to provide better explanation to the government's policy than the argument of fall in prices. Notwithstanding the government's ban on further planting, the people continued cultivation.

This official policy was a perfect illustration of using and subverting the colonial economy to the metropolitan one. It could also be argued that this attitude has to do with protecting the European synthetic rubber industry.

Post-Second World War Rubber Development

With the end of World War II, the colonial government abandoned the emergency program in Nigerian rubber, turning its focus to the preferred products of the Southeast Asian. But soon, the demands of the Korean war compelled the government to change its policy and encourage production in the Western Delta.

In 1952, the reversal of government policy on land alienation to foreigners was followed by the establishment of several large estates by foreign firms.[39] The production of crepe, a low quality rubber produced from lumps, increased and crepe factories were established in the same period. Prices rose and exports rose to record levels between 1950 and 1952. The new prices encouraged even further cultivation of plantations and production rose from 30,000 tons in 1955 and 38,000 tons in 1956.[40]

This period also coincided with the development of regionalization, the expansion of nationalist agitation and the involvement of nationalists in Nigeria's governance. The governments of the Eastern and Western Regions started to establish their own plantations. A rubber processing factory was established at Umutu and 3,000 acres of rubber estate at Utagba-Uno in Aboh division. When these rubber plantations began production in 1964, Nigeria replaced Liberia as the foremost rubber producing country in Africa.

In 1957, the Western Nigeria Ministry of Agriculture and Natural Resources launched the Rubber Improvement Campaign, the first major attempt by the colonial government to promote rubber production. The objectives of this campaign were to lower the cost of production, maintain Nigeria's competitive position in the world rubber market, and increase the income of the producers. The campaign was implemented through a training program in proper tapping and processing methods, supply of cloned seedlings, the establishment of processing cooperatives and technical advice given to the builders of small scale factories. There was an unprecedented increase in the production of crepe.[41] The expansion of crepe production could be attributed to the rapid growth of crepe factories and the rise in price of rubber lumps.

The Challenges of Indigenous Rubber Production

Rubber producers in the Western Delta were challenged by two major factors: Southeast Asian competition and the threat posed by the development of synthetic rubber. Low-priced and high-quality Asian rubber trade was more sought after by European and American merchants and industrialists than Nigerian rubber. The Asian rubber plantation-based system guaranteed better processes of production while the Nigerian rubber industry continued to use the wild and plantation rubber.

Processing was neither sophisticated nor mechanized. The standard of production was below approved regulations. This resulted in lower quality products, less preferred in the world market. In the organized plantation system, mechanized processes of production yielded products of high quality.

There were specific characteristics which made the Eastern products preferred in world markets like uniform thickness of the sheets, and high color purity. Nigerian rubber, on the other hand, was processed by a number of small producers using different methods, resulting in products which varied in quality and appearance not only from sheet to sheet, but often even within a single sheet.[42] These problems were due to lack of capital to build smoke houses, and establish other necessary processing infrastructure.

The Nigerian government and commercial firms seemed to have shared a serious sense of uncertainty about the fate of the Nigerian rubber trade if the processes of production were not radically changed. It appeared there was a lack of confidence which surrounded Nigerian rubber industry. The second threat to the Nigerian rubber industry was the rapid growth of synthetic rubber which assumed great importance from the 1930's. This endangered the survival of natural rubber in the world market.[43] The shortage of natural rubber during the Second World War strengthened the importance of synthetic rubber even further. Among its advantages were uniformity and higher quality. In addition, it had the benefit of integrating producers with the users of the product, strengthened by the proximity between them. Natural rubber was produced far from the points of consumption and there was no direct relationship between producers and consumers.

The producers of natural rubber had no idea how rubber was used in manufacturing. It is possible that, if they had an idea of the application of rubber in industries, they might have applied better processing methods, and come up with higher quality products. At the same time, manufacturers had no idea what was involved in the tapping and processing of rubber in the Nigerian system. This gap in understanding created major difficulties for both producers, agents, traders, and manufacturers.

It is important to emphasize that synthetic rubber is a more stable product, to the extent that it is graded according to specific technical properties. Therefore, producers of synthetic rubber could control their production because they can determine exact amount of elements involved in production. On the other hand, natural rubber products are prone to fluctuations in terms of quality. Producers have no full control over the exact composition of the product, since they cannot control the quality or quantity of the latex from the rubber tree. In addition, producers lacked adequate knowledge of the implications of the chemicals used for the processing of the latex. Because of the advantages of synthetic rubber and preference for Southeast Asian rubber, the colonial government failed to adopt a consistent policy toward the Nigerian rubber industry.

In concluding this section, the major differences in government's attitude to palm produce and rubber will be highlighted. While the government pursued a consistent, dynamic policy regarding palm produce, it pursued an inconsistent policy toward rubber, thus impeding the growth of the industry. Also, in the palm produce industry, there was no period of prohibition and restriction when producers were left on their own. The Department of Agriculture worked consistently and closely with the palm farmers while the rubber producers were left on their own and they exhibited a higher sense of initiative and enterprise.

Land appropriation and increased mechanization of palm produce were supported by the government. Such benefits were not enjoyed by rubber farmers. The inability of palm producers to purchase hand presses compelled the government to decide to build Pioneer Oil Mills for use in strategic locations. Both the government and the UAC undertook significant initiatives to promote the mechanization of the palm produce industry. The UAC supplied improved seedlings and machinery to ensure high quality production. This joint commitment was not evident in the case of the rubber industry.

The difference in attitude may be explained in large measure by the fact that unlike palm produce, natural rubber was competitive with synthetic rubber. The improvement and mechanization of the estates could enhance the quality of Nigerian rubber and could pose a threat to the growing synthetic industry. It is also important to note that in an international system where specific functions are ascribed to various areas, the colonial authorities considered it more profitable to promote rubber in Southeast Asia rather than promote mechanization and expansion of rubber in Nigeria.

On the other hand, palm produce had been the major item of international trade between Nigeria and Britain. Many firms and industries had been associated with the trade in which large sums of money were expended. It is no wonder that the UAC, the largest trading company in Nigeria, was committed to the growth and development of palm produce. Palm produce was a crucial product to the industries and growing urban population of Britain, Europe and North America. Palm produce was an essential source material for producing essential food items and vital detergents (soap). The rubber industry did not have similar implications.

Despite these differences, both rubber and palm produce remained peasant industries. Besides the provision of rudimentary machines, the colonial government and its agents made minimal efforts to revolutionize the means of production. Thus, qualitative changes did not match quantitative growth. This corroborates the contention of Rodney that "Capitalism in the form of colonialism failed to perform in Africa the tasks it had performed in Europe in changing social relations and liberating the forces of production."[44]

In the international capitalist system dominated by the economies of the colonizing powers, the concerns and interests of the colonies are decidedly peripheral. The rubber industry in the Niger Delta aptly demonstrates this. But rubber industry became more popular with the people than palm produce. A possible explanation relates to the higher prices of rubber, and higher earnings which accrued and assisted the people to meet financial demands of the new system. There were certain imported products, associated with improved social status and identity. These items included bicycles, radios, imported clothing and shoes.[45]

Another important development of this period was the ability of some rubber farmers, middlemen and agents to purchase corrugated iron sheets for roofing their houses. Increasingly, thatch houses gave way to more iron roofed and concrete homes. People worked hard in the rubber production to earn cash to improve their homes, educate their children and satisfy other socio-economic needs of the cash economy, including the payment of taxes. School children working as part-time tappers were able to earn money and subsidize their parents' incomes and expenses for their education. Women also earned cash from part-time tapping, thus augmenting family income.

The contentions of McPhee, Myint and Helleiner that the colonial government and its agents, including missionaries, were solely responsible for increase in production of cash crops does not apply to rubber. Without the enthusiasm and sustained interests of the people, the fluctuating policy of the colonial government and their agents would have destroyed the rubber industry in Nigeria. Therefore, it could be argued that it was not external demand and the efforts of the colonial administration, but the response of the local community which continued to promote and guarantee the required production for overseas export. It appears, however, that the palm produce industry did not have similar effects on the people.

Notes

1 P. Schidrowitz and T. R. Dawson, *History of Rubber Industry* (Cambridge, 1952); also William Woodruff, *The Rise of the British Rubber Industry* (Liverpool University Press, 1958).
2 *Ibid.*
3 C. Cuthbert, *African Rubber Industry*, (London, 1911), p. 1; also K.B. Dickson, *A Historical Geography of Ghana*, (Cambridge University Press, 1968), p. 162.
4 O. Omosini, "The Rubber Exporter Trade in Ibadan 1893-1904", *Journal of Historical Society of Nigeria*, 10:1 (December, 1979) pp. 21-42.
5 *Ibid.*
6 W. I. Ofonagoro, *Trade and Imperialism in Southern Nigeria, 1881-1929*, (New York: Nok Publishers, 1979), pp. 219-222.
7 Ofonagoro, *op. cit.*, p. 219.
8 *Ibid.*, pp. 220-221.
9 C. Cuthbert, *The African Rubber Industry and Funtumia Elastica*, (London: Bale & Sons and Danielson, 1911), pp. 13-14.
10 E. D. Morel, *Nigeria, Its Peoples and Problems* (London: Smith Elder and Co., 1911), p. 69.
11 Ofonagoro, *Trade and Imperialism in Southern Nigeria*, p. 219.
12 J. Mars, "Extra-Territorial Enterprises", in M. Perham (ed), *Mining, Finance, Commerce in Nigeria*, (London: Faber and Faber), Vol. II, p. 59.
13 N.A.I., War Prof. I, File No. 11857, Vol. XXX-XIII, Annual Reports of Warri Province, 1923-1935.
14 J.K. Helleiner, *Peasant Agriculture, Government and Economic Growth in Nigeria*.(Homewood: Ill.R.D. Irwin, 1966) p. 122.
15 *See* TABLE IV.
16 Anschell, *op. cit.*
17 Anschell, *op. cit.*, Chapter 4; Helleiner, *op. cit.*, p. 120.
18 *Ibid.*
19 Interview with Mr. Akpan, Personnel Manager, Pamol Estate, Sapele, May, 1987.
20 *Ibid.*
21 C. Ake, *A Political Economy of Africa*, (London: Longman, 1981), p. 43.
22 Alan McPhee, *The Economic Revolution in British West Africa*, (London: Routledge & Sons, 1926), p. 104.
23 J. Okitikpi, interviewed at Sapele, May 1987, states that the main firms were Spiropolous, Caiaphas Brothers, D.C.C. British Bata Shoe Company.
24 N.A.I., War Prof. I, File No. 11857, Warri Province Annual Report, 1938.
25 Anschell, op. cit., Chapter 4.

26 Sapele Dist. 1/1 199.
27 N.A.I., Kwale Dist. I. File 72C, Rubber Production.
28 *Ibid.*
29 In 1937, 500 acres were cultivated; 500 in 1938, 520 in 1942, 960 in 1943, 307 in 1944–Kwale Dist. I. File 72C, *op. cit.*
30 N.A.I., For 3647, Annual Report Warri Province, 1939.
31 Interview with Mr. G. O. Onomesa at Abraka, April 1987.
32 Kwale Dist. I Files 72B and 72C, *op. cit.*
33 Anschell, *op. cit.*, Chapter 4.
34 *Ibid.*
35 See *Wild Rubber Production* - issued by Agricultural Department, (Lagos: Government Printer, 1942).
36 N.A.I., Kwale Dist. I File No. 73C, Rubber Production.
37 N.A.I., Ughelli Dist. File No. 729, Vol. I, Rubber Industry.
38 N.A.I., Ughelli Dist. I File No. 729, *op. cit.*
39 K.R. Anschell, "Economic Aspects of Rubber Production in Mid-Western Nigeria:, (Ph.D. Dissertation, Michigan State University, 1965) Chapter 4. He states that three large plantations were established by a consortium of Malayan firms and one by Dunlop.
40 Helleiner, *Peasant Agriculture,* p. 121.
41 Anschell, *op. cit.*, Chapter I.
42 N.A.I., WAR Prof. I, File 557.
43 Anschell, op. cit., p. 34.
44 Walter Rodney, *How Europe Underdeveloped Africa*, (Washington, D.C.; Howard University Press, 1974), pp. 215-6.
45 Interview with Mr. P.A. Onemu at Irri (Isoko) in April, 1987. Mr. Onemu, age 65, is a retired rubber dealer and is at present engaged in retailing of general goods.
46 Alan McPhee, *The Economic Revolution in British West Africa*, (London: G. Routledge & Sons, 1926), p. 27. Also Hla Myint, "The Classical Theory of International Trade and Underdeveloped Countries" *Economic Journal* 68 (June, 1968), pp. 317-337 and G. K. Helleiner, *Peasant Agriculture Government and Economic Growth in Nigeria,* (Homewood: Illinois, 1966), p. 12.

Chapter 7

Commercial Firms, Trade and the Response of the People, 1929-1960

Trade and expansion of markets were the moving forces behind British colonization of Nigeria. By the late nineteenth century, some members of the British cabinet, Joseph Chamberlain, in particular, advocated colonization to promote and expand British trade.[1] They believed that colonization would develop the "underdeveloped estates," that is the overseas markets, in the interest of British commerce and industry. Lord Lugard stated "it is in order to foster the growth of trade of this country that our far-seeing statesmen and our commercial men advocate colonial expansion".[2]

The *Pall Mall Gazette* in 1899 supported this view by stating that," nor have we gone to the equatorial regions for religious or humanitarian motives . . . Still less have we sought out the African in order to endow him with the vices of Western civilization . . . the dominating force which has taken . . . for trade".[3]

Hopkins strengthens this contention by claiming that,

> the main reason why Britain decided to move into the interior of Lagos was because the officials and politicians who were responsible for colonial policy gave way to commercial pressure groups and to the local administration both of which favoured expansion of trade in order to solve the economic problems . . . which had become acute in the 1880's.[4]

Ake accepts the view that the principal objective of colonizing imperialism was the search for outlets to solve the inherent contradictions of growing capitalism.[5] Ihonvbere and Falola strengthens this claim that the need to win strategic advantages over other imperialist powers through cheap sources of raw materials and ready markets for manufactured goods provided the reason for the British imperial thrust and colonization efforts of the late nineteenth century.[6]

Lord Palmerston observed that "trade ought not to be enforced by canon balls but on the other hand, trade cannot flourish without security and that security may be unattainable without the exhibition of physical force"[7].

African-Europeans trade had two dimensions; the export of raw materials from the colonies and the importation of manufactured goods into the colonies. The two aspects of this trade were highly interdependent and the advancement of one influenced the growth of the other.

The commercial firms acted as intermediaries between the industrialists of Europe and the peasant farmers of the colonies. From this middleman position, they ensured that there was a favorable balance between the two parts of the trade system. The establishment of strategic locations in the interior did not only stimulate greater productivity but also expedited the delivery of goods to trading stations for export.

In the absence of adequate road infrastructure, waterways provided the main trade routes, being less difficult and cumbersome than the tedious roads. Consequently, most firms were established along the Niger and its river network. But head portage was inevitably used to convey goods from boats to warehouses and markets. Though slow and tedious, it remained the most common form of directly conveying goods on land.

Prior to 1929, the most important firms in the region were the Niger Company, Miller Brothers, Maclver, Thomas Welch, African and Eastern Trading Company, Le Bas West Africa Ltd., John Holt and the British West African Timber Company. Following the First World War, the French firms of Societe Commerciale de l'Ouest Africaine (SCOA) and the Compagnie Francaise de l'Afrique Occidentale (CFAO) joined the trade of this area.[8]

Both French firms were squeezed out in 1929 with the merger of all of the British firms and the formation of the United African Company (UAC). Only John Holt stood out of the merger. From then on, trade in the area was controlled by the UAC and John Holt. The implications of the merger on Africans is that they lost the choice of being able to deal with any firm of their choice. However, they had not really been able to play one firm against another because the firms often established standard prices.

In Aboh division, both the UAC and Holt Company established stations at Igbuku, Ashaka, Iselegu, Aboh, Sanubi, Obiaruku and Umutu. More stations were established at Ganagana, Aseh, Asaba Assey and Patani in Western Ijo and at Okpari, Otedo, Frukama and Ivrogbo in Urhobo division. In Jekri-Sobo, stations were built at Warri, Ogbe-Sobo, Sapele, Ajagbodudu, Asagba, Okpara, Kokori, Ogharefe and Koko.[9]

Most of the trading stations were located in centers which had been strategic commercial centers and whose structures were simply expanded by European firms. Some of the stations also became Christian mission centers.[10] In some cases, administrative headquarters were located in the stations, in order to maximize the benefits of the various activities.[11] For instance, the town of Warri served as the headquarters of the Southern Nigerian Protectorate.

Then, with the creation of provinces in 1914, Warri township served as the headquarters of Warri province, an area which coincides with the entire Western Delta. Warri township also served as the headquarters of the Sobo-Jekri (Urhobo-Itsekiri) division following the 1930 administrative rearrangements. Being a port town, Warri became the headquarters of John Holt Company and Holt Transport Services and of the Benin Division of the UAC.

Trade expanded in the first decades of this century primarily because of an increase in prices. Prices of palm oil rose from £23 per ton in 1914 to £43 in 1920.[12] After World War I, there was a decline in trade as a result of the Great Depression. From 1930-1945, trade stabilized, with a considerable increase from 1937. During the Second World War and after, there was a general boom in trade and production.[13]

The principal warehouses in Warri and Sapele served the inland stations and the middlemen agents in the urban centers. The middlemen sold imported items to retailers, who in turn, sold to shop keepers and petty traders. The people then made their purchases from these traders in local markets. General trade could affect volume of local production, depending on prevailing prices. In exceptional cases, producers boycotted trade in an effort to force up prices of cash crops. The price situation could also compel farmers to switch from producing one crop to another. Depression in palm oil prices resulted in a switch to producing rubber on account of more attractive prices.

Some imported articles of general merchandise, such as bicycles, were significant incentives for increasing production. For sub-agents, petty traders, and middleman, it was a status symbol which facilitated communication, travel and the collection and delivery of goods. Owning a bicycles was seen as an improvement in one's social and economic status. Producers and agents were forced to work hard to earn enough cash to purchase bicycles due to their attraction. Imported clothing and radios also had a similar attraction.

The volume of production for each household was low because farming was done on a very small scale on small family plots. Also farm operations were manually undertaken with rudimentary implements. The farmers and petty traders having low purchasing power could only buy wares in small quantities at any one time. This explains why small monetary denominations began with one-tenth of a penny, as the smallest unit.[14]

The UAC played a prominent role in the textile trade, followed after 1945, by the Indian firm of K. Chellarams. The mode of dressing of the people in the area was affected by the textile imports from India.[15] It is important to note that Alice Obahor and Agnes Agbaza, two female agents, of the firm of K. Chellarams played a strategic role in representing the aesthetic values of their people through Indian textiles. Through this strategy, they related the dress-forms and values of their people to those of the Indians. The Indian textile industry also became aware of the aesthetic sensitivity of the people of the Delta.

Female agents undertook direct importation of textiles through K. Chellarams. Specifically, they introduced the patterns and designs that are attractive to their people to the firm of K. Chellarams. The latter submitted such patterns to Indian textile mills for production. This practice ensured regular customership between the agents and the firm.

Increasingly, the activities of the trading firms became an integral part of the socio-economic life of the people. Some of the major items of trade became basic requirements in the daily lives of the people. For example kerosene, medicine, salt, sugar and matches became essential goods. Any disruption or fluctuations in the balance of trade had serious effects on the people. There was a growing sophistication in the variety of goods imported to meet the increase in the people's tastes for foreign goods. The firms imported goods that were attractive enough to stimulate people toward greater production.

Greater production was considerably in the interest of the firms because it assured stable supplies of cash crops.[16] Most of the imported goods were substitutable items which increasingly replaced indigenous types. The most significant impact of this type of trade on the people was that they ceased to appreciate and make their own products.

Reliance on imported goods is the root cause of a consumer culture which has become so characteristic of the people of this area much as those in other parts of the country. Apart from facilitating the erosion of indigenous industries and skills, it is clear that this type of culture does not promote savings without which investment in productive activities is difficult to attain. Post-colonial experience shows a continuity of this trend.[17]

Problems of Trade

As Nigeria became transformed into a formal colony, its economy and society became increasingly dependent on the interests of the British. The pattern of relationship was one of "unequal inter-dependence."[18] Ofonagoro gives support to this contention by claiming that in a colonial situation that emerged largely out of a desire to entrench British economic and political domination, nothing else could result. Equitable exchange can not take place under conditions of compulsion.[19] He adds that transaction can no longer be dignified by the term "exchange" or "trade." The term extortion seems more appropriate in this situation, he claims.[20]

It is largely against this background that the problems of the colonial trade will be discussed. The problems of trade centered on price policy, which as S. Leith-Ross points out, was the "hub around which the economic, and consequently, the social wheel, of the vast majority of Nigerians revolved."[21] The colonial situation which deprived the people of freedom to decide or choose made it impossible for producers to get a fair price for their products.

The economic laissez-faire attitude of the colonial administration guaranteed that expatriate firms had a free reign in determining the price policy. In order to maximize profits with minimum inputs, a price policy was established which tolerated low and indiscriminate prices for producer's goods and high prices for imported articles. This goal was realized through mechanisms such as "market sharing" and "pooling agreement" by the trading firms.[22] Through this, they schemed to pay low and fixed prices to the producers.

It was easy for the firms to do this because in the colonial economy, they had a symbiotic relationship with the colonial administration which ensured that the firms establish a commercial regime characterized by monopolization.[23] By 1929 merging of the trading firms, competition was highly reduced if not almost eliminated. The UAC became four times the size of its rival, the John Holt Company. It was part of the Unilever, Anglo-Dutch conglomeration. Within a few years the UAC established its commercial hegemony, assuming a predominating position in the trade of all West Africa not just Nigeria.

The people faced double control from the firms and the administration. At any time they had to battle against a double-edged sword of regulations with regard to trade.[24]

The export trade was just one side of the coin. Producers were driven into greater difficulties because the same firms controlled the import trade and its main distribution network.[25] From this vantage position the firms were able to determine the types and prices of imports which could be made available to African consumers. Through this tight control over both import and export trade conditions, they were able to enjoy much larger profits than otherwise in a competitive market situation.

On the other hand, Africans did not possess effective counter measures on a collective or individual basis. They lacked, and were unable to develop, collective bargaining power to counteract the seemingly formidable barriers of the firms. Their situation was aggravated by the tactics of the middlemen, who in most cases, exploited the ignorance and weaknesses of the producers to maximize their own profits.

Producers did seek redress through some organization of trade hold-ups and boycotts aimed at forcing the firms to increase prices for their produce. In the Western Delta, there was a trade boycott by palm producers in 1927 because of depressed prices.[26] Though trade hold-ups were a common feature during the Great Depression, they were no match for the effective barriers and the limitations imposed by the firms and government. A more radical and violent reaction was the anti-tax agitation in the Western Delta throughout most of 1927. This event has been interpreted largely as a political act, although it appears that economic disaffection crystallized the agitation.[27]

The reaction occurred during the Depression, at a time when the prices for primary products were low and the prices of imported goods were increasing. This meant that Africans were earning far less from their output and were yet required to pay more for imported goods. No doubt this increased their socio-economic hardships which ultimately compelled the people to protest.

It was into this situation of general disaffection, that taxation was introduced in 1928. It was conceived by the people that such an exaction would further depreciate their already precarious financial positions. The colonial authorities also increased revenue by raising the rate of import duties, and consequently the prices of goods. The duty on tobacco, for example, rose from 1 shilling and 6d per lb. to 2 shillings per lb. during the depression years.[28]

In the Western Delta, it was common to find owners of rubber plantations who mortgaged their plantations to African middlemen or European firms in order to meet their financial and social obligations.[29] This situation did not necessarily arise from the uncertainty of price fluctuations but the manipulations of European trading firms. Producers were compelled to switch from one crop to another, or from cash crops to food crop production, in order to survive.

There was also the problem of the sale of shoddy imported goods such as inferior quality textiles, spirituous liquor and second-hand clothing.[30] This situation was enforced by government controls. Britain wanted to maintain its hold on Nigerian trade to ensure that Nigeria remained an "imperial estate"; a supplier of raw materials and a consumer of British manufactured items. In 1932, the British government imposed a stiff quota on cheap Japanese textiles in order to protect the British textile industry. Such measures restricted the choices available to Africans and forced them to pay higher prices for British textiles.

The pattern of trade was not favorable for local middlemen, who had become an indispensable part of the import/export trade. The middlemen agents played a crucial role in expanding the frontiers of European trade by finding new markets. In addition, they helped to integrate the trade in raw materials with the European firms. This was very important to the firms when one considers that production was on a small scale by a large number of producers in scattered communities.

The agents also enhanced product quality by sorting, blending, grading, treating and bulking products before sale to the firms. Their role was made more complex because they had to undertake the tedious task of scouring the interior markets, usually on foot. Wealthier ones could afford bicycles and lorries.[31] But this was a minute percentage of the total middlemen.[32]

Though the depression experience was a global phenomenon, the African middlemen were less advantaged to adapt to its damaging effects. Unlike the Europeans firms, they were caught unaware and little prepared to deal with the problems and lacked a "capital reserve" to help cope with the situation.

Their problems were more complicated by the intervention of both World Wars and the accompanying restrictions and demands. In both wars, Germany was expelled from the market, leaving Britain as the only trading partner.[33] It is generally believed that Nigerian middlemen, and especially those of the rubber area of the Western Delta, made huge profits. This claim is difficult to validate because of the absence of statistical data. In view of the cost of the middlemen's operations, the general impact of the depression and the pricing policy of the firms, it can be concluded that only a few made substantial profits from the trade.

Firms tightened their hold over middlemen through the credit system. Credit increased their dependency on the firms and reduced the chances of rebellion against their abuse. The middlemen could not openly criticize the firms, for any overbearing attitudes. They were further weakened by inability to purchase the required infrastructure to improve their productiveness.

The farmers suffered the most. Beside their inability to purchase the necessary equipment and infrastructure to enhance production, they could scarcely afford to educate their children, pay taxes or receive Western health care. Most school pupils had to tap rubber on a part-time basis in order to be able to buy books and pay fees. Financial incapacity of parents prevented many young people from attending school. The commercial regime failed to introduce the forces which would have enabled the growth of a capitalist society as it was experienced in the metropole.[34]

At least, it failed to develop a substantial level of indigenous capital. Or it reduced the capacity for growth of an indigenous capitalist class. But what was more spectacular was the continued use of crude implements in spite of increased production. It was apparent that the government and the firms were not concerned so much with means of production. What was crucial to them was volume of production.

Unintended Benefits of the Operations of the Expatriate Firms

The operations of the firms had some unintended benefits for the people. John Holt's and UAC transportation system introduced modern transportation system of the area. The use of steamboats and barges on the waterways was an innovative sight and they served as models of more effective and advanced transportation system. In the 1950's, and in particular, after the establishment of the Western Nigeria Development Board and Finance Corporation, there was a plan to overhaul the river transportation system.[35]

The plan was to introduce a faster and less difficult mode of transportation in place of the slow and tedious canoe system which had become inadequate for the level of economic activities. This was with a view to enhancing communications and trade.[36]

Expansion of trade into the interior and the trading stations in strategic locations helped to stimulate some infrastructural growth. There was some construction of roads and bridges. Some roads were built by communities and others by the colonial authorities, though with community labor, to link the trading stations with the major commercial centers and with the administrative headquarters.

These developments acted as further stimuli to enhance trade and cash crop production. But, infrastructural development also created some social distortion because communities outside of the stations were little served by these roads and remained largely untouched by this development.

Also, it may be contended that the expansion of firms into the interior and the establishment of inland stations there altered the balance of power among the various ethnic groups in the Western Delta. Urhobo-Itsekiri, Itsekiri-Ijo, Aboh-Isoko and Aboh-Ukwuani relations were all radically affected. The advantages which accrued to the Aboh and Itsekiri as middle men declined and the way was open for more equal opportunities for all the various groups.

The new commercial system eliminated established middleman positions. All groups were able to trade directly with European firms, instead of through specific middlemen as was the case prior to 1929. European traders began to deal directly with producers in the interior, rather than rely on coastal middlemen. This expanded the scope of commercial activities as many more people came into direct contact with the European traders in the interior. The feeling of inferiority and superiority among different groups because of contacts with Europeans began to disappear.

As will be examined in greater depth later, a trading population was attracted to Warri and Sapele to seek new opportunities created by trade activities of the firms, and their agents. The activities of this new trading population, acted as catalysts for greater socio-economic changes in urban areas. Urban centers served as a means of integrating different groups from within and outside of the Western Delta.

The involvement of women in the new urban trade marked an important development in the economic situation. Participation helped to broaden their activities beyond traditional ones. Also it empowered women to take advantage of the opportunities that were becoming open in the region. Women began to take initiatives and confronted new challenges. The effect was the increasing empowerment of women especially in the urban centers.

Notes

1 A. Wood, *Nineteenth Century Britain, 1815-1944*, (London: Longman, 1968), p. 379.

2 F. D. Lugard, *The Rise of our East African Empire*, (London: Blackwood, 1893), cited in B. Onimode, *Imperialism and Underdevelopment in Nigeria*, (London: Macmillan, 1982), p. 31.

3 G.N. Uzoigwe, *Britain and the Conquest of Africa: The Age of Salisbury*, (Ann Arbor: University of Michigan Press, 1974), pp. 27-28, cited in L. I. Izuakor, "Quest for Further Exploitation: British Colonial Occupation of Nigeria", in Toyin Falola, ed., *Britain and Nigeria: Exploitation or Development*, (London: Zed, 1987), p. 57.

4 A. G. Hopkins, "Economic Imperialism in West Africa: Lagos 1880-1890", *Economic History Review* 21:3 (1968), p. 603.

5 Claude Ake, *A Political Economy of Africa*, (London: O. U. P., 1981), p. 19.

6 J. Ihonvbere and Toyin Falola, "Introduction: Colonialism and Exploitation", in Toyin Falola, ed., op. cit., p. 26.

7 B. Porter, *The Lion's Share: A shot History of British Imperialism, 1850-1870)*, New York: Longman, 1977), p. 11.

8 *Ibid.*

9 N.A.I., Ughelli Dist. I, File 701, Annual Report.

10 Patani was an important missionary center of the Church Missionary Society from the early part of this century. Okpara was also an important center of the Catholic Mission as well.

11 Ughelli which was the headquarters of the Sobo Division was close to Okpara. Kwale/Obetim/Utagba Ogbe (those names apply to the same town) was the headquarters of the Aboh Division and is currently the headquarters of the Ndokwa Local Government Area (Aboh and Ukwuani Areas) of Bendel State of Nigeria. Warri was the headquarters of the Jekri-Sobo and the capital of the Delta Province (the area occupied by the Western Delta).

12 G. K. Helleiner, *Peasant Agriculture, Government and Economic Growth in Nigeria*, (Homewood: Illinois, Irwin, 1966), Table II - B - 2.

13 *Ibid.*, pp. 1-33.

14 W. Ofonogoro, *Trade and Imperialism in Southern Nigeria, 1881-1929*, (New York: Nok Pub., 1979, p. 289.

15 Interview with Mrs. C.A. Agodo at Warri, December, 1986.

16 Helleiner, op. cit., p. 12.

17 *UAC Statistical and Economic Review* 6 (September, 1950).

18 Claude Ake, *A Political Economy of Africa*, (London: Oxford University Press, 1981), p. 36, cited in O. N. Njoku, "Trading with the Metropolis: An Unequal Exchange", in Toyin Falola, ed., *op. cit.*, p. 124.

19 Ofonagoro, *op. cit.*, p. 401.
20 *Ibid.*
21 Quoted in O. N. Njoku, *op. cit.*, p. 126.
22 *Ibid.*, pp. 126-127.
23 Ake, *op. cit.*, p. 47.
24 Njoku, *op. cit.*, p. 127.
25 Rodney, *How Europe Underdeveloped Africa*, p. 172.
26 N.A.I., Warri Provincial, War Prof. I, Annual Reports 1928 and 1929.
27 Obaro Ikime, *Niger Delta Rivalry: Itsekiri-Urhobo Relations and the European Presence, 1884-1936*, (New York: Humanities Press Inc., 1969), pp. 220-230.
28 Donald Kingdom, *Reports of the Aba Commission of Inquiry*, (Lagos: Government Printer), p. 102 cited in O.N. Njoku, op. cit., p. 129.
29 N.A.I., Kwale Dist. I, File 72C, Rubber Production.
30 Interview with Mr. G. Tuedon at Ughelli, November, 1986. (Secretary in Warri Provincial Office, 1949-55).
31 *Ibid.*
32 Helleiner, Table II-B-2, *op. cit.*
33 *Ibid.*
34 R. Zahar, *Colonialism and Alienation*, (Benin City, 1974), p. 9.
35 N.A.I., Kwale Dist. I, File No. 344/9, Document Loans Applications; N.A.I., War Prof. I. WP 146/F/3 Loans and N.A.I., Ughelli Dist. I, File No. 1742, Chief J. A. Akiri Application for Loan.
36 *Ikime*, op. cit., pp. 44-68.

Chapter 8

Port Development, Growth of Towns and Social and Economic Change

Before 1914, several ports were established by expatriate trading firms on the coast and up the Niger and Benue rivers.These included Lagos, Koko, Sapele, Warri, Burutu, Forcados, Akassa, Brass, Bonny, Degema, Port Harcourt, Opobo, Calabar and Ikang. Ports were strategic locations for the promotion of import trade and export trade as well as for the expansion of British influence. By 1914, there was a decline in the number of ports to fourteen customs ports and by 1954 these had been reduced to seven; Lagos, Port Harcourt, Sapele, Warri, Burutu, Calabar and Degema.

During colonial period, official port policy was one of concentration on a few ports. The focus of port development was Lagos which became the premier port and Port Harcourt, the second largest port.[1] The concentration on Lagos and Port Harcourt spelt the decline of the other ports including those of the Western Delta.[2]

In the Western Delta, the ports of Warri, Forcados, Sapele and Koko were affected by the government policy. Forcados port was closed while the status of Koko was reduced. The others were saved by the activities of the commercial firms especially by the UAC. Certainly, it prevented their decay, even though, with the exception of Burutu, the others did not receive any major infrastructural development. Their natural advantages were maximally exploited but they were largely left unimproved.

Burutu Port

Burutu port was owned, used and managed solely by the UAC. It was in 1898 that Burutu replaced Akassa as the company's primary port. It was the center of the UAC river fleet, Niger Transport Services and the headquarters of its international shipping and commerce in Nigeria. The UAC located its major bulking plant also at Burutu. Burutu served all the areas of the company's trade which stretched as far northwards as Makurdi, Yola and Chad in Northern Nigeria. It handled a larger volume of exports than other ports apart from Lagos and Port Harcourt.

The UAC undertook a systematic improvement of the port facilities in Burutu. A 1918 fire destroyed the wharfs and jetties built in 1914. But the company undertook a modernization program by establishing bigger wharfs and bigger undercover warehouse space capable of accommodating thirty-five thousand tons of goods.[3]

By 1955, the company had erected four berths, bigger warehouses and improved handling facilities with forklifts and portable wharfage cranes on pneumatics for loading and discharging.[4] By 1960, the UAC had built a new powerhouse, introduced diesel tractors, heavy trailers and mechanical stackers for efficient shipping facilities.[5] These innovations provided adequate facilities for its river fleet and international shipping.

Port activities attracted a high level of migrant population from other parts of the Western Delta and outside of it. Burutu had been a small fishing Island community whose population was inadequate for the type of labor required at the port. The immediate neighboring people were not attracted to jobs with fixed wages. Of the migrants, the Isoko, the Ukwuani, the Urhobo and Ishan were the dominant groups.

Burutu grew from a fishing community to a commercial port town. It was designated a third-class township in 1928. By 1951, the port employed one thousand and fifty people and the population of the town rose to over ten thousand inhabitants.[6] The dynamics of an urban life induced the formation of new social relations which cut across ethnic loyalties. This was achieved through membership of social clubs, trade unions, and church associations. Therefore, the activities of the UAC had an indirect benefit of transforming small communities into commercial towns with diverse populations. This was an impetus which also enhanced social interaction and integration in new ways in comparison with the pre-colonial period.

The physical outlook of the town changed by the housing scheme of the UAC for its employees. The housing estate was modern with advanced facilities for the comfort of its workers. But the there was a marked distinction between the houses for the European staff and the African workers. The former had better facilities including refrigeration units which were denied to the African workers. By 1953, the company provided a free hospital, potable water system, a recreational area, electricity, a church and large refrigeration units. The latter only served the needs of the European population.

The African area was dramatically different from this enclave of modern housing system. This development supports the Marxist perspective that colonization created disarticulation in the society.[7] This is because the facilities which graced the UAC housing scheme made the difference between a modern and more financially powerful section and non-modern largely rural section. It should be noted that the objective of the company was to create a contented and more productive work force which was essential for ensuring maximum productivity, generating and sustaining profits. But though the UAC did not provide for the entire community, some indirect benefits accrued to the Africans who were allowed access to some of the services, like churches and hospitals.

In pursuit of improving the skills of its workers to be able to handle the expanding and complex commercial activities, the company established an Apprenticeship school to train new entrants. The activities related to the port fostered the growth of several serious businesses at the secondary and tertiary levels. Labor contracting was one of the important businesses. The most successful was that of Chief Martin Okorodudu, an Itsekiri. He established a viable labor contracting business with the UAC.[8] He became influential as he contributed to the economic growth of Burutu. He made such an impact on Burutu and its residents that a section of the town was named after him (Okorodudu town). This was an acknowledgement in recognition of his contributions to the development of Burutu.

In addition, the demands of the increasing population of Burutu resulted in the growth of Shop-keeping and petty trading. These became necessary to cater to the needs of the people. The Burutu market for food items expanded and its activities were controlled by women. Yams and fish were basic food items which dominated the markets.

Population increase became a major stimulus for the expansion of the scope of economic and social activities. The traditional form of transportation was challenged and there was urgent need for modernization of the transport system especially with the increase in the volume of traffic between Burutu and Warri. This was very important for the growing population of Burutu. Burutu, an island, five nautical miles from the sea on the Forcados River and as part of the salt water mangrove swamp lower delta, like the neighboring Ijo and Itsekiri is little suited for food production, let alone food surplus. Most of the food items, traded to Burutu came from the upper delta through Warri.[9] By the end of our period there was a positive response. A number of tug-boats owned by indigenous people operated between Warri and Burutu, carrying goods and people.

Sapele Port

Sapele port was not owned and managed by any firm even though it was an active center, used by many foreign and indigenous firms for international shipping. The central location of Sapele within deep waters of the confluence of the Ethiope and Jamieson rivers, made it a more advantaged port than Warri or Burutu, where access was complicated by huge sand bars. It had an additional advantage of being accessible by road and by water to other parts of Southern Nigeria.[10]

The port was the center of the timber business, being centrally located to receive logs from the forests of the Benin, Ife and Ondo regions. Also, it became the center of the rubber industry, attracting a large number of rubber producing and exporting firms.[11] Its natural advantage of deep waters for berthing was exploited by the numerous firms without any of them taking the initiative to improved on the port. None of the firms undertook any infrastructural development. None of the firms which operated there considered it necessary to improve on its conditions.

This port provides a striking contrast between rapid growth of commerce and industry and the underdevelopment of infrastructure. The African Timber and Plywood company only built two wharfs beside its timber and plywood factory to handle its shipping operations.[12]

Warri Port

Warri port was owned by John Holt. Unlike the UAC in Burutu, John Holt did not develop Warri port. The only infractructural development was the construction of two wharfes by the John Holt while other firms built their own jetties and berthing facilities. This was in spite of the fact that it did not have the same natural advantages as Sapele. The trade volume of John Holt was lower than that of the UAC. This probably explains why there were no major infrastructural improvements in the port.

Koko Port

Another illustration of the UAC involvement in port development is the case of Koko port. Further, it shows how the firms could become involved in the affairs of the communities in which they operated. The issue of Koko port demonstrates a mutual relation in which the UAC acted like a patron and advisor in trying to foster its interest and that of the people of Koko.

The UAC pressured the colonial government to reopen Koko as a custom port and point of entry after its closure in 1942.[13] The company argued that Koko had a fine harbor and was better naturally equipped for handling international shipping than Sapele and Warri. It was also centrally located to exploit the resources of the Benin, Ife and Ondo areas. Unlike Sapele, it did not have the disadvantage of a ferry crossing which caused great delays and extra charges.

The UAC also argued that the reopening of Koko would help de-congest Warri and Sapele, which had reached their limit of expansion, In addition such efforts would contribute to the overall development of the entire area.

The UAC showed a consistent interest in Koko. The firm of Miller Brothers established sawmill here, in 1917 and it was inherited by the UAC in 1929. It was transferred to Sapele in 1935. The Niger Company also established a bulk oil plant at the port in 1928. Koko was further improved by the establishment of the Cowan Estate at Ajagbodudu, by the UAC, in 1935. Although other companies, including John Holt, Compagnie Francaise de l'Afrique Occidentale (CFAO) and the British West African Timber Company operated in the port, its activities was dominated by the UAC.[14]

The UAC proposed that a road be built to connect Ajagbodudu to Koko and end its isolation which caused its closure in the first place.[15] The company was also convinced that the road would ensure the delivery of foodstuffs from the interior stations to Koko and the adjacent riverine areas. A resumption of trade in Koko was also deemed as a way of stopping the town's declining population.

The campaign to reopen Koko was supported by the Association of West African Merchants. But all the firms including Rowntree-Fry Company, Mandillas and Karaberis, C. S. Madrides, the Secony Vacuum and the Norken Lumber Company, CFAO, British Bata Shoe Company and G.B. Ollivant, a Czech-Nigerian export/import business, preferred to concentrate their economic interests on Sapele, rather than move or expand to Koko. The John Holt preferred to focus its interests on Warri.[16]

The UAC encouraged the people of Koko and Ajagbodudu to undertake a self-help project by building a trunk road between the two communities. Such an effort was expected to preempt government intervention and attract the necessary focus on the reopening of the port. The company contributed two pounds a month towards the trunk road project.[17] The UAC pressured the community to demand seven year's rent (50 British pounds) advance payments for the land acquired by the government in the area. The amount was to be entrusted to the UAC manager at Koko for regular disbursement for the construction of road project.

In 1948, the UAC was successful in getting the government to approve the sum of twelve thousand British pounds for the construction of the road between Koko and Ajagbodudu, which was expected to precede the opening of the Koko port as a custom port. Why was the UAC so interested in reopening the Koko port? It has been emphasized that the UAC was the most important commercial firm which handled more than forty-two percent of Nigeria's trade. Koko port would promote and support its extensive commercial and shipping interests especially those based in the Benin area.

The people of the Koko-Ajagbodudu area would also benefit from the reopening of the Koko port in many respects: the better road, increased commercial activities and potential attraction for more investing firms. Certainly the UAC needed such a vibrant community for the promotion of commerce.

Table VI which follows indicates the initial development of the ports by the various firms in the late 1920's. This trend continued until the 1960's.

In concluding this chapter, it could be argued that the port development relates to three major factors. The first is the need of the commercial firms to export primary products, the second relates to the strategic location of the ports and finally, the vibrant and positive responses of the indigenous inhabitants.

Table VI: Western Delta Ports and Palm Produce Export 1927-1930

Ports	1927	1928	1929	1930
Burutu	9,483	11,882	12,906	25,128
	26,836	19,928	25,386	29,502
Warri	8,629	11,667	9,430	4,571
	20,139	25,957	23,184	26,376
Sapele	3,375	3,991	2,755	1,274
	7,609	8,992	12,414	10,707
Koko	8,602	6,686	4,697	475
	16,935	14,084	6,692	8,014

Note: The upper figures are for palm oil exports and the lower ones for palm kernels.
Source: War. Prof. I, Annual report for 1928 and 1930.

The UAC as the largest commercial firm in Nigeria and the Western Delta, was compelled to undertake port development in response to its need to facilitate import-export trade. The Western Delta ports provided access to the interior and were strategically located to receive goods from the interior stations. Also they were important in receiving import trade. Consequently they served as convenient points for export of cash crop export and reception and distribution of imported goods.

The dynamism and enterprising spirit of the indigenous people energized the actions of the firms. Their responses and activities went a long way to transform the Western Delta ports into a "huge economic export machine."[18] The growth of the ports expanded trade and enhanced social and economic change. The most significant change for the history of the Western delta is the growth of towns. This constituted a dramatic change in a region that had no history of urban culture. Urbanization promoted scores of activities, helped to broaden the scope of the economy including independent economic pursuits.

In general, trade and port development were interrelated dynamics for economic and social development in the Western Delta. Trade created the demand and challenge for port development on the one hand. On the other hand, activities at the ports acted as stimuli for expansion in the economy. Port development was, therefore, a serious catalyst for economic and social growth and for further expansion of commercial activities in the Western Delta. In spite of the patronizing attitude of the firms, their presence helped to bring considerable social and economic change which brought significant positive changes to the people. In particular, the port activities generated rural to urban migration, the growth and modernization of transportation systems and a new class of entrepreneurs.

Notes

1 B. Ogundana, "Seaport Development in Colonial Nigeria", in I. A. Akinjogbin and S. O. Osoba, eds., *Topics on Nigerian Economic and Social History*, (Ile-Ife: Ile-Ife University Press, 1980), p. 164.
2 Nigerian Ports Authority 'Ports' prepared by the Development Division, Nigerian Ports Authority, Lagos, 1938, p. 2.
3 *Ibid.*
4 N.A.I., War Prof. I, File No. 146/L, Development Proposals, Western Ijaw Report, 1956.
5 Ake, *op cit.*, Chapter 3.
6 Interview with Mr. T. Bekeme (former employee of UAC Port, Burutu) at Burutu, December, 1986.
7 *Ibid.*
8 N.A.I., War Prof. I, File No. WP 1130, Volume I, Koko Development.
9 *Ibid.*
10 V.E.E. Ika, "The Port of Burutu in Nigeria", *Institute of Transport Journal*, Vol. 32, 1968, pp. 390-394.
11 Nigerian Ports Authority 'Ports" *op. cit*, p. 8.
12 *Ibid.*
13 *Ibid.*
14 *Ibid.*
15 *Ibid.*
16 *Ibid.*
17 *Ibid.*
18 Annual Report of the Nigerian Marine, 1952-53.

Chapter 9

The United African Company (UAC) and the Establishment of Agro-Allied Industries

It has been stated that one of the most complex issues during the colonial period was the question of industrialization. To the British, encouraging industrialization would defeat the principal objective of colonialism, preserving Nigeria as a market for British manufactures and as a source of cheap raw materials.

Furthermore, the British were ill-prepared to introduce ideal industrialization because according to their conviction it was not part of their mission.[1] They believed instead that "they were destined to guide Africans along the path of progress while contemplating the time when Africans would on their own volition manufacture themselves instead of remaining dependent on European factories."[2] It was better, therefore, to preserve Nigeria to absorb their trade[3] It is claimed that "various colonial policies were introduced and enforced not only to suppress local industries but to encourage increased consumption of British manufactures".[4] The British were also convinced that,

> It is for the distant future to determine and we may safely leave posterity to deal with the problem if and when it arises. . . . Our present task is clear . . . we are shaping policies for the future . . . of the colonies in political, material and moral progress.[5]

This view is supported by Helleiner in his contention that,

> Beyond offering the peasant farmers a vent for their potential surplus production the foreigner did next to nothing to alter the technologi-

> cal backwardness of the economy. Since production functions were left largely untouched, he cannot be accused of introducing an export bias to the economy. All that he did was to dangle sufficiently attractive prices before the producers' noses to persuade them to convert potential into actual surpluses by increasing their inputs.[6]

This contention is further corroborated by other writers such as Falola, who supports the claim of Nkrumah that,

> in the process of creating "development" in the colonies . . . the direct and indirect actions of the colonial state not only ensured that the colonies were converted into non- manufacturing dependencies but also ensured that they were prevented from acquiring the knowledge of modern industries.[7]

In general, the company's activities were determined by enlightened self-interest. They provided facilities to enable them exploit the resources much more profitably. The ultimate goal is to expand commerce and increase profits. So, the commercial firms provided these facilities where they felt their economic interests were most at stake. It is impossible, however, to compare the cost of construction of the facilities with the profit accrued to the companies. It is necessary to have all the figures on cost input in providing the facilities and on trade income and profit to be able to accurately ascertain whether or not there had been exploitation of the people and to what degree.

From 1929, the United Africa Company Limited controlled 42% of the total export/import trade of Nigeria.[8] From its predominating commercial position, the company played a pioneering role in the process of what may be considered token industrialization of Nigeria. It pursued a consistent policy in the mechanization of the palm produce industry, the bulking of palm oil for export and the industrialization of the timber industry.

Mechanization of the Palm Produce Industry

The challenge to the Nigerian palm produce industry by the plantation system in Southeast Asia and the Belgian Congo has been discussed in Chapter five. Also the initiatives of the colonial administration and the United African Company in mechanization of production processes has been addressed in the same chapter.

By 1939, the Engineering Department of the UAC designed the Miller Hand Press along the lines of an old cylinder press, and presented 250 of them to the Department of Agriculture in its efforts to promote the mechanization of the palm produce industry. This was done ostensibly as a goodwill gesture to the people of Nigeria.[9]

With the approach of the Second World War, the UAC and the colonial government became apprehensive about supplying the Duchscher press from Germany. The UAC produced the Miller Hand Press which replaced the German-made Duchscher. This was a significant effort to promote high quality production even though it is evident that it was done essentially in self-interest. Increased production of higher grades meant higher profits for the firms. But it also began to sensitize the people to new production processes.

More research by the UAC led to the design and creation of a larger extracting machine known as the Pioneer Oil Mill, which was presented to the Nigerian government for its research stations. As the demand for higher oil increased at the beginning of the World War 1, it was considered necessary to have a larger extracting machine to enhance production and export. The mill was capable of extracting 85% of the fruit's oil with a free fatty acid content of less than five percent, as shown in the Table below.[10]

Table VII: Method of Palm Oil Production and Quality

Total Oil Processed (tons)	Extracted Rate (percent)	Total Oil Produced (tons)	Free Fatty Acid Content (percent)
Traditional Method	55%*	276,000	9-40%
Hand Presses	65%	20,000	1.5%
Pioneer Mills	85%	3,250	4.5%

*the highest rate by traditional methods
Source: *UAC Statistical and Economic Review* 7 (March, 1951).

The mill had the advantage of processing greater quantities of palm fruits by handling up to half a ton an hour. The cost of its construction ranged from £1,500 to £2,000 and no producer, many of whom were small-scale producers, could afford to buy it.

The government therefore encouraged the establishment of mills at strategic locations for the producer's use. The government was concerned that each mill be established within a six-mile radius of a palm producing community capable of producing sixteen tons of fruits a day.[12] The government anticipated that the farmers would form palm oil processing cooperatives but they continued to process their palm fruits individually and in the traditional manner. It was expected that the Pioneer mills would remain under European management for some time until local people could be trained with the necessary skills.[13]

In addition to the location requirement of a dense surrounding of palm trees, the site also needed to contain an uninterrupted all year-round, easily accessible water supply. Unlike the hand presses, processing with the palm oil mills involved the loss of the palm kernel to producers. Specifically, it interfered with the role and responsibility of women in the palm produce economy as well as their incomes. The processing of palm kernels had always been women's responsibility. Consequently, they were hard hit by the operations of the Pioneer mill which involved loss of kernel and income.[14] Not only were women's income affected but also the entire family finances were jeopardized.

Like the hand press, the major operational problem was in obtaining a regular supply of fresh fruits to ensure the production of the highest quality oil. This problem was even more serious with the Pioneer mill because of its size and locational disadvantage. Even though it was located at the epicenter of a six mile radius of the palm producers, there were serious complaints about the difficulties involved in transporting the fruit to the mill. Most producers could not afford bicycles, and head portage was slow and uneconomical. Motor transportation was not available to farmers in the rural communities. This left them with no other options open other than trekking and head portage.

In installing mills, the Department of Agriculture focused attention on hard oil producing areas in Benin and Warri provinces.[15] It was hoped that the mills would help to encourage the production of soft oil which was preferred by the industrialists. Its introduction involved problems of land acquisition and compensation.[16] The installation of pioneer mills did not, however, preclude the use of hand presses. The hand press did not have the complexities and complications of the pioneer oil mill, and required very little technical skill. It was designed and made for a minimal level of technology and enjoyed the advantage of mobility. The pioneer oil mill which was motor-driven, demanded a higher degree of technical skill from its operators. None of the producers could operate it.

Towards the end of the period under investigation, the response of the people changed from rejection to acceptance. Only in the Isoko area did the Pioneer mills fail to gain acceptance and popularity. In Urhoboland, some communities applied for the installation of a mill without compensation for the land.[17] This attitude also coincided with the increasing surge of nationalist agitation for independence. The nationalists pushed ahead with an expanded package of socio-economic development programs which focused on the people's demands.

The Western Nigerian Production Development Board and the Western Nigeria Finance Corporation were established early in the late 1950's, to enhance the production of crops and to fund agro-allied projects. For the palm produce industry, this was implemented through the promotion and adoption of Pioneer Oil Mills. Cooperatives were encouraged to take over existing mills or apply for new ones. It was perceived by the government that this would encourage popular participation and control and de-emphasize the government's role. In the Western Delta, this plan led to many applications from communities and individuals for loans planning to establish plantations and install mills. But only a few loans were actually granted.[18]

In spite of the fact that only a few mills were approved, it is important to to stress the change in the responses of the people to innovations and quality production. This reflected a progressive development in production attitudes. After 1960, the economy experienced a relative decline. This was the period of civil and political disorder which culminated in the Nigerian Civil War of 1967. There is no doubt that the civil war disrupted the general trend of growth, especially in the Western Delta, which was a battle ground. The war undermined the progressive acceptance of the Pioneer mills.

With the end of the civil war in 1970 and the explosion of the petroleum industry, the Pioneer Oil Mill scheme suffered set-backs from which it is yet to recover. The exploration for crude oil set off several socio-economic activities which detracted from agricultural production. It should be noted that the Western Delta is second only to the Eastern Delta as a petroleum oil producing region. The petroleum industry virtually drained labor from the palm oil industry and from then onwards the industry suffered neglect and decline. From being an exporting country, Nigeria began to import her palm oil requirements, beginning in the late 1970's.

However, it is important to note that until 1955, the UAC and colonial government made profits from the introduction of Pioneer mills and hand presses. There was an unprecedented production of a higher quality, as can be shown in Table VII below.

This level of production led to greater commercial activities and higher profits for the UAC.[19] For the government, it meant higher revenues and increased taxes and export duties. There was a considerable degree of mutual interest between the UAC and the colonial government up to 1960. European firms had a high degree of control over the economy and were left to determine the direction of vital economic sectors, such as agriculture.

Table VIII: Percentage of Total Purchases of Improved Palm Oil, 1948-1953

Free fatty acid content	1948	1949	1950	1951	1952	1953
< 4.5%	–	–	0.2	6.3	29.6	50.0
4.5%, < 9%	65.9	66.4	61.3	70.8	56.3	38.0
> 9%	34.1	33.6	38.5	22.9	14.1	12.0
Total	100%	100%	100%	100%	100%	100%

Source: Nigerian Oil Palm Marketing Board Annual Reports to 1952, 1953 estimated.

Bulking Plants and Oil Bulking

Bulking was an intermediary stage between the period of purchase of oil from middlemen agents and shipping of product overseas to Britain and other international buyers. In general, its aim was to reduce the cost of shipping and improve the quality of the palm oil in order to enhance its marketability. This meant that bulking was an essential stage in the processing of oil export since it minimized impurities and enhanced the quality of the product. Other stages of the processes included storage, cleaning and purification, handling of bulk loading and delivery of the oil into tanks of ocean liners for shipment. The UAC established a monopoly of bulking services in Nigeria during this period.[20]

The Niger Company, the founding firm of the UAC had established the first bulk oil installation at Burutu in 1927 and the second at Koko in 1928.[21] By the early 1930's, there were five bulking facilities in Nigeria at the export centers of Apapa, Port Harcourt, Degema, Opobo and Calabar as shown in Map 6. Cleaning and purifying processes inevitably involved a loss of oil. But they helped to remove dirt, water and some free fatty acids from the oil as illustrated in Table IX.

The quantity and grades of oil bulked at each bulk oil installation in 1951 and 1953 is shown in Table X.

The figures above show the quantity of oil bulked at each installation, but this does not mean however that the oil was produced in the neighborhood of the bulking point.

To transport bulk oil,the UAC utilized the services of Palm Line Shipping Company, one of its subsidiaries, whose ships were designed and fitted for the purpose. Before the introduction of bulking, oil was exported in drums and casks and freighted in ships. But bulking involved rolling casks of oil

Table IX: Nigeria: Bulk Oil Installations*

Tons	1950	1951	1952	1953	Total
Total Oil Bulked	158,600	136,100	176,000	198,000	669,000
Impurities Removed	1,145	1,047	1,197	1,200	4,589
Oil Lost	700	750	685	816	2,951

* Estimates based on twelve month figures to end of November, 1953.
Source: *UAC Statistical and Economic Review 13-16 (1954).*

Table X: Quantities Bulked, 1951-53*

	Special Grade <4.5% f.f.a		Grade I >4.5%-9% f.f.a.		Grades > 9% f.f.a.		Total '000 Tons	
	1951	1953	1951	1953	1951	1953	1951	1953
Apapa	–	–	0.9	–	1.2	1.1	1.9	31.1
Abonemma	–	5.2	18.5	16.9	6.8	3.1	25.3	25.2
Burutu	–	–	6.1	10.2	8.7	7.4	14.8	17.6
Calabar	–	6.9	18.4	24.2	7.6	3.7	26.0	34.8
Koko	–	–	0.2	1.8	6.2	7.9	6.4	9.7
Opopo	–	–	10.0	15.7	1.3	0.1	11.3	15.8
Port Harcourt	7.2	85.3	40.9	7.4	2.3	0.9	50.4	93.6
Total	7.2	97.4	94.9	76.3	34.1	24.3	136.2	198.0

* 1953 is calculated until November of that year.
Note: Any discrepancies in totals are due to rounding off.
Source: *UAC Statistical and Economic Review* 13-16 (1954).

onto ships, removing its bung and allowing oil to run out into containers in the ship. These processes involved a great deal of time and labor. The extra time involved in processing, contributed to increase in the free fatty acid content. But on the whole bulking helped to reduce the cost of labor and ocean freight charges much more than the handling of drums and casks.

Most of Nigeria's exported palm oil was bulked at UAC bulking installations from 1943 onwards. In 1949, the Palm Produce Marketing Board was established as the sole controller of the Nigerian palm oil trade and the UAC became its chief agent. The UAC bulked all the Board's oil under a specific arrangement. Table XI shows the charges paid by the Marketing Board under this agreement.

How did bulking affect the inhabitants and their economy? First, it provided an additional source of livelihood and helped

Table XI: Bulking Charges (nearest £100)

	1950	1951	1952
Leasing charges for installation and land	49,300	23,300	56,000
Operating and overhead expenses	93,200	123,000	166,600
Total Bulking charges	142,500	176,300	222,600

Source: *UAC Statistical and Economic Review* 13-16 (1954).

to expand the economic activities of the area. Bulking activities attracted migrant labor to the bulking stations and energized the immediate communities. For Burutu, the migrations increased its population and contributed to raise it to third class townships status by 1928. Urban activities contributed to the growth of secondary and tertiary activities. Therefore though bulking was established in the self-interest of the UAC, it had some benefits for the people and the society. These were some of the unintended benefits of the operations of the colonial economy.

Timber Industry: African Timber and Plywood

Perhaps a better illustration of UAC's pioneering effort in industrialization in Nigeria and the Western Delta in particular is the establishment of the African Timber and Plywood factory at Sapele in 1948 by African Timber and Plywood company, a subsidiary of the United African company. It was the largest timber factory in West Africa. It processed at least thirteen species of timber as shown in Table XII.

Table XII: Estimated Percentage by Volume of Total Extraction of Logs

	African Timber and Plywood Limited	Total Fellings, High Forest Concession
Abura	5	2
Afara	4	3
Agba	18	6
Antaris	2	1
Daniella	2	1
Gedunohor	3	3
Guarea	4	4
Idigbo	2	1
Iroko	1	2
Mahogany	10	27
Mansonia	3	4
Obeche	26	33
Others	8	7
Walnut	4	2
Total	100	100

Source: Annual Report of Forestry Administration, 1949-1950.

Timber Industry

The people of the Western Delta used trees for canoes construction, firewood, wooden utensils, furniture, doors and other wooden products. The people did not engage in the commercial exploitation of the forest for timber in pre-colonial times. The bulk of the timber came from the forests of Benin, Ondo and Ijebu north of the Western Delta Region came from outside of it in the Ondo and Benin forests.
Sapele port with a deep natural harbor and accessible by river, creek and road, was strategically situated on the edge of the rain forest to serve as a depot and port for the forest products of Ondo and Benin.

The logs were rafted down the rivers or transported by lorries, to Sapele, where they were received, prepared and stored for export as shown in Map 7. This figure illustrates Sapele's role as a depot and port for trade in timber. The timber industry was an expensive business. It required considerable capital and technical skills for its wide-ranging operations. These involved acquisition of forest concessions, forest operations, transport of the timber to the sawmill and preparation for export. It also include other actions such as road building and maintenance, forest maintenance, supervision and housing for forest workers.

This accounts for why many Africans could not establish timber operations. Indigenous timber business was limited to logging, a less expensive level of the industry.

Early History of African Timber and Plywood

The African Timber and Plywood Company which owned the African Timber and Plywood factory in Sapele was a subsidiary of the UAC. The Miller Brothers who were the pioneers of Nigeria's timber export trade had established a small sawmill at Koko around 1917.[24] This mill passed on to the African Timber and Plywood which became a subsidiary of the UAC in 1929. The UAC inherited the saw mill in the same year and relocated it to Sapele in 1935.[25] After World War II, the African Timber and Plywood company embarked on a modernization scheme, building a plywood factory on the same Sapele site in 1948. In 1951, the old sawmill was completely replaced by a modern unit. The activities of the factory included forest operations, saw-milling and the manufacture of plywood and veneer.

Forest Operations

Felling trees was followed by log sawing. Deformed or defective logs were removed in a process of selection and grading. This was followed by classification of logs by logging assistants who divide the logs into those required for plywood and for the sawmill.[27] Each log was given an identification number at the loading point which accompanied it until its final destination.[28]

Transportation was undertaken at two levels. The first was by lorries (logging vehicles) from the forests to the waterside where they were rafted to Sapele. Before the use of diesel engine tug boats, the logs were rafted down-stream to Sapele. This took take up to five weeks from the Ondo and Ife forest areas. But with the use of tug boats, the voyage rarely took longer than a week.

Reception at Sapele

Upon arrival, each raft was checked and discharged from the tug master to the beach master who undertook the further classification of the logs. The best logs were usually reserved for export. The ones for plywood came out of this category while the ones for the sawmill came out of the ones not designated for export.[29] The preparation of logs for export (rounding and squaring) took place either on the beach or in the sawmill. The timber was treated with chemicals to protect them from damage. About four and a half million cubic feet of logs were extracted from the Ondo, Ife and Benin forests, every year, from 1952-1962.[30] Table XIII analyzes the relative importance of each tree species, and the way in which it was processed.

Table XIII: Log Utilization, 1949-50 ('000 cubic feet)

	Floater (f) Sinker (s)	Export	Plywood	Sawmill	Total
Abura	f/s	225	–	–	225
Agba	f	255	–	578	833
Antaris	f	95	3	–	98
Daniella	f	82	–	6	88
Gedunohor	f	46	22	55	123
Guarea	s	52	30	81	163
Idigbo	f	39	–	37	76
Iroko	fs	20	–	21	41
Mahogany	f	50	235	174	459
Mansonia	f/s	95	–	38	133
Obeche	f	344	415	445	1,204
Others	–	220	7	121	348
Sapelewood	f	138	130	103	37,371
Walnut	f	95	–	86	181
White Afura	f/s	51	150	–	201

Source: *UAC Statistical and Economic Review* 9-12 (1952-53).
Also Annual Report of the Forestry Administration, 1949-1950.

Sawmill

The sawmill not only processed sawn timber, but also prepared logs for export. Both timber and logs were dried, treated with chemicals and graded before export, and local sales.[31] There are two noteworthy features of the sawmill. The first was the use of individual electric motors for powering each of the machines; and the second was the use of compressed air to operate the conveyor machines.[32]

Plywood Production

The establishment of the plywood factory marked a major stage in the industrialization of the timber industry. The first stage in the timber industry was export of logs. The second was processing logs into sawn timber and finally the manufacture of timber into plywood.

The plywood factory was set up with the intention of producing a hard quality plywood of the highest quality according to world standards. When it began production, it was an industrial establishment without precedence in West Africa. In fact, along with the sawmill, it was one of Nigeria's largest establishments which made Sapele one of the principal industrial centers of Nigeria and the whole of West Africa.

Plywood is made up of three or more layers of wood (veneers) securely glued together in a manner that gives the product equal strength and stability across its height and width, an advantage not enjoyed by solid wood. The factory manufactures flush doors, blackboards and other wood products of increasingly greater diversity.[33]

Until 1960, the UAC produced more plywood for export than for the local market. About eighty percent of its products were exported while about twenty percent were for local markets.[34] Exports went mainly to the United States, United Kingdom, South Africa, Canada and other Commonwealth countries.[35] The demand for tropical wood grew with the decline of the production of temperate woods. The trade witnessed a boom between the 1950's and 1960's.[36] Though the quality of Nigerian timber was among the highest in the world, its price was relatively low. Numerous types of wood were also exported. Tables XIV and XV outline the growth in demand for Nigeria's plywood, logs and sawn timber.

Table XIV: Plywood and Veneer Products, 1951-63

Year	Quantity ('000 m^3)	Value N '000	Value per '000 m^3
1951	11.01	822	74.65
1952	12.77	1,046	81.91
1953	12.94	1,082	83.61
1954	13.25	1,754	132.27
1955	15.12	1,510	99.86
1956	15.07	1,852	122.89
1957	12.18	1,494	122.66
1958	14.61	1,820	124.57
1959	14.98	1,900	126.83
1960	19.09	2,194	114.92
1961	10.33	2,378	116.69
1962	21.78	2,592	119.00
1963	20.53	2,072	100.92

Source: A. D. Little, Jr., Chief Conservator of Forests, *The Feasibility of Expanding Production of Plywood and Veneer in Nigeria: Report 60 to the Ministry of Commerce and Industry*, Federal Republic of Nigeria, September, 1964.

Table XV: Nigerian Timber Exports

	Logs			Sawn Timber		
Year	Volume '000 m³	Value N '000	Value N / '000 m³	Volume '000 m³	Value N '000	Value N / '000 m³
1951	477	10,156	21.29	27	956	35.40
1952	218	4,306	19.75	26	1,014	39.00
1953	334	6,446	19.29	32	1,254	39.18
1954	290	5,562	19.17	36	1,452	40.33
1955	410	7,456	18.18	42	1,762	41.95
1956	300	5,102	17.06	49	1,974	40.28
1957	367	6,652	18.12	53	1,838	34.67
1958	434	8,286	19.09	62	2,418	39.00
1959	547	9,754	17.83	63	2,364	37.52
1960	629	11,856	18.84	59	2,222	37.66
1961	576	10,958	19.02	62	2,486	40.09
1962	459	8,748	19.05	66	2,602	39.42
1963	528	10,890	20.62	77	2,724	35.37

Source: A. D. Little, Jr., Chief Conservator of Forests, *The Feasibility of Expanding Production of Plywood and Veneer in Nigeria: Report 60 to the Ministry of Commerce and Industry*, Federal Republic of Nigeria, September, 1964.

Initially, most of the local sales were made to government departments, especially the Public Works Department (PWD). Plywood was used for construction of industrial, educational and residential buildings. Most of the offices and residences in the modern sector constructed by the government before 1960 were built of wood. Almost all the buildings in the government reserved areas (GRAs) in the old regional and provincial headquarters were also built of wood produced largely by the African Timber and Plywood company. The rise in the number of government constructions during the period under investigation, created a large local market for the factory's products. There was increased demand in 1947 when John Holt formed a partnership with Costain to participate in the 1947 ten-year plan.[37] The plan called for numerous large-scale construction projects which created a big demand for timber products of the African Timber and Plywood.

In 1953, the UAC convinced the British construction firm of Taylor Woodrow to come to Nigeria to participate in the construction enterprise. Taylor Woodrow established three furniture factories in 1953, 1955 and 1958. In 1954 it established a concrete product company which became one of the principal local customers of African Timber and Plywood because of its requirements for construction projects.[38]

Aside from the demand created by these large firms, the demand from smaller consumers also contributed significantly to the growth of the timber trade. Local demand continued to grow as the economy and the political situation changed with increase in nationalist agitation for independence in the late 1950's.

Table XVI estimates the local consumption of plywood by subtracting exports from total production.

Increasingly, the proportion of the products reserved for the local market could not meet the local demand. As a consequence, the commercial firms began to import plywood and veneer. Table XVII shows the estimated consumption of plywood and veneer in Nigeria from 1956-1961.

It is important to mention that wood was not the basic material for construction in Nigeria, the way that it was in Europe and the United States. In these countries, wood was consider-

Table XVI: The Feasibility of Expanding Plywood and Veneer Production in Nigeria, 1956-1963

	Production		Exports		Local Consumption	
Year	cu. ft.	sq. ft. '000	cu. ft.	sq. ft. '000	cu. ft.	sq. ft. '000
1956	657,874	31,578	522,952	25,102	134,923	6,476
1957	627,751	30,132	413,455	19,846	214,296	10,286
1958	679,809	32,631	495,124	23,765	184,683	88,865
1959	717,137	34,423	522,495	25,080	194,642	9,343
1960	828,756	39,780	673,660	32,336	155,096	7,444
1961	935,974	44,927	730,000	35,040	205,974	9,887
1962	974,491	46,776	794,000	38,112	180,491	8,664
1963	1,006,962	48,334	754,000	36,192	252,960	12,142

Source: A. D. Little, Jr., Chief Conservator of Forests, *The Feasibility of Expanding Production of Plywood and Veneer in Nigeria: Report 60 to the Ministry of Commerce and Industry*, Federal Republic of Nigeria, September, 1964.

Table XVII: Estimated Consumption of Plywood and Veneer, 1956-61

	Production		Exports		Local Consumption	
Year	cu. ft.	sq. ft. '000	cu. ft.	sq. ft. '000	cu. ft.	sq. ft. '000
1956	134,900	6,476	28,600	1,373	163,000	7,849
1957	214,300	10,285	51,000	2,448	263,000	12,734
1958	184,700	8,865	103,800	4,982	288,500	13,847
1959	194,600	9,343	120,700	5,794	315,300	15,137
1960	155,100	7,444	190,000	9,120	345,100	16,564
1961	206,000	9,887	313,700	15,058	519,700	24,945

Source: A. D. Little, Jr., Chief Conservator of Forests, *The Feasibility of Expanding Production of Plywood and Veneer in Nigeria: Report 60 to the Ministry of Commerce and Industry,*

ably used for paneling, sub-flooring, sheathing and in concrete floors. In Nigeria, concrete was the most important building material in urban areas while mud and bricks were extensively used in rural areas.

Today, the company's products have become varied, sophisticated and specialized. This demonstrates the adaptability of the Plywood factory to changing socio-economic demands. Also there appears to be a continuity in major customers of the factory's product. For example, Vono Company, another UAC subsidiary which specializes in home furniture had patronized the factory products for a long time. Since the growth of off-shore crude oil exploration in the 1970's, the African Timber and Plywood developed a product known as "systems building" or a complete wooden building used as residence by expatriate staff in the oil rigs off-shore.

Eternit, a large construction company based in Sapele, is also another major user of the factory's products. In recent times products of the company currently range from particle boards, the ceiling boards, tables, wardrobes, police batons, flooring blocks, decorative veneer, paper baskets and dressing hedges for doors. The operations of the company generated new forces of change in Sapele and the immediate community.

Benefits of the Activities of the African Timber and Plywood Factory

Educational Benefits

The requirements of its engineering and maintenance divisions created an urgent need for vocational training. It established a training school for training apprentices for a period of five years. The training school program was extended to the students of the Government Trade Center. Upon completion, the graduates were qualified to register for the City and Guild of London Institute or the Nigerian Ordinary and Higher National Certificates. Thus, the company contributed to the growth of skilled manpower at the levels of technicians and tradesmen.

The company paid higher wages to its employees in comparison to the public and other private sectors. The relatively high wages and fringe benefits was a strong attraction to job seekers. But more significantly, the wage situation enabled the company to maintain a stable staff and permanent work force.

The provision of modern housing and other social facilities including health care, a theater house, a general store, boxing facilities and a playground enhanced the comfort of its diverse labor force, which reached three thousand in 1959. With the exception of the senior managerial staff which was European, the company workers came from almost every group in Southern Nigeria and even the Northern parts of the country. The Igbo formed the largest group of workers, followed by the Yoruba. Other important groups represented were the Benin and the Ishan.[39]

The Integrative consequences of inter-ethnic interaction have been discussed in this work. The formation of social clubs based on considerations other than ethnicity helped to strengthen inter-ethnic relations. Labor unions pulled together people of different, ethnic, economic and class backgrounds.

The large labor of the factory contributed to the growth of the population of Sapele. Other commercial and industrial businesses especially those connected with rubber and general trade also drew migrant labor into the town which grew to become a highly mixed community. But of all the employers of labor, the African Timber and Plywood was the single largest not only in Sapele but the whole of Nigeria.

Sapele grew from 15,000-20,000 in 1939 to 40,000 by 1955.[40] The presence of Europeans, Lebanese, Greeks added greater diversity to the population. Intermarriages across ethnic and racial groups were quite common. One of the consequences of this was the emergence of a new racial category known as mulattoes. Sapele gained the status of a grade two township by 1956. Foreign and indigenous businesses established schools, hotels, hospitals, cinemas and sports clubs during this period. The urban council market established in 1945 expanded to meet the growing needs of the population.

In concluding this chapter, it could be argued that the activities of the UAC and other businesses stimulated the social and economic growth of Sapele and its environs. Increasing social interrelationships among diverse groups is a progressive consequence for the people and society in the Western Delta. In this case, the presence of the commercial firms and the colonial administration generated progressive forces which improved the welfare of the people.

Notes

1 A.A. Lawal, " Industrialization as Tokenism". in *Britain and Nigeria: Exploitation or Development.* (London: Zed. 1987) P. 114

2 ibid.

3 ibid.

4 i bid.

5 F. J. D. Lugard, *The Dual Mandate in British Tropical Africa,* (Reprinted London: Frank Cass Ltd., 1965), p. 509, cited in A. A. Lawal, "Industrialization as a Tokenism", in Falola, ed, op. cit., p. 509.

6 G.K. Helleiner, *Peasant Agriculture, Government and Economic Growth in Nigeria,* (Homewood, Illinois: R.D. Irwin, 1966), p. 12.

7 K. Nkrumah, *Towards Colonial Freedom: Africa in the Struggle Against World Imperialism,* 1979 p. 10. cited in Falola. *ed.* op. P.19

8 J. Mars, "Extra-Territorial Enterprises", in M. Perham, ed., *The Economics of a Tropical Dependency,* (London: Faber and Faber, 1941), p. 232.

9 CSO 26/36546, *op. cit.*

10 *UAC Statistical and Economic Review* 7 (1951).

11 Western Nigeria Ministry of Agriculture File 21095.

12 Forde, op. cit., p. 240.

13 *Ibid.*

14 *Ibid.*

15 *Ibid.*

16 *Ibid.*

17 Ughelli Divisional, Ughedist. I, File 1530, Oruworun Development Project.

18 Interview with Mr. A. Asidi (Secretary to Isoko District Council from 1952-63), at Iyede, December, 1986.

19 N.A.I. , Nigerian Oil Palm Marketing Board, Annual Reports up to 1952, 1953 estimated.

20 P. Kilby: *Industrialization in an Open Economy: Nigeria, 1945-1966,* (Cambridge University Press, 1969), p. 67.

21 Warri Province, War Prof: I, WP 1130, Vol. 1, . . .

22 *UAC Statistical and Economic Review* 13-16, *op. cit.*

23 *Ibid.*

24 N.A.I., Warri Prof. I, File 340, Koko Township, Papers.

25 F.A. Well and Wermington, *Studies in Industrialization: Nigeria and the Cameroons,* (Oxford University Press, 1962), p. 26.

26 *Ibid.*

27 *UAC Statistical and Economic Review* 10 (1952).

28 *Ibid.*

29 Interview with Chief O. Ilebe (former employee of the A.T. & P.) at Sapele, December, 1986.

30 *Ibid.*
31 Interview with Commercial Manager, Mr. O. Oraka, A.T. & P. Factory, December, 1986.
32 Sapele Urban District Annual Report, 1955 NAI.
33 Little, *op. cit.*, p. 6.
34 Kilby, *op. cit.*, p. 67.
35 *Ibid.*, p. 70. See Map VI.
36 Interview with Mr. Oraka, *op. cit.*
37 Wells and Wermington, *op. cit.*, p. 36.
38 Interview with Mr. Udoh Udoh, Personnel Manager, A.T. & P., Sapele, December 1986. Wage scale was 5 1/2d an hour for unskilled labor or £1.2.0d for 48 hours a week; process workers 6 l/1d an hour or £1.6.0d a week; clerks–£120 per annum. These wages were paid before 1960.
39 Wells and Wermington, *op. cit.*, p. 35.
40 Sapele Urban District Annual Report, 1955. *op. cit.*

Chapter 10

The Growth of Indigenous Entrepreneurs and Entrepreneurial Activity in Palm Produce Trade

The Growth of Indigenous Entrepreneurs

There is considerable evidence to suggest that the term "entrepreneur" and the ascribed role of the businessman predated the writing of Max Weber and Joseph Schumpeter, who are regarded as the pioneers of the concept of entrepreneurship.[1] Some writers trace the origin to the works of Richard Cantillon and J.B. Say[2]

Weber's thesis sought to identify the historical conditions under which industrial capitalism rose and flourished and the decisive role which religious values played in the formation of effective entrepreneurs. Specifically, he ascribes the rise and growth of capitalism to the Calvinist doctrines of the Puritan Movement of the sixteenth and seventh century Europe.[3] Despite its apparent plausibility, the thesis has evoked much criticism and debate. It is valid, in part, by the contention that capitalism predates Protestantism. Webers's critics claim that the several factors that gave rise to capitalism can be traced back to the Middle Ages, more specifically to the period of the Crusades.

It appears that capitalism of Weber's thesis is fundamentally different from the capitalism of today, especially in in terms of how he defines "motivation". Even if, he is correct in his analysis of the beginning or escalation of capitalism in the eighteenth century Europe, his findings have little application to the problems of capitalist development in the modern period, it is said.[4]

Schumpeter also attempted to account for the development of capitalist economies. To him, entrepreneurship is the decisive factor in the process of economic development. He equates entrepreneurship with the innovation which he describes as the "creative response".[5] Unlike Weber, he posits that the primary factor behind entrepreneurial activity is the profit motive, although other considerations such as the desire to found an "economic empire" could also be a motivational force. He has been seriously criticized for his concept of defining entrepreneurship as the "fountain head" of critical innovation and capitalist development. Many critics agree that the entrepreneur is the central figure in the modern economy, but they contend that he is not always the unique economic actor as Schumpeter claims.

Since the second world war, there has been a growing scholarly interest in the subject of entrepreneurship. These works examine entrepreneurship as an inclusive factor within an overall economic development.[6]

In relation to Nigeria, Akeredolu-Ale identifies some historical situations which have significantly influenced the growth and development of entrepreneurial activity since the Second World War.[7] He claims that the "environment" which promoted the development of entrepreneurs did not start inNigeria until after the Second World War.[8] He adds that it was not until 1946, that the colonial government took major steps toward the launching of programs whose effects stimulated significant change in the economy. In that year, the colonial government launched a Ten-Year Program of Development and Welfare which turned the attention of the investing world on Nigeria.[9] This was a social and economic package aimed at improving the welfare of society. The measures led to an increase in the registration of companies, expansion of economic activities in the private sector, and a surge in the number of modern economic organizations.

In addition to government provision of "appropriate substantial infrastructure," Akeredolu-Ale stresses the role of population changes, urbanization and markets, as fundamental factors which affected the growth of indigenous entrepreneurs in Nigeria.

In the post-Second World War period, the most dynamic force which affected the Nigerian society was politics. Nationalist agitation for independence dominated the scene. Many front-line nationalists were modern professional elites and they saw independence as an eventual means of controlling the economy.

The role of indigenous businesses in the nationalist movement was minimal. Indigenous entrepreneurship was little developed in the colonial period. A number of reasons explain this situation. But the most fundamental were the dominance of the expatriate commercial firms and the stifling trade regulations which prevented indigenous business people from developing capital. While emphasizing the role of the government in promoting entrepreneurial growth, Akeredolu-Ale and Helleiner describe the colonial government as the most important sources of initiative and the most dynamic element in the Nigerian economic experience.[10] They claim that the government not only provided appropriate substantial infrastructure, but also, participated directly in agricultural and industrial activities as well as introduced measures enabling the private sector of the economy to expand and become modernized. Most of these measures had as their goal, the stimulation of indigenous entrepreneurship.

Akeredolu-Ale also suggests that population changes and urbanization were closely related to the growth of markets and to entrepreneurship. He asserts that although the actual size of the Nigerian population remains unknown, the size of her domestic markets is one of her principal assets in her struggle for economic growth. Entrepreneurial activities in the urban areas acted as a "pull" force for migration, he posits. This perspective differs from some studies of urban unemployment in Nigeria that state that migration occurred due to "push" forces in the rural areas, not from attraction in the urban areas.[12] There is a strong reason to believe that the growth of urban areas did provide a strong impetus to the development of entrepreneurship. Urbanization created an almost elastic supply of two types of laborers. The first was unskilled laborers who were paid subsistence wages, the second, a vast pool of school leavers who were recruited for more skilled operations. There is no doubt that population growth and urbanization did, indeed, provide additional incentives for entrepreneurial growth.

The Growth of Indigenous Entrepreneurs in the Western Delta

This study recognizes that there were indigenous entrepreneurs who actively participated in the Nigerian economy, including that of the Western Delta, prior to British colonization. A considerable amount of entrepreneurial activity took place before 1946, the point at which Akeredolu-Ale claims the government began to encourage entrepreneurship. For example, substantial activity in palm produce, rubber and trading predate the end of the second world war.

The individuals discussed in this study were a new breed of indigenous entrepreneurs whose business operations were determined by the dynamics of the activities of the expatriate commercial firms. The stimuli for their actions, were derived from the forces generated from their interaction with expatriate commercial firms.

The growth of entrepreneurial activities in the Western Delta corresponds with the concept of Akeredolu-Ale to some extent. Population changes and urbanization provided a large domestic market for merchant activities. To this extent, the majority of the entrepreneurial activities took place in the major urban areas of Warri and Sapele.

It is difficult to apply the "crucial role of government thesis" to the development of entrepreneurial activity in the Western Delta. In this region, entrepreneurial activities were more in response to internal dynamics. The local demand for imported goods in the Delta and beyond it, in addition to the challenge of a monetized economy which created the major impetus for increased entrepreneurial interests.

For the purpose of this study, entrepreneurial activity in the Western Delta will be classified according to palm produce, rubber, general merchandize and logging. These categories can hardly be considered to be a definitive categorization because most entrepreneurs undertook multi-faceted pursuits. Many palm produce traders were also involved in the rubber trade, general merchandise and transportation. Doing business in palm produce or rubber necessitated trade in general merchandise because collectors needed imported goods to sell to producers in return for palm oil, palm kernels or rubber. The demand for imported items lent continuity and permanence to the palm and rubber trades. The transportation business developed as a concomitant feature of logging, rubber, palm produce, and to some extent, general merchandise. Vehicles were required to deliver products to the export centers and take imported goods from them. Despite their interrelatedness, it is possible to discuss such activities as separate entities in the case of palm produce, rubber, logging and general merchandise.

It has been stated that the colonial government provided a conducive "environment" for economic growth. In fact, entrepreneurs in businesses like rubber as will be demonstrated were discouraged, not encouraged by government policy. It is the operations of the commercial firms which impacted more positively on the people, in terms of providing the immediate stimuli for entrepreneurial growth in the Western Delta. This is inspite of the fact that the government and the firms enjoyed a symbotic relationship.

It should be emphasized that the change in the taste of the people and the resultant increase in the demand for imported goods intensified commercial activities in the Western Delta. The urgent need for cash in the new economic situation for payment of taxes, procurement of essential commodities, other financial responsibilities including school fees for children and church dues enhanced the need for the establishment of large scale business activities. This situation posed the decisive challenge inducing the entrepreneurs discussed in this study to undertake effective independent enterprises.

The nature of trade, and, in particular, the challenge of undertaking and ensuring regular supplies of export products to the commercial firms, thrust great responsibilities on the agents. They were compelled to undertake serious initiatives which culminated in entrepreneurial activities. The agents organized subagents who "combed" the communities directly for palm produce or rubber. The need to reprocess and recontain products called for decisions which challenged the need to establish organized large scale businesses.

Some common features were evident in the development of entrepreneurs in the Western Delta. For example, frequent exposure to European traders made the agents to become more acquainted with modern business strategies. With few exceptions, most of the entrepreneurs received a Western education, such as was available to them at that time.[13] Western education controlled by the Christian missions exposed them to Christian ethics and capitalist values. No doubt, such exposure enabled them to broaden their world view and to imbibe the Christian and European "spirit of capitalism" based on individual enterprise and profit-making.

The third factor which affected the development of the indigenous entrepreneurs is their parentage and family backgrounds. All the entrepreneurs discussed in this study came from trading families. One or both parents were traders with a considerably long history of wealth. In most cases, they were agents to European trading firms or connected to trade. In general, such families owned considerable land and fishing waters, which provided significant sources of wealth. In view of their economic power, they were able to wield considerable political and social influence in their communities, enhancing their patronage. Thus, the entrepreneurs considered here, had adequate training and financial bases on which they founded their business activities.

Indigenous Entrepreneurial Activitity in the Palm Produce Trade

Three entrepreneurs are discussed in this chapter. They are Chief William Eboe Otobo, 1903-1978; Chief Ovedhe Mazoje, 1910-, and Chief Jefia Obori, 1905-1969.

William Otobo was born into the wealthy and influential family of Chief Otobo of Uzere in Isokoland. His father served as a councillor at the Uzere Native Court in the Isoko area and also operated as a produce agent and a general trade, in which his wife, the mother of William, was involved. As a boy, William Otobo attended the Church Missionary Society (C.M.S) Primary School and the Dennis Memorial Grammar School both in Onitsha. He began his working career as a court clerk at Ase from 1927-29, after which he moved to Ughelli to serve as a clerk at the Urhobo Divisional Council. He also served as an interpreter and rose to the position of secretary to the divisional officer. Later he became treasurer of the council.

He retired in 1949 to become the first vice-president of the Federated Urhobo/Isoko Court of Appeal in 1950. He officiated as president of the Customary Court at Ughelli until he retired again in 1974. He began trading, in palm produce in the mid-1930's, rubber in the 1940's and operate a transportation enterprise in the 1950's. His business activities were limited to the Urhobo and Isoko areas. These businesses were undertaken simultaneously with his official responsibility.

William Otobo received a good education, having attended one of an the best missionary secondary schools in Nigeria during his time. He studied outside his area, an experience which exposed him to other people and cultures. Onitsha, where he was educated is the largest market in West Africa. This level of education was rare for his time. In his days, the First School Leaving Certificate was the most common level of educational attainment, thus he was considerably well educated for his time. Also there is no doubt that the business environment of the town affected his business ambitions. His varied life experiences among the Ijo, Urhobo and Igbo broadened his perspective on life which impacted richly on his activities.

In addition, his official positions and experience made him knowledgeable about government regulations and their implementation. But, his official responsibilities restricted his ability to expand his business outside his working environment. Why did Otobo establish businesses in spite of his job? This can be attributed to a number of factors. Family tradition was a major determining factor. His family background and early social environment contributed to his business interests. The resources of the Otobo family provided financial stability and a psychological edge for him. His business establishments were a continuation of his family tradition.

The salary of a Council employee was not sufficient to meet the basic needs of a polygamous family. Earning more cash became a necessity. Specifically, the cash requirement of the new social and economic situation also added to his determination for business undertakings.

Chief Jefia Obori, 1904-1969

Chief Obori was born in Jeremi in Urhoboland. His father was a wealthy trader in palm produce and imported goods. Obori received an education of less than Standard Six. Through his dynamism and the advantages of family resources and name, he became president of the Jeremi Customary Court in eastern Urhobo. He was the *Olorogun* (High chief) of the Jeremi clan in which capacity he represented his community in the Native court system. He began his business in the palm produce industry in the late 1920's and established an extensive trading network; Obori operated outside the Western Delta as far as Agbor. Even within the Delta, his business stretched from Burutu, Forcados in Ijoland to Obiaruku in Ukwuaniland. The informant who discussed Chief Obori claimed that the focus of the business, however, was in the Urhobo/Isoko areas.[14] It was an important strategy for networking different levels of relationships, social, economic and political, across the region and beyond. Very few other factors could have created such linkages during this period.

Chief Ovedhe Mazoje, 1906-

Chief Mazoje was born about 1905. Ovedhe had no formal education. He was born at Oyede in Isokoland, but migrated with his mother to Iden on the Niger, in Abohland. His mother was engaged in general trade between Iden and Onitsha. He claimed to have learned the art of trading from his mother, who also gave him the initial capital to enter the palm produce business. He was not involved in the "Native" Court system in any capacity, unlike the previous entrepreneurs. Like Obori, he entered the palm produce trade in the late 1920s.

Mazoje was the only one in this group with no formal education. But he was very industrious. He established a wide trading network of on the lower Niger at strategic locations. He established sixteen stores along the Niger and its distributaries. He operated primarily among the Isoko, Aboh and Ijo, unlike Otobo who traded primarily among the Urhobo and Isoko.

Although there was an advantage in multi-business operations, specializing in one product or aspect ensured greater efficiency and guaranteed the advantages of specialization. Mazoje said he concentrated on palm produce to such a degree that his name became synonymous with produce trade. His relations with the UAC became highly successful. He claimed that the UAC "trusted" him. His people respected him to the extent that they honored him with a chieftaincy title which recognized his high degree of success in the produce trade.[15] He is titled *Osisiego* which literally translates as *Tree of money*.

Nature of Business Operations

All three men operated as major agents to European trading firms. Most firms established trading stations at strategic locations in the hinterland, along the Niger and its distributary network.[16] They operated on a cash and credit basis with the European firms and established stores and shops in strategic locations for both retail and wholesale businesses in palm produce.[17] Running the shops was a great responsibility which required a good deal of hard work, commercial acumen and organizational ability.

Commercial activities were expanded beyond ones ethnic borders. Shops were established in areas where it was relatively easy to obtain produce and to market imported good. Activities connected with the shops promoted inter-group social and economic relations and created new linkages in the interior.

The challenges of operating in relatively unfamiliar environments seemed to have compelled these men to engage in inter-ethnic marriages. These marriages helped to expand social relations and promote security. Also they fostered support for the growth of business. Wives were engaged as supervisors and managers of the shops of their spouses. The use of family labor in traditional businesses was common. The difference here is that it assumed a new dimension in the expanded commercial environment. New opportunities became open to women at different levels.

But on the whole, a substantial labor force was required to operate stores and shops, man the canoes and carry the bags of kernels and containers of oil, serve as guards, attendants and messengers. For the most part, they drew on traditional labor facilities. The most dependable and significant was family labor which included relatives, wives, children and dependents. Others included persons seeking to acquire skills in trade and were willing to serve as apprentices. In most cases, this category came from the entrepreneur's own community.

The concept and practice of The African extended family system facilitated this type of labor. Relatives were satisfied to work for successful and influential members of their families and community. The economic power, the socio-political influence of these successful businessmen provided substantial support and protection for those who depended on them. A mutually advantageous relationship came to determine the nature of the labor force used in these indigenous businesses.

The larger the household, the larger and more profitable the labor force. It is no wonder then that the number of wives of the men described here was between ten and fifteen and the number of children in each family, fifty or more. However, it is not customary to number the children of the African chief.[18]

Unlike in the formal economic sector, fixed wages were not attached to labor output. Reward was usually paid "in kind" rather than in cash. But the workers enjoyed "unlimited" social and economic advantages and protection from their employers.[19] These included free housing and feeding, payments for health services and meeting the financial costs of marriage. In addition, they received some minimal allowances.

It is difficult to argue that the method of remuneration was exploitative. Rewards were usually paid in "kind" rather than cash. The laborers enjoyed "unlimited" social and economic advantages and protection from their employers, normally referred to as "masters". The wealth that grew was sown back into the communities, to the advantage of its members. The benefits were enjoyed by relatives and non-relatives of the agents alike because their patronage was broad and profound. This was true when one considers that most villages were sparsely populated in this period.[20] In most cases, the benefits received were more substantial than cash payments. African traditional values and institutions were being adapted to the new commercial system. There are contradictions between European work ethics based on instant financial remuneration and the African system in which workers did not expect immediate financial rewards from their superiors. To what extent was the combination of these different work values and systems compatible? This study shows that there were no major contradictions in the adaptation of both systems in the business operations of these entrepreneurs.

In a largely oral culture, it is not surprising that the entrepreneurs hardly kept the records and statistics of their business activities. They claim they kept their records mentally. They argued that they did not require extensive documentation. The oral method may seem a simplistic method of accounting to those not accustomed to the dynamics of oral cultures but the fact is that these entrepreneurs were highly intelligent people who kept abreast of their businesses in an articulate manner. Nevetherless, it is difficult to understand the lack of documentation given the high educational levels of many of the entrepreneurs, the growing literacy and the increase in the pool of educated people capable of clerical duties. One of these entrepreneurs said that he deliberately did not keep the records of his trade and the extent of his wealth.[21] He added that records could be exposed and could create a serious problem.

On the average, the entrepreneurs sold about ninety barrels of oil and seventy sacks of palm kernels a year. This volume increased during times of good harvests and high prices. They did not directly participate in the government programs of quality improvement in palm produce, as outlined in chapters four and seven. But in general, they claimed that they were able to meet market demands, although there is no doubt that they were influenced by fluctuations, depressions and price increases as described in chapter six.

The entrepreneurs claimed that though the relationship between the firms and the entrepreneurs was based on the mutual understanding of promoting trade, it was basically an unequal relationship in which power and discretion lay with the firms. Merchandise was made available upon delivery and sale of the produce. Though the entrepreneurs agreed that there was generally no serious difficulties with maintaining the required volume of produce, they complained about arbitrary fixing of prices of both cash crops and imported items without due consultation with them. The cost of production in terms of land use, time, labor and energies was much higher than prices fixed for the produce. They attributed their financial difficulties to the price level and the uncertainty connected with fluctuating prices.[22]

The entrepreneurs operated with the support of sub-agents.[23] Sub-agents made purchases directly from the producers and sold to the entrepreneurs. The latter then sold directly to the commercial firms. But before delivery to the firms the middlemen/entrepreneurs cleaned, sorted, regraded and rebagged palm kernels, while palm oil was put in better containers to ensure acceptance to the firms. These processes reduced impurities and enhanced quality on delivery to the firms.[24] Subagents operated mainly on a credit basis with the entrepreneurs, receiving goods in trust for a regular supply of produce.

Often the producers and subagents created difficulties for the entrepreneurs in produce trade. Produce was adulterated in many cases in their bid to increase the quantity of oil or kernels supplied. This increased the responsibility of the entrepreneurs who adequately checked all deliveries to avoid the problem of rejection of adulterated items by the firms. Rejections involved loss of time and money, not to mention emotional frustrations.[25] There were problems with an inconsistent supply of produce from the subagents. During bad harvests and low price the supply became inconsistent. Sub agents often argued that they had no control over the volume producers could offer for sale. They also had to deal with the boycotts of producers who were attempting to force up prices; the only weapon the producers had to ensure price increase.

The entrepreneurs were compelled to engage in more than one line of business because the commercial firms required cash crops and in exchange sold imported items to them. Therefore sale of imported items became intrinsically linked to produce trade. They became highly skilled in commerce because of the experiences gained from interrelated businesses. Losses in one business were offset by profits from another.

Transportation for movement of goods and people was generally slow and uneconomic. Head portage was the most common and least profitable. In the riverain areas, use of canoes and tug-boats were the most common. It was only after the second world war, that trucks or tippers became visible in transportation in the Western Delta. In spite of this development, transportation was difficult and restricted trade and movement of people.

It is important to highlight some of the difference among the entrepreneurs. Otobo was one of the most exposed and educated among these entrepreneurs, an advantage that enabled him to have a successful career in the Divisional Council service. Mazoje with no formal education was a hard worker, focused only on palm produce trade, used all opportunities available to him to establish most extensive palm produce business in the Western Delta. But he lacked the political advantage of Jefia Obori and the education of Otobo. Inspite of this, he did not appear to have suffered any serious limitations in his business.

Of the three entrepreneurial activities, Otobo's business was least extensive because of the constraints of a full time government job. But like Obori and unlike Mazoje, he had interrelated businesses in addition, being involved in the rubber trade. He was the only entrepreneur who managed a public transport services.[26] In these cases, a loss in palm produce revenue was offset by profits in rubber trade. But Mazoje reaped the rewards of concentrating on a single business, becoming so efficient and proficient in the palm produce trade. Obori' network of trade was more extensive than Mazoje's business which was concentrated in the riverain areas of Isoko and Aboh.

Obori extended his trade all over the Delta region, from Isoko to Burutu and Forcados and beyond it to Agbor outside of the Delta though the focus of his business was the Isoko/ Urhobo area.[27] He had less education than Otobo but more than Mazoje. But his political influence and dynamism enabled him to achieve a lot. Of all of them Mazoje had the least political influence, not having been involved in Council administration or politics. He was the most private of all the three.

Notes

1 A.H. Cole, " Entrepreneurship as an area of Research", *Journal of Economic History*, 2, (December,1942), pp.118-126; F.Redlich, " The Origin of the Concept of " Entrepreneur" and the creative entrepreneur", *Journal of Entrepreneurial History.* 1, 2. (February 1949); B.F. Hoselitz, "The Early History of Entrepreneurial Theory", *Exploration in Entrepreneurial History* , 3 (April 1951)

2 J. B. Say, *A Treatise on Political Economy.* London 1921. A. H. Cole, "An Appraisal to the study of Entrepreneurship" *Journal of Economic History*, 6, Supplement (1946).

3 Max Weber, *The Protestant Ethic and the Spirit of Capitalism.* (New York: Charles Sarbner and Sons, 1930).

4 H.M. Robertson, " A Criticism of Max Weber and His School," *Aspects of the Rise of Economic Individualism*, (Cambridge University Press.1933)

5 J. A. Schumpeter, The Theory of Economic Development. (Cambridge University Press, 1949).

6 J. W. McGuire, *The Theories of Business Behavior,* (New Jersey: Prentice Hall Inc., 1964). E.T. Penrose, *The Theory of the Growth of the Firm.* (Oxford: Basil Blackwell, 1959)

7 E.O. Akeredolu-Ale, *The Underdevelopment of Indigenous Entrepreneurship in Nigeria*, (Ibadan: Ibadan University Press, 1975), Chapter 3.

8 E. O. Akeredolu-Ale, *op. cit.*, p. 35.

9 Government Printer, *A Ten-Year Program of Development and Social Welfare for Nigeria*, (Lagos, 1946).

10 P. Kilby, *Industrialization in an Open Economy: Nigeria.1946-66* London: OUP. 1969

11 Akeredolu-Ale, *op. cit.* P.35

12 I.I.U. Eke, " Population of Nigeria: 1952-1963". *Journal of Economic and Social Studies*, 8, 2. July 1966.

13 Primary Education was the most common and Standard Six Leaving Certificate was the highest educational level at that time.

14 Interview with Lydia Obori, wife of Jefia Obori at Jeremi, May 28, 1987.

15 Interview with Mazoje, *op. cit.*

16 *Ibid.*

17 Chief O. Mazoje owned 16 shops; Chief J. Obori owned 6, and Chief W. S. Otobo 6.

18 Each of them had about 20 wives on the average.

19 Some lived freely with their masters. They were given some money when they had new babies or were helped to pay brideworth for potential wives. At ceremonies and festivals they received gifts from their masters. A faithful worker could also receive a loan and or credit to start his own business. The master often helped workers build a house in their

own home communities. Interview with O. Mazoje at Oyede in Isoko, June 9, 1987.

20 War Prof.1. WP 809/1.

21 Interview with O. Mazoje, *op. cit.* June, 1987.

22 For details on price problems, see chapter 6.

23 Each had about 10 sub-agents at a time.

24 There were two main grades of palm oil; Grade I and Grade II–interview with Chief O. Omuvbie at Sapele, April 1987.

25 Interview with Chief O. Omuvbie, *op. cit.*

26 Chief William Otobo's Personal Files.(He owned three lorries).

27 Interview with Lydia Obori, wife of Jefia Obori at Warri, May 28, 197

Chapter 11

Indigenous Entrepreneurial Activities in Rubber, General Merchandise and Logging

Indigenous Entrpreneurial Activity in Rubber Business

Entrepreneurial activity in rubber industry covered a large area including most of the Urhobo/Isoko and Ukwuani areas. Sapele, was the focus of rubber trade while palm produce export centered around Warri. Warri which served as the main port for palm produce export because its proximity to the major production area, was accessible by a network of waterways and was the headquarters of one of the most important commercial firms that operated in the Western Delta, the John Holt. Sapele, on the other hand, was closer to the main rubber producing areas, such as the Benin forest and Ukwuaniland. Consequently, it attracted numerous rubber processing and purchasing firms. It became the major rubber exporting port not only in the Western Delta but also in country.[1]

The indigenous entrepreneurs connected with the rubber business in this chapter are *Chief Iwegbue*, *Chief Oki*, *Chief Oghene* and *J. A. Thomas*. Their careers will be analyzed in the same manner their counterparts in the palm produce trade were looked at.

Chief Otunuya Iwegbue, 1907-1982

Chief Iwegbue was born in 1907 into the influential Iwegbue family of Emu in Ukwuaniland. He began his career as a market master under Warri Council Authorities from 1926-28, after obtaining his First School Leaving Certificate.[2] At the end of 1928, he was employed by the Native Authority Administration and established Native Authority offices at Abraka and Amai between 1932-33. He rose to become treasurer of the Aboh Divisional Council at Kwale, the post from which he retired in 1964. He began trading in rubber in 1940-41.[3] Like Otobo, he combined official work with business.

Chief Fentu Oki 1898-1979

Chief Oki was born into a rich Ijoh family of Patani. His father was a wealthy produce trader based at Patani in the Ijo and Isoko border area. He was trained by a C.M.S. missionary, Reverend Henry Proctor, at Patani, where he also acquired his elementary education.[4] He began his career as a teacher in 1917-18, and later became an employee of John Holt. He also served as a manager at several John Holt stations including Asaba Aseh on the Niger. His last station was Ashaka which was the Aboh Divisional Headquarters of Holt businesses in the Western Delta. He remained here as manager until he retired in 1975 after which he served as the Patani customary court president. From 1960-63, he was a member of the Western Regional House of Assembly in which he represented Western Ijo Division.[5] Chief Oki began trading in rubber in the 1940s.

Chief Daniel Oyibo Oghene 1910-1987

Chief Oghene hails from Elume in the Okpe area of Urhoboland. After his primary education at the Elume Baptist school, he joined the G. B. Ollivant firm at Sapele as a clerk and rose to the rank of supervisor and ultimately an accounts clerk.[6] He retired from this post in 1958 in order to establish an independent rubber business in the same town. Chief Oghene established a plantation of 6425 acres (2600 hectares) at Elume in 1959.

In 1961, Chief Oghene established a "modern" rubber factory in Sapele. The factory produced Grade I rubber because of the application of more sophisticated and mechanized processing methods. The products of his factory were able to compete with those of the European firms.[8] Not every rubber producer attained the sophistication of Oghene's operation.

Oghene obtained the capital he used to establish his factory from personal savings.[9] Between 1958-61, he operated as a middleman. He bought rubber from producers and small-scale agents and sold to rubber purchasing firms. Through these undertakings, he was able to accumulate enough capital to build his factory which undertook direct export in 1961. Part of his success can be attributed to his location at Sapele, the center of the rubber trade.

J. A. Thomas 1895-1965

James Thomas was born at Ugbuangue in Itsekiriland. He came to Sapele in the first decade of this century and joined the firm of Miller Brothers, the first firm to establish a rubber estate in Nigeria. Thomas left Miller Brothers in 1912 and established the first indigenous rubber estate which undertook direct export.[10]

Nature of Business Operation

These rubber entrepreneurs owned their own plantations and also leased plantations from people who lacked capital to engage in commercial tapping. In addition, they undertook the collection of lumps and sheets from producers and small-scale agents. All of them owned and operated plantations not only in their own native lands but also outside their own ethnic communities. Outside their ethnic group, they were referred to as "native foreigners", persons who leased, purchased or planted rubber trees outside of their native areas.[11]

The acreage of each plantation ranged from ten to fifty. (Rather exceptional was the case of Oghene whose acreage, as noted above was quite huge). The bulk of their planting was done in the late 1930's and the 1940s. The high price for rubber in this period encouraged cultivation and increased production despite government regulations to the contrary. Each of them had an average of twelve plantations, of various sizes, both owned and leased.[12]

The major problem which faced the rubber industry was the lack of basic facilities and equipment for the production of improved rubber sheets and crepe. These entrepreneurs, however, had enough capital to cope with this challenge. They were able to afford large ovens and purchase rolling machines and chemicals required for processing and consequently, they were able to meet government standards. One of the informants claimed that it was difficult to produce Grade I rubber not because the tappers did not want to follow regulations but because they were poor and could not afford to set up modern factories.

As with the palm produce industry, all the entrepreneurs in the rubber industry had sub-agents. Most of the sub-agents operated on a credit basis with the middlemen. They collected lumps and sheets from primary producers and delivered them to the stores of the middlemen located in urban areas. In the stores, the products underwent further treatment and reprocessing; drying, grading and repacking in order to improve quality of the rubber products and make them more satisfactory to European firms.

Here also, the absence of records made it impossible to have accurate figures of production. These entrepreneurs claimed that each plantation could produce about forty sheets of rubber a day and that each middleman sold an average of five lorry loads five times a year to European firms.[13] The nature of the rubber industry demanded that each major agent possesses his own means of transportation to facilitate the collection and the delivery of product. It is important to note that the bulk of the rubber products was transported by land, while the majority of palm produce was transported by water.

The labor employed in the rubber industry were more skilled than that of the palm produce industry. Apart from great physical strength, some minimum skill was required to operate the rolling machines and heating systems adequately. Proper Tapping also required some specialized skill to prevent recklessness and shortening the tree's life-span. Unlike in the palm produce industry, labor was not necessarily recruited from among relatives.[14] The Igbo from the region east of the Niger river formed the bulk of the rubber tappers.

Some school children tapped on a part-time basis, as did some women.[15] Remuneration was different from that of palm produce. Laborers were paid according to their output. Men and women received equal amounts of six pence per sheet while children received less.[16] In some cases, plantations were leased to tappers and the profits were shared in agreed proportions. On the whole, the relations between laborers and entrepreneurs were much more formal in the rubber industry than in the palm produce business.

The entrepreneurs can be classified into two groups; Iwegbue and Oki in one and, Oghene and Thomas in the other. Those in the first group were employees of native authorities while operating as business men. They did not operate as full-time businessmen, yet their positions allowed them to be more familiar with governmental policies and programs than the others. They were able to harmonize their roles as native authority employees with viable business enterprises in rubber and imported goods.

The second group of entrepreneurs had worked in commercial firms before setting up their own businesses. They had more business experience having worked with expatriate firms. Like the first group they obtained the initial capital for their businesses from their own savings. With the exception of Oki, all of the entrepreneurs lived in Sapele which had become the major industrial town in the whole of the Western Delta. The business environment of the town had a positive effect on their business. The Thomas and Oghene businesses engaged in direct exporting, the others sold their rubber products to the European firms. Oki and Iwuegbue were limited by their full time jobs while Oghene and Thomas devoted all of their time to their businesses. This gave them the opportunity to expand and compete with European rubber firms.

The Problems of Rubber Business

The first problem was the shortage of regular labor. The Igbo tappers did not operate on a permanent basis and they were reckless. The second was the risk of fire created by heating and drying systems. This was dreaded all the more because fire services and insurance facilities were not available. The entrepreneurs were confronted with the third problem of adulterated products supplied by sub-agents. Reprocessing of adulterated products involved extra cost and labor. Most small-scale producers paid little attention to the quality of their products. This made reprocessing a serious investment. Pilfering by relatives and workers also constituted a nuisance to the owners of businesses.[17]

The fourth problem was the shortage of materials such as tapping knives and chemicals which created delays in production. It may be argued that in spite of the difficulties and problems which confronted these entrepreneurs, they were not only able to produce high quality grades of rubber as the expatriate firms but were able to undertake direct export.

Entrepreneursial Activity in General Merchandize and Logging Business

The four entrepreneurs studied below include two women who contributed significantly to the development of the textile business in the Western Delta. They are *Chief Alice Obahor, Chief Agnes Lady Agbaza, Chief T. J. Sokoh and Chief Wilson Odibo.*

Chief Alice Obahor, 1910-1984

Chief Alice Obahor was born into a trading family at Effurunto in Urhoboland where she received her primary school education.[18] She acquired her trading skills from her parents who were wealthy traders in palm produce and general goods. She lived briefly with her husband who was a marine engineer at Lokoja, a confluence town of the Niger and Benue rivers. On the death of her husband, she moved to Warri and began to trade in general goods in 1930. She started as an agent to the Compagnie Francaise d'Afrique Occidentale (CFAO) and the Societe Commerciale Ouest Africaine (SCOA) in 1934.[19]

Chief Obahor was exceptionally dynamic and progressive. In 1957, she was appointed a Director of the Board of John

Holt as a demonstration of the large volume of trade and considerable credit she had with the company. None of the other indigenous entrepreneurs discussed in this study attained this level of achievement.

Chief Agnes Agbaza, 1921-

Chief Agbaza was born in 1921. She is the daughter of Chief Jefia Obori of Jeremi who was an entrepreneur in palm produce business. She began her career as a school teacher and then became a clerk in John Holt at Warri.[20] Between 1952 and 1953, she began her business in textile as an agent of the Indian firm of K. Chellarams in Warri.

Chief T. J. Sokoh, 1908

Chief Soko was born in 1908 and received his primary education at Ovwian and Lagos.[21] He worked as a fisherman and a carpenter. In 1937, he began a trading business with his own savings. Sokoh bought general goods at Onitsha and sold them at Ovwian. He moved permanently to Warri in 1939. In 1947, he became an agent of the CFAO, and claims that was when his "fortune" began.[22]

Chief Wilson Odibo, 1923-

Chief Odibo was born in 1923 and began his business career in 1947 after receiving a primary school education at Egini in Udu clan.[23] His father was a rich produce dealer and his mother, a trader in general goods. He began by traveling to Onitsha and Aba to buy general goods for sale in Warri and its suburbs. In 1949, he became an agent for CFAO and G. B. Ollivant.[24]

Nature of Business

Reference has already been made to the importance that general trading had in the palm produce and rubber trades. The entrepreneurs discussed here claim to have concentrated solely on general trading. This quasi "mono-economic" activity can be explained by the fact that they began business on a very small-scale. Two began by buying goods from Onitsha on a retail basis while the other two began as sub-agents of CFAO. As the largest open wholesale market in the lower Niger districts, Onitsha was a focus of trade where high profits could be realized.

Trade in general goods was intensive and highly profitable. These entrepreneurs began their businesses during the Second World War. Also, the war created a high demand for general goods, most of which had become necessities. Some of the essential items included kerosene and matches. The colonial economy had become consolidated and there were conspicuous social changes affected by the growth of christianity and Western education.

During the war, they were appointed as agents/customers to almost all the firms which operated in Warri. To be qualified for distributorship, a business person was required to have own a considerable capital and the necessary infrastructure like stores and transportation. These entrepreneurs had substantial savings which they accumulated through personal savings and family financial support.

Agency with all the firms was necessary because each of the firm specialized in different types of merchandise. The demand for a broad variety of goods in expanding markets demanded that they register as agents with the different companies.[25] UAC brands were more popular with the people. The UAC, the oldest and biggest company which operated in the area, had established a reputation. The people had an aversion to change and preferred to continue using the same types of goods. It held a monopoly over some essential goods, such as kerosene.

The entrepreneurs operated on a cash and credit basis with the firms. There were two forms of credit: monthly credit and permanent credit.[26] With the monthly credit, the entrepreneurs received commissions after sales. With the permanent credit, the commission was accumulated as savings with the firms. The savings gave the entrepreneurs greater confidence. Also, the firms considered such savings as guarantees for business expansion. Such savings enhanced mutual trust between the agents and the firms. The monthly credit was preferred by new entrepreneurs. But as confidence increased, permanent credit became more desirable.[27]

The entrepreneurs lived and operated at Warri, the main commercial center of the Western Delta. Warri, also developed as the educational and cultural center with a growing christian missionary activity after the second world war.

Warehouses and stores were established as centers of business transactions in Warri. Of all the entrepreneurs, only Alice Obahor uniquely expanded her trade business to other parts of the Western Delta and Benin province. Each of the entrepreneurs owned at least three warehouses and two stores in Warri township for both wholesale and retail trade. Wholesale trading was preferred to retailing businesses because the goods were sold much faster. Customers for wholesale trade came from all over the Western Delta and beyond even as far as Aba in Eastern Nigeria.

Business expansion reached new heights in the 1950's as the UAC and other important trading firms began to give up general trade in preference for manufacturing. This change provided the opportunity for these businesses to expand and consolidate their commercial activities. They took over general trade from the firms and became the major operators of wholesale and retail trade in the Western Delta. The next stage in the growth of the entrepreneurs was their appointment as the major distributors for the manufacturing companies in the Delta and neighboring regions. This helped to increase and diversify their businesses. In order to be qualified for a distributorship, a businessman or woman was required to own considerable capital and the necessary infrastructure for operations. By the late 1950s and the early 1960s, they had the necessary financial and physical infrastructure to do so.

Their relationship with the commercial firms was based on mutual trust. They built up substantial capital to earn that respect. Their major complaint concerned their inability to influence the fixing of prices. But, they claim to have had high volumes of trade and made reasonable profits.

However, Obahor specialized in a special design of cloth popularly known as D. K. G. and Jackal, as well as head-ties called "Haze." These types were the most expensive and attractive types of cloth and head-ties.[28] Agbaza specialized in the type of cloth called "George", or Indian Madras, which was less expensive than the D.K.G. Both of them placed orders directly through the firm of K. Chellarams. Obahor made her orders to the United Kingdom while Agbaza made hers to India. Buyers had a choice from the variety of textile materials which became available. Agbaza concentrated on her textile trade with the firm of K. Chellarams but Obahor engaged in both textile and other forms of general merchandise with all the firms.

Labor

The labor used in these businesses was informal labor. It was considerably different from that of the formal modern sector. These entrepreneurs did not recruit specialized skills in the early stage of their businesses. People were engaged as apprentice traders. Initially, labor was recruited from family relations and other dependents. But as the business became more complex, labor was recruited from available sources for specialized duties.

Hausas from northern Nigeria and the neighboring Chad republic, generally considered more martial, were engaged as night guards to prevent burglary in warehouses and shops. Some Igbo and Yoruba were hired as petty contractors for special duties. For apprentices who were recruited from families, the conditions of remuneration were the same as those described in the palm produce industry in Chapter 4. Non-family members were paid wages of about £3 per month in the 1950s and this rose to £10 in 1960. Though actual wages were lower than those received in the public sector or in European firms, the workers enjoyed other benefits which brought their real wages close to those of the public sector and European firms.[29]

Problems of Trade

Apart from the problem of price setting referred to above, relations with sub-agents contained serious problems for the entrepreneurs. In some cases, the sub-agents failed to render correct accounts and diverted money for other purposes. This made the entrepreneurs to suffer financial losses. Also the sub-agents failed to supply the exact volume of produce agreed upon with the entrepreneurs. This affected the entrepreneurs' supplies and contracts with the firms.

As the businesses expanded, they increasingly had problems with adequate land and water transportation. Lorries and trucks were scarce and expensive. Transport owners complained that their vehicles were expensive to maintain because roads were in poor condition and spare parts were rare and expensive.[30] The large number of applications to the Western Regional Government for loans made by businessmen in the Western Delta to establish transportation business in the late 1950's can be attributed to the expansion of trade and high demand for transportation.[31]

The two women entrepreneurs profiled are distinct compared with their male counterparts, specifically, in their contribution to the growth of aesthetical values of their people. It is interesting to note their commercial acumen and initiative. Not only did they purchase textiles from the trading firms, but also, they imported directly from Britain and India. These women were the leading agents of textile trade, introducing unique designs attractive to the people.

Both organized their own designs and patterns, reflecting the aesthetic values of their people. These patterns were adopted by textile factories in Britain and India for manufacturing African prints. Hence, they demonstrated a sense of cultural independence, initiative which projected African cultural values and art to the outside world.

In addition, their initiative made imported textile more attractive to the people of the area. They were able to identify more closely with the people and their values more than the male entrepreneurs. It may be argued that the female entrepreneurs demonstrated a greater sense of initiative, innovation and dynamism which enabled Alice Obahor to surpass all of her male competitors. Through the activity of both women, the people of the Western Delta began to share similarities in textile materials with the people of India.

These women became role models for many people, especially women. They were married with families. Having families did not pose obstacles to their business endeavors rather they were supportive. On the whole, more men were involved in businesses because the colonial system and economy favored men in the formal and modern sector. For the women discussed in this chapter, it was a double struggle against colonial as well as traditional patriarchy.

Entrepreneurial Activity in Logging

Three entrepreneurs will be examined in the timber industry. I.T. Palmer(1899-1966), J.Asaboro(1900-1970) and Chief Odili Ibuaka, 1921-. Palmer and Asaboro were Yoruba migrants to Sapele during the inter-war years, who lived there until their deaths. Palmer had received primary education but Asaboro received no formal education. Both began logging in the later 1930s. Ibuaka, an Aboh was the most educated having obtained what he referred to as "Senior Cambridge Certificate" in 1949. (This was the Cambridge Overseas Certificate) He began his career as a clerk with the UAC and later with Palm Line Shipping, from 1949-51. He started logging in 1951 with the capital which accrued from his personal savings.[32] Ibuaka owned two logging sites, which employed about twenty laborers.It is affirmed that Palmer was the first African in the area to undertake the export of timber to Great Britain. He owned large timber concessions in Sakpoba (Benin) forests, while Asaboro owned large concessions in the Benin and Owo forests. Ibuaka claimed he did not own any concessions.

Nature of Logging Business

Unlike the other enterprises discussed in this work, family labor did not play a significant role in the labor requirements of the logging business. Logging did not often involve other business as palm produce, rubber and general merchandise did.

The bulk of the logs was exported. Prices of logs for export were higher than the ones for the local markets. Consequently, the desire was to produce for export. The demand for local sales was unimportant as the overseas demand could hardly be met. The boom period was 1950-54, followed by a period of low prices and a reduction in production.[33] In the boom period, it was difficult to meet overseas orders. But, often, it was possible to purchase timber from other non-exporting log merchants. As the nearby forests were depleted, it became more problematic to obtain regular supplies, because obtaining timber from the more distant forests was fraught with serious difficulties.[34]

All the entrepreneurs undertook direct export and did not rely on European firms for exports. None operated as an agent of expatriate firms as was the case with many of the entrepreneurs discussed in previous chapters.

Shipping of logs did not pose too much of a problem because there were always ships at the Sapele port to transport logs overseas. Sapele had become an important port for the export of timber, rubber, palm produce and other cash crops such as cocoa since the 1920's.

A major problem which confronted the logging business was theft of the logs, especially during the boom period. This was addressed by an increase in the number of guards employed, in addition to a stricter and more effective system of log identification for easier detection.[35]

Often the entrepreneurs were disappointed by forest owners who did not meet orders for logs. Ibuaka claimed that it became necessary to provide some equipment and transportation to forest owners to facilitate their operations.[36] It was imperative to own lorries for transporting timber from the forest areas to the port.[37]

It was difficult to recruit the required labor because of the hazards involved in the business which included rafting logs all day and night along the rivers and creeks. Labor for the industry was recruited from the local area, Igboland and other parts of Nigeria. Hausas from the north were employed as guards. Benin and Ijo were hired to raft logs. Ethnicity did not affect economic pursuits. People sought their livelihood where it could be obtained, and gave their expected input.

Palmer and Asaboro obtained most of their logs from their own forest concession, but Ibuaka purchased his from forest owner as he had no forests concessions. They all owned their own lorries which transported timber from the forest areas to the port. Ibuaka had previous experience with the European firms before engaging in his own business. Palmer and Asaboro established larger business than Ibuaka , not because they entered the industry earlier, but because they exploited their cordial relationships with communities in Ondo, Owo and Lower Benin River areas. Apart from getting him a job with the UAC, Ibuaka's education does not appear to given him an advantage over the other two entrepreneurs.

The logging business served as a model business and its success provided an incentive to many people to venture into the timber business. It is important to stress that logging was dominated by men. There has been remarkable continuity in the timber business in Sapele. In recent years, there has been a proliferation of sawmills in Sapele and its surrounding vicinity which remains the center of the timber industry in Nigeria. In fact, it is now the most important business, employing the largest number of people in the Sapele area. The entire area of Sapele known as Waterside is occupied by sawmillers and sawmills.

Notes

1 These include Miller Brothers(UAC,1929); Pinnock, Bey and Zimmer; D.C.O. Spiropolous(Harriman), Caiaphas Brothers; Bata Shoe Company, K.B. Omatseye; D.O. Oghene and Sons. Interview with Okitikpi at Sapele, June 6, 1987
2 Interview with Dr. Godwin Iwegbue, Lagos, March. 1987
3 *ibid.*
4 Interview with Venerable B.P. Apena, Irri, March 1987.
5 Interview with Blessing Oki, New York, December 1995
6 Interview with Peter Oghene, Sapele, April 1987.
7 *ibid.*
8 Interview with S. O. Okitikpi, Sapele, April 1989.
9 Interview with Peter Oghene, *op. cit.*
10 *ibid.*
11 *Ibid.*
12 Okitikpi. *op. cit*
13 Dr. Godwin Iwegbue, *op. cit*
14 Peter Oghene, *op. cit*
15 Interview with Chief Omuvwie, Sapele, March 1987.
16 *ibid.*
17 Chief Omuvwie, *op. cit.*
18 Interview with Christy Agodo, Lagos, May 1987
19 *Ibid*
20 Interview with Chief Agnes Agbaza, Warri, April 1986.
21 Interview with Chief T.J. Sokoh, Warri, May 1987
22 *ibid.*
23 Interview with Chief Wilson Odibo, Warri, May 1986
24 *ibid*
25 U.A.C.–Kerosene, K. Chellarams,–Textiles, John Holt–Hardware, G.B. Ollivant–Bicycles, C.F.A.O./S.C.O.A.–general goods.
26 Interview with Chief W. Odibo at Warri, May 20, 1987.
27 *Ibid.*
28 Interview with Mrs. C. Agodo, daughter of Chief Mrs. Alice Obahor, at Warri, May 22, 1987.
29 Interview with D. Ogboko who worked for F. Oki between 1952-55 at Oleh, May 5, 1987.
30 Otobo Personal Files, *op. cit.*
31 Ughelli Dist. I, File Nos. 1747, War Prof. 2, WP 344/9, War Prof. I, WP 146/F/3. N.A.I.
32 Interview with Chief Ibuaka himself at Sapele, June 10, 1987.
33 *Ibid.*
34 ibid.
35 *Ibid.*
36 ibid.
37 *Ibid.*

Chapter 12

The Contributions of the Indigenous Entrepreneurs to the Modernization of the Western Delta Communities

Indigenous Entrepreneurs as Exploiters or Agents of Development

The Marxist perspective claims that the indigenous entrepreneurs colluded with expatriate commercial firms to exploit their own people and contributed to the underdevelopment of their communities. This chapter questions this assertion by evaluating the use of indigenous wealth. How did the indigenous entrepreneurs use their wealth, accumulated, from participation in the economic activities associated with operations of the expatriate commercial firms and the colonial administration. This is in view of the fact that they did not repatriate profits overseas. Did they use their wealth for the improvement of their communities or did they simply accumulate wealth for self-enhancement and maintenance of a wealthy class with privileges.

The view of the Marxists also contends that the entrepreneurs as agents of commercial firms were collaborators who assisted the perpetuation of exploitation.[1] Available information and empirical observation do not support this contention. Rather a critical analysis of the activities of the entrepreneurs indicate that they used their wealth to initiate the development and modernization of their communities. The contribution of these entrepreneurs is classified into urban infrastructure, rural social infrastructure, economic infrastructure and venture capitalist activities.

Contribution to the Development of Urban Social Infrastructure: Modern Housing

One evidence of the use of wealth is their investment in the development of modern housing complexes/estates in Warri, Sapele and Ughelli where population growth, modernization and urbanization created an increasing demand for modern housing. Population of towns like Warri and Sapele expanded in the late 1950's.

Other less significant towns like Oleh and Kwale also gained population with expansion of economic and educational opportunities. Increasingly, the towns had serious attractions for the people because only the towns had social facilities including electricity, potable water and theater houses. These lured many people from the rural areas where similar facilities were non-existent. This is a reality of the imbalance of the colonial society. However, this experience not only underpopulated but also increasingly turned the villages into "enclaves of underdevelopment".

Exploration of oil became important during the end of the 1950s. The oil industry engaged a large number of foreign skilled workers from Europe and the United States. The labor demands of the oil industry created the need for modern houses of international standards.

Initially, there was scarcity of such houses in the area and consequently, most expatriate personnel lived in imported mobile homes near the site of oil exploration. Demand for modern housing became high. The development of the oil industry and the consequent explosion of population in the towns, thus, provided the impetus which compelled the entrepreneurs to venture into the real estate business which had become the most lucrative investment.

The indigenous entrepreneurs seized the opportunity to invested their profits in the real estate business. Odibo, Sokoh, Agbaza, Obahor, Mazoje are familiar names in Warri housing estate business. At least each has more than two housing estates. Obahor alone has twelve.[2] The houses were of high standards and quality approved by government and of international quality. Thus, they responded to the challenges of change.

Specifically, they became agents of modernization, contributing significantly to the growth and improvement of urban areas, especially with reference to provision of modern housing.

The provision of modern housing appears to confirm locational imbalance and social class divisions created during colonization. Modern housing could also be viewed as having contributed to class consciousness. It is correct to state that the provision of modern housing was for the upper class and middle class, not necessarily for the lower class.

What is important for this study is that the wealth of these entrepreneurs was ploughed back into society for developmental purposes. The question of class is a normal experience, associated with growth in many capitalist oriented societies globally.

Closely associated with modern housing were investments in modern hotels, supermarkets, and restaurants. Activities connected with these institutions provided job opportunities for the people of the area. Apart from being features of a modernizing society, these institutions broadened the scope of the economy and turned the towns of the Western Delta into convenient destinations for foreign workers and indigenous businesses. Obviously, the activities of the indigenous entrepreneurs were at the center of this social and economic progress. These developments invalidate the contention that the indigenous entrepreneurs were "collaborators of imperialist commercial firms" who assisted the perpetuation of exploitation.

The concentration of modern housing in the urban areas and the neglect of rural areas, however, created distortions in the overall development of the region. It tended to divide the area into two sectors, a powerful attractive urban sector and a neglected, powerless and underdeveloped rural one. But, it must be emphasized that the demand for modern housing was not urgent in rural areas.

Rural Social Infrastructure: Housing

Like other successful urban dwellers, these entrepreneurs built modern homes as private residences in their communities. Modern housing was an index of modernity, personal success and achievement. They promoted and transferred new housing values and designs to rural communities. Although the number of these houses is small, it can be said they contributed to altering the general outlook of the villages.

Schools, Churches, Health Institutions and Town Halls

The term contribution as applied here implies financial input, leadership role and mobilization of people to act as well as putting pressure on the government to approve and, in some cases, assist in the completion of programs.

Chief Daniel Oghene founded and built the Okpe Grammar School at Sapele in 1960, and handed it over to the government without seeking compensation.[3] He regarded it as a contribution to the advancement of education in the Sapele area. Today, Okpe Grammar School is one of Delta State's Grade A schools, and among the best equipped in the Sapele area.

On his own, Chief Odibo founded the Egini Secondary School in Udu clan. Otobo contributed to the establishment of Uzere Community Grammar School and compiled the Intelligence Reports of the Isoko clans.[4]

Chief Sokoh contributed to the founding and building of the Ovwian Grammar School to which he awards five scholarships annually to deserving students who are indigent. He states that, this is to ensure that deserving students are not denied the opportunity of receiving secondary education on account of poor parentage.[5]

Fentu Oki contributed to the founding of Okproza Grammar School at Patani, Mater Dei and Ashaka Grammar Schools as well as a number of primary schools in the riverain areas.[6]

Why did it become necessary to found schools? This was because the government did not regard education of the people as a priority. Christian missions which pioneered education in the Western delta did not establish schools in every community. As a result, many areas were starved of schools and the responsibility of establishing schools especially at the secondary level fell on the people. Each of these entrepreneurs also donated trophies to schools to promote competition in athletics.

Churches

Connections with their communities were also made through the church. The churches constituted communities within the larger societies. Building of churches was considered both a duty to God and the people. Consequently, a number of churches were built with donations by the entrepreneurs. Oki assisted in the building of the C.M.S. Church at Ashaka, and the rebuilding of the C.M.S. Church at Patani, as did Odibo in the building of the "modern" C.M.S. Church at Egini.[7]

Economic Infrastructures: Roads and Bridges

The colonial administration did not develop roads and bridges commensurately with the level of productivity in the local economy. Many areas were neglected. Consequently, the responsibility for the development of such infrastructure lay with the people of the communities themselves. The need for this became urgent with increased commerce and trading activities.

Chiefs T.J. Sokoh and W. Odibo contributed to the construction of the Udu Bridge which links the Udu clan with Warri commercial center.[8] The Udu are essentially farmers and they supplied food items to the Warri urban population. Trade between Warri and the neighboring Udu clan was active and significant. The urban population depended on food stuffs from Udu farmers. Today, the bridge provides a major access between Warri and the steel industry at Ovwian-Aladja in Udu.

Fentu Oki contributed to the construction of the Patani-Ughelli road whose extension and modernization resulted in the new Ughelli-Patani-Port Harcourt highway.[9] William Otobo contributed to the construction of the "difficult" Uzere-Oleh road.[10] These roads were innovations as well as catalysts for socio-economic growth, facilitating the movement of goods, people and services.

Agbaza helped in the construction of a new town hall in Otibio-Oweh in Isoko area as Obahor did in Effurunto in Urhobo area. Townhalls are sensitive social buildings of great significance to all people in their communities.

Their Role as Venture Capitalists

As traders in imported goods, they served as agents for the flow of new products, new values and new skills to rural areas. As employers of labor, they provided sources of livelihood for a large number of people. The entrepreneurs acted as financiers to people desiring to set up businesses of their own. Many of such people grew to become sub-agents and small-scale middlemen.[11]

Their offices and shops became training schools for people desirous of entering into the business of general trade. It is common to find people who began as apprentices and later obtained loans from these entrepreneurs to start their own businesses. Always around them at any time were a host of dependents who looked to the entrepreneurs for training, guidance and necessary support.[12]

The Significance of Chieftaincy Titles and Honors

As chairmen and presidents of community development associations, the entrepreneurs took active part in making crucial decisions which affected the social and economic and political growth and development of their various communities. It is no wonder that they were honored with chieftaincy titles in recognition of their achievements and appreciation of their contributions to the communities.

These titles obviously made them effective heads of clan and village councils. Otobo was honored with the title of Odion-Ologbo. This made him the most important titled chief in his area. In this capacity, he became the executive head of the clan and the president of the Uzere Improvement Union. Otobo actively supported the struggle for an independent political status for Isokoland, separate from Urhoboland, a goal attained in 1963 with the establishment of the Isoko Divisional Council with headquarters at Oleh.[13]

Oghene was titled *Eni of Okpe* which literally means the "elephant" of Okpe. By this title, he was the most prominent chief of the Okpe people. In 1960, Obahor was honored with an unusual chieftaincy for women, that of Olorogun of Effurunto literally translates as war leader.[14] This entitled her to become the head of all the chiefs in Effurunto and hold a premier position among the people. This is an unprecedented honor for women and a rare one, even for men. In addition, she became the "mother" of the community and patron of several associations.[15] No woman has since been honored with this title in any of the communities in the Western Delta. This placed her in an exclusive social position infact above of both titled and non-titled males.

Odibo is titled the *Oyivwi of Udu* for his role in the construction of the Udu Bridge. Oyivwi in Urhobo language means one who dares. The construction of the Udu bridge was a daring act in the minds of the people because before its construction, communication across the river was difficult especially for transportation of commercial goods.

The bridge has vital economic importance for the Udu people because it helped to overcome on headpoterage and dependence on use of canoes to cross the Udu River to Warri township. Trade with Warri has crucial significance for the people of the area. The bridge stimulated expansion of trade and allied activities. It eliminated the physical barrier between the Warri commercial center and the adjoining areas.

Sokoh was titled "unbeatable" meaning one who undertakes unprecedented act of philanthropy and loyalty to the welfare of a community. In addition to founding an orphanage, school and award of scholarships, he finances the care of the oldest man in Ovwian community.[16]

Almost all of the entrepreneurs were patrons of many socio-economic and cultural organizations. For example, Alice Obahor was a patron of fifteen women associations. Their advise is sought and their guidance is highly valued. In addition, they made financial contributions toward the development of these associations. Most of these associations are improvement unions dedicated to modernization of communities.

What was the significance of these titles? Reference has been made that the titles represented the community's recognition of the achievements of the entrepreneurs. This made them role models in their communities. It may be argued that this appears to be the real significance of the honors and titles.

The desire to achieve and excel inspired people regardless of gender to place emphasis on hard work. Merit and individual enterprise became the hallmark of social recognition and mobility in these communities. This is a positive impact as they stimulated people to compete for high honors in their respective pursuits.

The communities were not biased in award of titles. Men and women received titles according to their levels of achievements, contributions and merit. What does this say of traditional societies? Certainly, it points to a sense of gender equity in the evaluation of merit and honor. Cosequently, though women were marginalized in the formal public sector, they made substantial contribution in the informal sector where they were accorded earned respect and recognition.

One can emphasize that the economic power of the entrepreneurs enable them wield tremendous social and political influence. They were enlightened and alert about political developments. Apart from serving in the "native" courts and councils (Otobo, Iwegbue, Obori, Oki), they acted as major influences on political developments in the area. Some of them were appointed to councils by government authorities in order to channel the development efforts of the people toward meaningful goals. In this respect, Otobo, Oki and Iwegbue helped to resolve some problems relating to land use and taxation in their respective communities.

It is important to state that though many of them were not directly involved in politics, they sought to protect their political interests through active support for candidates running for seats in the federal and sate assemblies.[17] Obahor was patron of the National Convention of Nigerian Citizens (NCNC). Otobo was in the forefront of the struggle to attain an independent political status for Isokoland, a goal attained in 1963 with the establishment of the Isoko Divisional Council.

It can be concluded that these indigenous entrepreneurs utilized their wealth and resources to the advantage of their communities. Their position gave them social, economic and political power and influence. In return, they provided security, support and guidance for their people.

Their contributions are significant for the improvement of the welfare of the people and modernization of the societies. This is in view of the fact that the development of rural areas was neglected by the colonial government. Though they are clearly upper class people, they freely associated with majority of the people in a highly functional manner and did not necessarily create distinct class lines with special privileges. Therefore the entrepreneurs can be described as facilitators of socio-economic growth. They responded effectively to demands of their people and challenges of change introduced by the colonial situation. Since much of their wealth was utilized to increase the well-being of the people, they can hardly be regarded as exploiters or collaborators.

Notes

1 *See* Chapter I.
2 Interview with Christy Agodo, Lagos, May 1987.
3 Interview with Peter Oghene at Sapele, April 1987.
4 Interview with Chief Guy Otobo at Warri, April 1987.
5 Interview with Chief T. J. Sokoh at Warri, May 1987.
6 Interview with B. P. Apena at Irri, December 1986.
7 Interview with Chief Wilson Odibo at Warri, May 1987.
8 Interview with Chief T. J. Sokoh and Wilson Odibo, *Op. Cit.*
9 Interview with Blessing Oki at Warri, May 1987.
10 Interview with Guy Otobo, *Op. Cit.*
11 *Ibid.*
12 Interview with Onome Odhegba at Warri, June 1987.
13 Interview with B. P. Apena, *Op. Cit.*
14 Interview with C. A. Agodo at Lagos, March 1987.
15 *Ibid.*
16 Interview with T. J. Sokoh, *Op. Cit.*
17 Chief Otobo personal Files, *Op. cit.*

Conclusion

My reading of the evidence available for the Western Delta suggests that the colonial economy is not synonymous with economic revolution as the imperialists contend. Nor is it synonymous with underdevelopment, and retardation as the Marxists believe. While each view has its merits, it is the conclusion of this study that the colonial economy contributed to the growth and progress of the people of the Western Delta in some sectors, while inhibiting and distorting it in others. Specifically, the dynamics for achieving the goals of the expatriate commercial firms produced the effects which in some sectors of the economy were beneficial and contributed to the welfare of the people and their society. In other sectors, they did not have similar effects, but rather resulted in distorting progress. This is clearly demonstrated by the example of the production and production techniques in the agricultural export sector and the role of the commercial firms. Also, the colonial economy affected trade, urban and port development in different ways compared with food production and physical infrastructure.

Trade

Equitable exchange did not take place between the European traders and the African producers of palm produce and rubber, which were the major exports of the Western Delta. Under the conditions of monopoly created by the firms, backed by governmental controls, African producers and middlemen did not receive a fair share in the trade. The prices paid for cash crops were not commensurate with labor inputs and yet Africans were forced to pay relatively high prices for imported goods. The gap between earnings and expenditures kept producers at low financial levels and therefore they were unable to afford basic improvements for their businesses and their lives.

It was a major objective of the firms to offer low prices for cash crops and charge high prices for imported goods, thereby establishing the unfair conditions of trade. The pricing policy of high prices for imported goods and low prices for cash crops retarded the incomes of the producers and affected their ability to be effectively involved in the modernization process. In fact, it became almost impossible for the people to save and to develop their own capital. This constituted a major disadvantage which did not advance the local economy. The positions of the farmers was worsened by their inability to form producers'cooperatives to counteract the formidable barriers created by the commercial firms and the government. In most cases, the barriers restricted the choice of goods available to Africans who had to purchase British made goods, even if cheaper and higher quality goods were available elsewhere.

It is important to note the contribution of island stations established by European trading firms in redressing the balance of socio-economic power between the people of the Upper and Lower Delta. Also important is their role in stimulating commercial activities and broadening the base of the economy. Prior to the colonial period, the Itsekiri and Aboh were powerful middlemen that controlled import and export trade, exploiting the advantages of their strategic locations. Earlier contact with European traders and civilization apparently gave credence to their claims of superiority over their neighbors. The situation changed radically as non-coastal peoples became exposed to Europeans. This created competition between the various groups for the import and export trade, helping to mitigate the feelings of ethnic superiority.

Trading stations served as easy points of exportation aiding the maximization of exploitation by middlemen, provided opportunities for increased productivity in the agricultural sector and enhanced commercial activities in the retail trade which led to growth of markets. All this helped to minimize dependence on the agricultural sector for livelihood, even though it remained the basis of the economy.

The establishment of the stations also created an upsurge in entrepreneurial activity, especially in general merchandise. A remarkable feature of this development was the increased involvement of women. While women were active in the precolonial economies, they were restricted to the opportunities available in their local environments. But, the activities of the commercial firms and the increased internal demands expanded the economic base available to women at the level of wholesale and retail trading. Markets of the interior became increasingly dominated by women and many migrated to urban areas (some with husbands, others without) to participate in general trade and eventually dominated the markets there as well. The colonial economy enlarged the scale and number of activities available to women, in this case, colonialism was not exploitative.

Production and Production Techniques in Agricultural Export

The colonial administration, supported by the UAC, introduced improved seedlings and higher yielding varieties of oil palm and rubber trees. Through plot development and grove replacement, the farmers began to regard the trees as commercial crops which could be cultivated and nourished rather than as wild plants. This was a considerable improvement on the conception of the oil palm and rubber trees in the traditional socio-economic system. The program was a modernizing one and it was conspicuously successful. However serious socio-cultural and economic constraints hampered a more effective adoption of innovations(plot development and grove replacement) which would have provided major improvements in the palm industry. This indicates that some of the difficulties in the sector were internally induced while external ones like the installation of Pioneer oil mills accounted for others.

Better cultivation techniques were also introduced, following the research conducted by the UAC and the Department of Agriculture, emphasizing the trees as commercial crops. Of particular significance in the palm produce industry was the introduction of produce inspectors in 1929 and mechanized oil extraction. These were aimed at improving the quality and quantity of Nigerian palm produce. It was hoped that this would enhance the marketability of the Nigerian oil and sustain its position in the world market especially in view of the serious challenge posed by the plantations in Southeast Asia and the Belgian Congo. Although, it can be contended that the efforts were in the self-interest of the firms and the government, they, nonetheless, helped to improve the quality of the Nigerian palm industry and raise a new consciousness about oil palm products.

It is not being argued here that there was a revolution in the palm produce industry. The producers were not able to afford the purchase of hand presses and the Pioneer oil mills were not widespread enough to cater to the needs of many producers, even those in a high density palm producing area. Consequently, even though there was an increasing appreciation of the Pioneer mills by the end of the period of this study, the level of production technology remained generally low. Though the people were sensitized to new methods of production, they did not experience serious technological change in their production processes which remained basically traditional. The level of production and volume of export was not commensurate with changes in the methods of production.

The lack of a revolution is even more apparent in the rubber industry where there was no equivalent of Pioneer Oil Mill. It could be argued that government policy was insensitive to the concerns of indigenous rubber farmers as demonstrated by the inconsistent policy towards rubber cultivation. Producers could not afford to purchase the necessary equipment and machinery to set up even basic infrastructure like rolling machines and ovens hence substandard methods of production continued. This accounted for the inability of producers to produce Grade A rubber. Lack of financial ability was not because the people did not work hard enough but because of the price policy as already noted.

The increasing volume of exports had been attributed to external factors, according to Myint's vent-for-surplus production and Helleiner's contention concerning the primacy of the colonial government in enhancing production and exports. But, as it has been illustrated, the colonial government adopted an inconsistent policy toward rubber production, and in some cases, it was decidedly anti-expansion and discouraged farmers from cultivating large plots, all of which tended to retard growth in the industry. In spite of this, production increased and expanded largely due to the dynamism of the people.

In the case of palm produce, poor world prices until 1946, failed to discourage production, though in some instances, it led to reduction in output. People continued to produce palm oil, kernels and rubber in spite of the external factor because they were used to producing the products. More significantly, farmers continued to produce to satisfy the demands of a cash economy. Underlying this, was a sense of enterprise. The people had few alternative economic activities that would provide them with economic satisfaction and cash.

In relation to production, the role of prices cannot be ignored. Better prices for rubber were caused by external demands, creating a competitive advantage which caused many to switch production from palm produce to rubber, and food production in some areas. Thus, external factors were largely responsible for the rise in prices and an increase in production , while increased exporting was a response to internal stimuli.

Some of the innovations did not seriously consider the dynamics of traditional methods of production. The reaction to the pioneer oil mills was initially one of cold indifference or outright rejection because the mill system did not consider the nature of traditional palm collection which included the difficulties of head portage over long distances and climbing of trees. Rejection of palm fruits by mill officials because they were unsuitable was a serious loss financially and emotionally to the farmers.

Perhaps the most negative impact of the pioneer mill was the loss of kernel to the mills. This affected women's activities and incomes since processing of kernels was women's business. The policy of retaining kernels was affected by the values of Western family system in which husbands and wives have common family income.

On the contrary, in the African family system women were independent financially and men did not share incomes with their wives neither did the women make their incomes freely available to their husbands. Consequently, loss of incomes by women affected family incomes and financial arrangements. The loss of kernels amounted to disempowerment of women.

Activities of the Commercial firms: The UAC

The role of the commercial firms have been a subject of debate for some time. They have been criticized for the misuse of their freedom of action and for controlling vital sectors of the economy. But, it should be noted that the firms undertook infrastructural development when the government did not. In some areas, they complemented the role of the government. In either case, the initiatives were generally undertaken in the firms self interest with direct and indirect benefits for the people.

The expatriate firms had a symbiotic relationship with the colonial administration which functioned to the disadvantage of the people in almost all cases. They supported each other's interest and colluded against the interests of the indigenous people in ways which suited their interests. The people were constrained in their actions and choices and definitely did not have allies in the colonial establishment.

However, the activities of the expatriate commercial firms indirectly brought significant positive changes to the people. This was evident in the expansion of trade and commerce, the growth of towns, the emergence of indigenous entrepreneurs and the development of ports.

Port Development

The colonial government undertook a policy of port concentration during the period and consequently focused on Lagos and port Harcourt. The ports of the Western delta: Warri, Burutu, Sapele and Koko were neglected. The development of the Delta ports fell on the commercial firms which required them for servicing their import/export trade and trading networks. Of the ports, Burutu, owned by the UAC was more developed than Sapele which was not controlled by any one firm. Despite the considerable commercial and industrial activity that necessitated the development of Sapele, its resources remained underdeveloped. Though this reflects a significant imbalance between the contribution of the commercial firms and the exploitation of natural resources, the ports of the Western Delta would have lapsed into decay were it not for the efforts of the firms. The vitalization of ports by the firms had favorable effects, producing dynamic forces that energized the society and economy.

Although it could be argued that the growth of towns contributed to rural neglect, it was a progressive development in the evolution of the Western Delta society which did not have a tradition of towns before colonization. Towns provided important catalysts for the growth and development of the area as well as interaction of people. In these developments, the implications of the presence and actions of the firms were undoubtedly beneficial.

Industrialization and Growth of Towns

The colonial administration did not undertake industrialization in the Western Delta. The UAC made significant efforts in industrialization. Although its industrialization policy has been criticized, it can be argued that establishment of the African Timber and Plywood Factory radically altered the timber industry, the use of forest resources and helped to popularize African forest products in the world market. In any case, African entrepreneurs lacked the capital and the technical skills necessary to construct such a factory.

The direct benefits in the agro-allied industrialization of palm produce has been outlined. Indirectly, their operations helped to induce socio-economic changes which helped to broaden the base of the economy and consequently the progress of the people. The requirement for labor provided employment opportunities and contributed to urban growth(Warri and sapele) and development of ones(Burutu and Koko). Urbanization also occurred from the establishment of administrative headquarters in places like Ughelli and Kwale.

The urban environment stimulated growth in economic activities such as transportation, retail trade, general stores, hotels and restaurants. Urban centers also provided a forum for ethnic interaction and integration among various ethnic groups from the Western Delta and other parts of Southern Nigeria. The towns were also places of large-scale multiculturalism with the appearance of Europeans and Asians as well. Intermarriages among these groups created a racial hybrid referred to as mulattoes who became numerous in Warri and Sapele.

Urbanization opened new opportunities to women in the informal sector. And even though women were marginalized in the formal modern sector of the economy, they controlled the informal economy especially in the supply of food items. The colonial economy empowered women in the informal sector and empowered men in the formal and modern sector. But the modern sector is the powerful sector while the informal sector is the disadvantaged and powerless sector of economy. Consequently women were considered weak and powerless. However, some female entrepreneurs showed that women could organize large-scale businesses with tremendous capacity for innovation and ability to compete effectively with men. This was in spite of the fact that these women faced the challenge of double patriarchy, of both the male dominated traditional society and white male dominated colonial society.

Also related to population movement was rural-rural migration which was induced partly by the firms. Plantation labor and the labor requirements of the inland stations involved the movement of people from one location to another. Plantation labor was organized in estates or around the plantations which exposed them to new social amenities. The Isoko and the Urhobo undertook rural-rural migration to the Ijo and Aboh areas of the Niger and its distributaries, and to the Ondo, Ife, Ilesha, Ekiti and Ijebu Yoruba areas in search of oil palm trees to exploit. The search for fertile palm trees was closely associated with the export trade in palm produce. While many urban centers continued to grow, some rural areas experienced considerable depopulation.

The firms and the government have been criticized for causing dislocation in society. The provision of amenities and infrastructures in new urban centers created a gulf between them and the rural areas. Transportation and communication development which was focused on the urban areas further contributed to the problem. It seems to me that these criticisms fail to understand the objectives of the firms and the colonial mission. All the institutions and structures created by the colonial administration were aimed at controlling, expanding trade and enhancing profits. It must be emphasized that neither the colonial administration nor the expatriate commercial firms came to develop the Western Delta or the colonies in general. To argue whether they developed or did not develop the colonies amounts to mixing causes with effects. The principal objective of the firms was the maximization of profits through optimum resource utilization, including human resources. Thus, in the minds of the managers of the firms, the provision of the amenities for their labor force was aimed at helping to maximize productivity. By the logic of capitalist development, profits are to be accumulated for further development. Thus, providing infrastructure for the larger society would be a significant deviation which could lead to the demise of the system on which Western society and civilization depended. Yet, some of the services provided by the firms like health facilities, training schools, churches, roads and pipe borne water were extended to the larger society as a goodwill gesture by the UAC. In other words, they did for the people what the government should have done for them.

Consumer Economy

The economy which emerged from in this period was a consumer economy. As it has already been stressed, neither the government nor the firms(perhaps with the exception of the self interest efforts of the UAC) tried to encourage manufacturing since it would negate the very essence of the colonial mission in providing raw materials and markets for manufactured goods from Europe. This was the case in spite of the claims of the imperialists that the conditions were not right for industrialization. The pattern of economic relation led to the decay of local industries, decline of local skills and significantly, the ability of the people to industrialize. Secondly, the situation turned the people into endless consumers of imported goods.

The consumer culture of the Nigerians has continued to develop. Preference for imported goods, even when local substitutes are available, dates back to the colonial culture of compulsory purchases and consumption of imported goods. What was initially an imposition on the people turned into a passion which did not only corrupt the taste of the people but also affected the way they perceived themselves and their society. The lack of appreciation for indigenous products affected the way people viewed their communities and culture. Increasingly the perspective of the indigenous cultures as inferior cultures became internalized by the people themselves. In spite of the post colonial governments' efforts to industrialize and to broaden the base of the economy, the economy remains geared towards the production of primary goods for the export market and the importation of manufactured goods.

The Role of Indigenous Entrepreneurs

The growth of indigenous entrepreneurs and their contribution to the welfare and improvements of the societies is an appropriate example of the beneficial consequences of responses to the presence of the commercial firms. This is in spite of the fact that indigenous entrepreneurs faced serious problems associated with the prices, subagents supplies to the firms and loss of income.

It should be emphasized that the entrepreneurs had no serious education on the nature and complexities of capitalism and capitalist economy. In spite of this, they responded vigorously to the opportunities offered by the presence of the commercial firms, dealt with the challenges and made significant accomplishments in their businesses. Their contribution to the improvement of their communities and the welfare of their people was strategic to the growth and development of the society. The contributions were of fundamental significance because the colonial administration did undertook very few development programs to improve the rural areas and conditions of rural dwellers. The application of their wealth in this manner reflects the spirit of sharing and community self-support system in African traditions.

A critical analysis of the available evidence available supports the conclusion that the dynamics of the colonial economy involved two different value systems. At one level, was the European capitalist culture and spirit of individual enterprise, expansion of profit and accumulation of wealth based on investment and reinvestment in ever-expanding markets. It was also a system which regarded the entire world as its potential market. At the other level, was the traditional African value system based on the supremacy of the community and interdependence within mutually interrelated social groups which emphasized sharing, collective ownership of property and wealth, with less emphasis on self, individual investment and reinvestment for profits in an endless manner.

The African society is a highly spiritualized one, in which spirituality dominates the thinking of people. Therefore the dynamics of capitalism, embodied by the expatriate commercial firms were in most cases at variance with basic values of the people. The people were not necessarily schooled or familiar with the fundamental principles of capitalist economy and the European values which determined it. It may be argued that the people of the Western Delta and the managers of the expatriate commercial firms interrelated from two different cultural perspectives. The apparent fundamental differences no doubt affected relations between the two. Even today, cultural contradictions still affect relations between African bureaucrats and political leaders and their counterparts in Western societies and institutions.

The positive responses of the people energized the activities of the expatriate firms. Without the application of their productive energies, the export trade could not have developed at the level that it did and therefore the goals of the firms and colonial administration would not have been realized. Consequently, positive changes in port development and growth of towns, expansion of markets and the growth of women's activities, contributions of the indigenous entrepreneurs to improvement of their communities were all necessarily the result of the dynamic responses of the people to change induced by the activities of the commercial firms and the colonial administration. In spite of the loss of sovereignty and controls on the activities of the people, the local economy was vibrant at the end of the period and the Western Delta became one of the most crucial economic regions of Nigeria with meaningful improvement on the lives of the people.

There were considerable positive changes evident in the growth of towns, growth and contribution of indigenous entrepreneurs, vitalization of ports, expansion of trade, monetization of the economy, expansion of economic opportunities and enhanced roles of women. To this extent, it could be argued that the presence of the expatriate firms and the presence of the colonial administration helped to facilitate serious improvements in the welfare of the people and advancement of the communities. These were significant improvements in the history of the Western Delta.

Symbiosis of the Private and Public Sectors

The issue of conjunction of interests between the commercial firms and the colonial governments, the private and public sectors continues to evoke debate and criticism. It is important to note that in the history of economic development, with the exception of the Soviet Union and the communist states, development has been the function of both the private and public sectors. The public sector usually provides the basic infrastructures like roads, ports, and other forms of transportation and communication while the private sector supplies the capital, technology, management and technical expertise. In some cases, the private sector has borne part of the cost of economic development. Thus the criticism that the colonial government permitted the UAC to undertake initiatives in the vital sectors of the economy is unfair.

In the Western Delta, where the government failed to develop ports, the responsibility fell on the UAC, and to some extent John Holt. It is difficult to measure the degree of exploitation of the firms given their contribution to infrastructural development. Supplying amenities and infrastructure seems to be an extension of a similar policy in Europe where workers were provided with such benefits as housing. The housing scheme of the Action Group government of Western Nigeria in 1955 was a replication of such efforts. If the post independence government had fashioned their housing policy to make provisions for both the urban and rural sectors, many of the present social difficulties associated with housing would have been obviated.

The argument against the symbiotic relationship of the private and public sectors and the capitalist mode of production appears to emanate from the opponents of the capitalist system. The argument seems to be based largely on the disparity between the metropoles and the former colonies and on the general perspective of African development. This is done without considering specific sectors and areas. It also appears that the critics neglect to apply a cost-benefit analysis to the colonial situation. The path towards economic development is not restricted to only one approach. It is argued that since Nigeria has not experimented with a socialist or other alternative forms of economic development, it is difficult to assess its impact on the country and its people. The claim that capitalism is bad is a matter of ideological preference. What is important is development and positive change for the progress of the people.

After 1960, as a reaction to the criticism of capitalism, successive governments of Nigeria introduced economic packages in which the public sector took over large sectors of the economy and restricted the involvement of the private sector which was not in a powerful position in any case. Twenty-seven years after independence in 1987, the government reversed its economic policy and has allowed for the privatization of socio-economic development and encouraged the private sector to undertake infrastructural developments, even in vital areas like agriculture. This seems to suggest that perhaps there is something to learn from the colonial experience after all.

Bibliography

Primary Sources

1) Official papers

Nigerian National Archives files from the following series:

Warri Provincial papers including Annual Reports from 1960-1975.

District papers (Sapele Township, Warri Township, Koko Township,

Kwale District, Sobo District, Western Ijo District and Sobo-Jekri District 1960-1975)

Chief Secretary's Office papers relating to Agriculture

Commerce and Forestry

Western Region Ministry of Agriculture papers

UAC documents, treaties, and administrative papers

University of Lagos Library (The Ghandi Graduate Library)

Annual Reports of the Nigerian Marine, 1951-55.

Annual Reports of the Federal Department of Inland Waterways, 1957-58

Annual Reports of the Forestry Department, 1951-60

Nigerian Year Books, 1952-58

Nigeria Ports Authority, Lagos Marina

Annual Reports of Nigeria Ports Authority, 1956-57

2) Private Papers

Chief W. E. Otobo papers

3) Select List of Informants

Name	Age	Occupation	Status	Place of Inter-view	Date of Inter-view
Chief Mrs. Agbaza	55	textile dealer	Chief + member of Otibio Improve-ment Union	Warri	May 2, 1987
Mrs. C. A. Agedo	50	general trader	general trader	Warri	March 7, 1987
Chief O. Ibuaka	55	transporter + sawmiller	Aboh Chief of Utuechi	Sapele	April 4, 1987
Dr. G. O. Iwegbue	45	medical doctor	Director of Memisor Clinics, Lagos; Chief of Emu	Emu 1987	March 10,
Chief O. Mazoje	90	retired businessman	Chief of Oyede (Isoko)	Oyede 1987	June 10,
Mr. G. Okitikpi	90	retired trader	Community Elder	Oghara	June 6, 1987
Chief W. Odibo	60	general trader	Chief in Egini	Egini and Warri	May 11-12, 1987
Mr. P. Oghene	40	trader	trader	Sapele	April 3, 1987
Mr. C. Otobo	42	rubber merchant	rubber merchant	Uzere	June 13, 1987
Chief T. J. Sokoh	75	general trader	Chief in Ovwian	Warri	May 13, 1987
Chief O. Umuvhie	65	produce dealer	Chairman of Produce Dealers, Bendel State	Sapele	April 6, 1987
Arch-deacon V. P. Apena	99	clergyman	retired arch-deacon of Anglican Church	Irri-Isoko	Dec. 25, 1986

Name	Age	Occupation	Status	Place of Inter-view	Date of Inter-view
Mr. N. Obaro	68	fisherman	Chairman of Fishermen Association	Bomadi	Dec. 22, 1986
Dr. A. Ifie	40	professor	senior lecturer	Ibadan	Jan. 1987
Tekena Tamuno	65	professor of History	retired	Ibadan	March 1987
Chief Unoka	70	Business-man	active businessman	Sapele	Februa ry 1987
James Ogboko	66	Clerical worker	Former employee Offentu Oki	Irro	May 1987
Chief Enuesike	86	retired John Holt employee	retired	Issele gu	Februa ry 1987
Godwin Inomiesa	40	professor of economics	professor	Abraka	March 1987
Paul Onuemu	65	rubber dealer	general trader	Oleh	June 1987
Idolor onemu	70	Native healer	Native healer	Irri	June 1987
Chief T. Bekeme	62	former UAC employee	trader	Burutu	April 1987
Onome Odhegba	61	Business-wo man	Business-wo man	Warri	June 1987
Chief F. Ojobo	69	trader	retired	Burutu	Decem-ber 1986
Chief G. Tuedon	66	Secretary	retired	Ughelli	Decem-ber 1986
Mr. A. Akpan	43	adminis-trator	personnel manager	Pamol Estate Sapele	May 5, 1987
Mr. A. Eda	68	trader	prominent trader	Sapele	May 7, 1987

4) Unpublished Works

Anschell, K. R. "Economic Aspects of Peasant Rubber Production in Mid-Western Nigeria." Ph.D. Dissertation, Michigan State University, 1965.

Egboh, E. O. "British Forest Policy in Nigeria: A Study in Colonial Exploitation of Forest Produce 1897-1914." Ph.D. Dissertation, University of Birmingham, 1975.

Ekhuerare, B. U. "The Influence of Colonial Policy on the Nigerian Economy with Special Reference to Foreign Trade Sector." M.S., University of Ibadan, 1972.

Erivwo, S. "Christianity in Urhobo and Isokoland." Ph.D. Dissertation, University of Ibadan, 1972.

Jawando, G. A. "The Role of Agriculture in the Economic Development of Nigeria." Ph.D. Dissertation, University of Minnesota, 1968.

Ofonagoro, W. I. "The Opening up of Southern Nigeria to British Trade and its Consequences: Economic and Social History, 1881-1916." Ph.D. Dissertation, Columbia University, 1967.

Ogendengbe, K. O. "The Aboh Kingdom of the Lower Niger, 1650-1900." Ph.D. Dissertation, University of Wisconsin, 1971.

Ogundana, B. "Some Aspects of Changing Port Concentration in Nigeria." M.Sc., London, 1966.

Okolugbo, E. O. "Christianity and Ukwuani Traditional Religion: A Study in Religious Encounter." Ph.D. Dissertation, University of Ibadan, 1972.

Stilliard, N. H. "The Rise and Development of Legitimate Trade in Palm Oil with West Africa." M. A. Thesis, University of Birmingham, 1938.

Ukegbu, B. U. "Production in the Nigerian Oil Palm Industry, 1900-1954." Ph.D. Dissertation, University of London, 1974.

5) Articles and Reports

Abiola, M. K. O. "Dilemma of Foreign Grip and Control on Nigerian Transport System" *Transport* 2, no. 1 (1982).

Afigbo, A. E. "The Warrant Chief System in Eastern Nigeria." *Journal of the Historical Society of Nigeria* 3, no. 4 (1967).

——— "Sir Ralph Moor and Economic Development of Southern Nigeria." *Journal of the Historical Society of Nigeria* 3 (Dec 1970).

Alagoa, E. J. "Ijo Origins and Migrations." *Nigeria Magazine* 91, (December, 1966).

——— "Long Distance Trade and States in the Niger Delta." *Journal of the Historical Society of Nigeria* 11, no. 3 (1970).

Aluko, S. A. "Agriculture and Economic Development in Nigeria." *Nigerian Journal of Economic and Social Studies* 1, no. 1 (1959).

Amin, S. "Underdevelopment and Dependence in Black Africa: Origins in Contemporary Forms', *Journal of Modern African Studies* 10, no. 4 (1972).

Anon. "What the Producer Receives for his Produce." *UAC Statistical and Economic Review* 1 (March 1948).

———. "Production of Palm Oil and Palm Kernels in Nigeria." *UAC Statistical and Economic Review* 1 (March 1948).

———. "The Company River Fleet and Port, Nigeria." *UAC Statistical and Economic Review* 2 (September 1948).

———. "The Produce Goes to Market, Nigerian Palm Produce" *UAC Statistical and Economic Review* 3 (September 1949).

———. "Some Financial Aspect of Trading in West Africa." *UAC Statistical and Economic Review* 3 (September 1949).

———. "Trading in British West Africa." *UAC Statistical and Economic Review* 5 (March 1950).

———. "Forcados and Escravos Bars." *UAC Statistical and Economic Review* 6 (September 1950).

———. "Palm Oil Production in Nigeria." *UAC Statistical and Economic Review* 7 (March 1951).

———. "Plantations in Africa." *UAC Statistical and Economic Review* 9 (1952).

———. "Timber in West Africa." *UAC Statistical and Economic Review* 9-12 (March 1952).

———. "The Processing, Storage and Transport of Nigerian Palm Oil." *UAC Statistical and Economic Review* 13 (March 1954).

———. "Marketing Boards and Licensed Buying Agents." *Economic Review* 14 (September 1954).

———. "Nigerian Palm Oil." *UAC Statistical and Economic Review* 13-16 (March 1954).

———. "Transport Economics in West Africa" *UAC Statistical and Economic Review* 15 (March 1955).

———. "Port Capacity and Shipping Turnaround in West Africa." *UAC Statistical and Economic Review* 19 (March 1957).

Bayer, P. B. and B. S. Young. "A Case Study of Response to Price in an Underdeveloped Country." *Economic Journal* 69, no. 276 (1959).

Blackenburg, P. "Rubber Farming in Benin Area: A Study of some Socio-Economic Factors Influencing Rubber Production", *Preliminary Report*, Nigerian Institute of Social and Economic Research, Ibadan.

Bohanan, P. "The Impact of Money on an African Subsistence Economy." *Journal of Economic History* 19, no. 4 (1959).

Cole, A. H. "Entrepreneurship as an Area of Research." *Journal of Economic History* 2 (December 1942).

Fieldhouse, D. K. "Imperialism: An Historical Revision." *Economic History Review* n. s. 21, no. 3 (1969).

Forster, W. P. "Pre-Twentieth Century Isoko: Its Foundation and Later Growth." *African Historical Studies* 2, no. 2 (1969).

Frank, A. G. "The Development of Underdevelopment." *Monthly Review* 18, no. 4 (September 1966).

Hayes, D. "Hong Kong." Marine Stores International (March 1966).

Ikime, O. "Western Ijo 1900-1950: A Preliminary Survey." *Journal of Historical Society of Nigeria* 3, no. 1 (December 1967).

———. "Chief Dogho: The Lugardian System in Warri, 1917-1932." *Journal of the Historical Society of Nigeria* 3, no. 2 (1965).

———. "The Anti-Tax Riots in Warri Province." *Journal of Historical Society of Nigeria* 3, no. 3 (December 1966).

———. "Native Administration in Kwale-Aboh 1928-1950: A Case Study." *Journal of the Historical Society of Nigeria* 3, no. 4 (June 1967).

———. "The Coming of C. M. S. into Itsekiri, Urhobo and Isokoland." *Nigeria Magazine* no. 68 (September 1965).

Little, A. D. Jr. "The Feasibility of Expanding Production of Plywood and Veneer in Nigeria.", *Report* to the Ministry of Commerce and Industry, Federal Republic of Nigeria, September 1964.

Lloyd, P. C. "The Portuguese in Warri." *Odu* no. 4 (1956).

———. "The Itsekiri in the Nineteenth Century." *Journal of West African History* 4, no. 2 (1963).

Manning, P. "Analyzing the Costs of Benefits of Colonialism." *African Economic History Review* 1, no. 2 (1974).

Myint, H. "The Classical Theory of International Trade and the Underdeveloped Countries" *Economic Journal* 68 (June 1958).

Ogundana, B. "The Fluctuating Significance of the Nigerian Seaport Before 1914." *Odu* 3 (1967).

———. "The Locational Factor in Changing Seaport Significance in Nigeria." *Nigeria Geographical Journal* 14 (1971).

Omoisini, O. "The Rubber Exporter Trade in Ibadan 1893-1904." *Journal of the Historical Society of Nigeria* 10, no. 1 (December 1979).

———. "Background to the Forestry Legislation in Lagos Colony and Protectorate 1897-1902" *Journal of the Historical Society of Nigeria* 8, no. 2 (1976).

———. "Alfred Moloney and His Strategies for Economic Development of Lagos Colony and Hinterland 1886-1891." *Journal of the Historical Society of Nigeria* 7, no. 4 (1975).

Oni, S. A. "Production Response in Nigerian Agriculture: A Study of Palm Produce, 1949-1966" *Journal of Economic and Social Studies* 2, no. 1 (March 1965).

Ryder, A. F. C. "An Early Portuguese Voyage in the Forcados River." *Journal of the Historical Society of Nigeria* 1, no. 4 (1959).

——— "Missionary Activity in the Kingdom of Warri to the Early Nineteenth Century" *Journal of the Historical Society of Nigeria* 2, no. 1 (December 1960).

Salubi, A. "The Establishment of British Administration in Urhobo Country." *Journal of the Historical Society of Nigeria* 1, no. 3 (December 1958).

Szereszewski, S. et al., "Agriculture and Economic Development in Africa : Theory and Experience, 1880-1914" in E. L. Jones and S. J. Wolf, eds. *Agrarian Change and Economic Development.* (London. Methuen. 1969).

Towofari, S. R. "Nigerian Waterways." *Docks and Harbor Authority* 64, no. 757 (January 1984).

Tukur, B. M. "Nigerian Ports Gateways to Economic Development" *Transport* (Official Journal of the Chartered Institute of Transport) 3, no. 2 (March/April 1982).

Ullman, S. "Is There a Need for a National Port Policy". *Ports and Harbors* 26, nos. 1-2 (January/February 1981).

Welch, J. W. "The Isoko Tribe". *Africa* 7, no. 2 (1934).

6) Books

Aboyade, O. *Foundation of an African Economy: A Study of Investment and Growth in Nigeria*. New York: F. A. Praeger, 1966.

Adeyoju, K. *Forestry and the Nigerian Economy*. Ibadan: Ibadan University Press, 1975.

Afigbo, A. E. *The Warrant Chiefs*. London: Longman, 1972.

Agboola, S. A. "Agricultural Changes in Western Nigeria 1850-1910" in I. A. Akinjogbin and S.O. Osoba, eds., *Topics on Nigerian Economic and Social History*. Ile-Ife: Ife University Press, 1980.

Ahazeum, J. O. and Toyin Falola, "Production for the Metropolis: Agriculture and Forest Produce" in Toyin Falola, ed. *Britain and Nigeria: Exploitation or Development*. London: Zed, 1987.

Ajayi, J. F. A. and M. Crowder, eds. *History of West Africa* vols. I and II. London: Longman, 1971.

Ake, C. A. *Political Economy of Africa*. London: Longman, 1981.

Akeredolu-Ale, E. O. *The Underdevelopment of Indigenous Entrepreneurship in Nigeria*. Ibadan: Ibadan University Press, 1975.

Akinjogbin, I. A. and S. O. Osoba, eds. *Topics on Nigerian Economic and Social History*. Ile-Ife: University of Ife, 1980.

Alagoa, E. J. *The Small Brace City-State: A History of Nembe-Brass in the Niger Delta*. Madison: University of Wisconsin Press, 1964.

——— *History of the Niger Delta*. Ibadan: Ibadan University Press, 1972.

Amir, S. *Imperialism and Unequal Development*. New York: Monthly Review, 1977.

——— *Neo-Colonialism in West Africa*. Harmsworth: Penguin, 1973.

Anene, J. C. *Southern Nigeria in Transition 1885-1906*. Cambridge University Press, 1966.

Arghiri, E. *Unequal Exchange*. London: Monthly Review, 1972.

——— *Essays on Political Economy of Africa*. London: Monthly Review Press, 1973.

Ayandele, E. A. *The Missionary Impact on Modern Nigeria*. London: Longman, 1966.

Bauer, P. T. *West African Trade*. Cambridge University Press, 1954.

Berry, S. *Cocoa, Custom and Socio-Economic Change in Rural Western Nigeria*. London: Oxford University Press, 1975.

Bradbury, R. E. *The Benin Kingdom and the Edo-Speaking People of South-Western Nigeria*. London: International African Institute, 1975.

Brett, E. A. *Colonialism and Underdevelopment in East Africa, 1919-1939*. New York: Nok Pub., 1973.

Buell, L. R. *The Native Problem in Africa*. New York: Macmillan, 1928.

Cliffe, L. "Rural Political Economy of Africa." in P. C. W. Gutkin and I. Wallerstein, eds. *The Political Economy of Contemporary Africa*. London: Sage Publication, 1976.

Cook, A. N. *British Enterprise in Nigeria*. Philadelphia: University of Pennsylvania Press, 1943.

Crowder, M. *West Africa Under Colonial Rule*. London: Hutchinson, 1968.

——— and O. Ikime, eds. *West African Chiefs*. Ile-Ife: Ife University Press, 1970.

Crowe, S. E. *The Berlin West African Conference*, 1884-85. 1940. Westport, Connecticut: Negro University Press, 1970.

Cuthbert, C. *African Rubber Industry and Funtumia Elastica*. London: J. Bale, Sons and Danielson, 1971.

Diejomaoh, V. *Economic Development in Nigeria, Its Problems, Challenges and Prospects*. Princeton, New Jersey: Princeton University Press, 1965.

Dike, K. O. *Trade and Politics in the Niger Delta, 1830-1885*. Oxford: Clarendon Press, 1956.

Egharevba, J. U. *A Short History of Benin*. Ibadan: Ibadan University Press, 1964.

Eicher, C. K. and C. Liedholm, eds. *Growth and Development of the Nigerian Economy*. Michigan State University Press, 1970.

Ekundare, R. O. *An Economic History of Nigeria, 1860-1960*. London: Methuen & Co., 1973.

Falola, Toyin, ed. *Britain and Nigeria: Exploitation or Development*. London: Zed, 1987

Fieldhouse, D. K. *The Colonial Empires: A Comparative Study from the Eighteenth Century*. London: Weidenfield and Nicolson, 1966.

Flint, J. E. *Sir Goldie and the Making of Nigeria*. London: Oxford University Press, 1966.

Forde, O. and R. Scott. "The native Economics of Nigeria." in M. Perham, ed. *The Economics of a Tropical Dependency*, vol. 1. London: Faber and Faber, 1946-1948.

Gann, L. H. and P. Duignan, eds. *Colonialism in Africa 1870-1960* vols. 1-5. Cambridge University Press, 1974.

Greary, W. N. M. *Nigeria Under British Rule*. London: Frank Cass, 1965.

Hence W. A. *African Economic Development*. London: Oxford University Press, 1958.

Helleiner,G. K. *Peasant Agriculture, Government and Economic Growth in Nigeria*. Homewood, Illinois: R. D. Irwin, 1966.

——— "Agriculture and Economic Development in Africa, 1880-1914." in E. L. Jones and S. J. Wolfe, eds. *Agrarian*

Change and Economic Development. London: Methuen, 1968.

Hertskovitz, M. J. and Harwitz. *Economic Transition in Africa*. Evanston, Illinois: Northwestern University Press, 1964.

Hill, P. *The Gold Coast Cocoa Farmer*. London: Oxford University Press, 1956.

——— *The Migrant Cocoa-Farmer of Southern Ghana: A study in Rural Capitalism*. Cambridge University Press, 1963.

Hobson, J. A. *Imperialism: A Study*. London: George Allen and Unwin, 1962.

Hopkins, A. G. *An Economic History of West Africa*. London: Longman, 1973.

Hubbard, J. W. *The Sobo of the Niger Delta*. Zaria: Gaskiya, 1948.

Igbafe, P. A. *Benin Under British Administration*. London: Longman, 1970.

Igbozuruike, M. *Problem-Generating Structures in Nigeria's Rural Development*. Uppsala: Institute of African Studies, 1976.

Ihonvbere, J. and Toyin Falola. "Introduction: Colonialism and Exploitation." in T. Falola, ed. *Britain and Nigeria: Exploitation or Development*. London: Zed, 1987.

Ikime, O. *The Merchant Prince of the Niger Delta*. London: Heinemann, 1968.

——— *Niger Delta Rivalry*. New York: Humanities Press, 1969.

——— *The Isoko People*. Ibadan: Ibadan University Press, 1972.

——— *The Fall of Nigeria*. London: Heinemann, 1972.

——— *Chief Dogho of Warri*. Ibadan: Heinemann, 1976.

——— "The Peoples and Kingdoms of the Delta Province." in O. Ikime, ed. *Groundwork of Nigerian History*. Ibadan: Heinemann, 1980.

——— "Changing Status of Chiefs Among the Itsekiri" in M. Crowder and O. Ikime, eds. *West Africa Chiefs*. Ile-Ife: University of Ife Press, 1970.

Irvine, F. R. *A Textbook of West African Agriculture* 2nd ed. London: Oxford University Press, 1958.

Jones, E. L. and S. J. Wolfe, eds. *Agrarian Change and Economic Development: The Historical Problems*. London: Methuen, 1968.

Jones, G. I. *Trading States of the Oil Rivers*. London: Oxford University Press, 1963.

Kay, G. *Development and Underdevelopment: A Marxist Analysis*. London: Macmillan, 1974.

——— "Manufacturing in Colonial Africa." in L. H. Gann and P. Duignan, eds. *Colonialism in Africa 1870-1960*, vol. 4. Cambridge: Cambridge University Press, 1973.

Kilby, P. *Industrialization in an Open Economy: Nigeria, 1945-1966*. London: Macmillan, 1969.

Kirk-Greene, A. H. M. *Lugard and the Amalgamation of Nigeria*. London: Frank Cass, 1968.

Knowles, L. C. A. and C. M. Knowles. *The Economic Development of British Overseas Empire*. London: Routledge and Sons, 1936.

Lawal, A. A. "Industrialization as Tokenism." in Toyin Falola, ed. *Britain and Nigeria: Exploitation or Development*. London: Zed, 1987.

Lenin, V. I. *Imperialism: The Highest Stage of Capitalism*. New York: International Publishers, 1963.

Leonard, A. G. *The Lower Niger and Its Tribes*. London: Sheldon, 1932.

Leubuscher, C. *The West African Shipping Trade*. Leiden: A. W. Sythoff, 1963.

Lloyd, P. C. "The Itsekiri" in R. E. Bradbury. *The Benin Kingdom and the Edo-Speaking People of South-Western Nigeria.* London: International African Institute, 1957.

Lugard, F. D. *The Dual Mandate in British Tropical Africa.* London: Blackwood, 1922.

——— *The Rise of Our East African Empire.* London: Blackwood, 1893.

——— and Lady Flora. *A Tropical Dependency.* London: J. Nisbet, 1905.

Magdoff, H. *Imperialism: From Colonial Age to Present.* New York: Monthly Review.

Mars, J. "Extra-Territorial Enterprises." in M. Perham, ed. *Mining, Commerce and Finance: The Economics of a Tropical Dependency*, vol. 2. London: Faber and Faber, 1946-48.

Martin, A. *The Oil Palm Economy of the Ibibio Farmer.* Ibadan: Ibadan University Press, 1956.

Mba, N. *Nigerian Women Mobilized: Women Political Activities in Southern Nigeria, 1900-1965.* Berkeley: University of California Institute of International Studies, 1982.

Mbaeyi, P. M. *British Military and Naval Forces in West African History, 1807-1914.* New York: Nok Pub., 1978.

Mcphee, A. *An Economic Revolution in British West Africa.* 2nd ed. London: Frank Cass, 1971.

Moore, W. A. *History of Itsekiri.* London: Frank Cass, 1979.

Morel, E. D. *Affairs of West Africa.* London: Macmillan, 1902.

——— *Nigeria: Its People and Problems.* London: Smith Elder and Co., 1911.

Myint, H. *Economic Theory and Underdeveloped Countries.* London: Oxford University Press, 1956.

——— *The Economics of Developing Countries.* London: Hutchinson, 1967.

Nicolson, I. F. *The Administration of Nigeria: 1900-1960.* London: Longman, 1970.

Nkrumah, K. *Neo-Colonialism: The Highest Stage of Imperialism.* London: Panab, 1971.

——— *Towards Colonial Freedom: Africa in the Struggle Against World Imperialism.* London: Panaf, 1979.

Ofonagoro, W. I. *Trade and Imperialism in Southern Nigeria, 1881-1929.* New York: Nok Pub., 1979.

Ogundana, B. "Seaport Development in Colonial Nigeria." in I. A. Akinjogbin and S. O. Osoba, eds. *Topics in Nigerian Economic and Social History.* Ile-Ife: Ife University Press, 1980.

Okurume, G. O. *Foreign Trade and Subsistence Sector in Nigeria: The Impact of Agricultural Exports on Domestic Food Supplies in a Peasant Economy.* New York: Praeger, 1973.

Oluwasanmi, H. A. *Agriculture and Nigerian Economic Development.* London: Oxford University Press, 1966.

Onimode, B. *Imperialism and Underdevelopment in Nigeria.* London: Macmillan, 1983.

——— *An Introduction to Marxist Political Economy.* London: Zed, 1985.

Osuntokun, A. *Nigeria in the First World War.* London: Longman, 1979.

Pedlar, F. *The Lion and the Unicorn in Africa: A History of Origins of the UAC, 1787-1931.* London: Heinemann, 1924.

Perham, M., ed. *The Economics of a Tropical Dependency*, vols 1-2. London: Faber and Faber, 1946-48.

——— *Lugard: The Years of Authority, 1898-1945.* London: Collins, 1960.

——— *Colonial Sequence, 1930-1949.* London: Methuen, 1967.

——— *Colonial Reckoning.* London: Fontana, 1963.

Perham, M. *Native Administration in Nigeria.* London: Oxford University Press, 1962.

Pim, A. *Colonial Agricultural Production.* London: Oxford University Press, 1946.

Robinson, R. and J. Gallagher. *Africa and the Victorians: The Official Mind of British Imperialism*. London: Macmillan, 1961.

Rodney, W. *How Europe Underdeveloped Africa*. Enugu: Ikenga, 1982.

Ryder, A. F. C. *Benin and the Europeans, 1484-1897*. London: Longman, 1969.

Schumpeter, J. A. *The Theory of Economic Development*. Trans. R. Opie. New York: Harvard University Press, 1949.

Sokolski, A. *The Establishment of Manufacturing in Nigeria*. New York: Praeger, 1965.

Suret-Canale. *French Colonialism in Tropical Africa 1900-1945*. London: Heinemann, 1978.

Szereszewski, R. *Structural Changes in the Economy of Ghana*. London: Weiderfield Nicolson, 1965.

Talbot, P. A. *The Peoples of Southern Nigeria*. London: H. Milford, 1926.

Tamuno, T. N. *The Evolution of the Nigerian State: The Southern Phase, 1885-1906*. Cambridge University Press, 1965.

Usoro. *The Oil Palm Industry*. Ibadan: Ibadan University Press, 1974.

Uzoigwe, G. N. U. *Britain and the Conquest of Africa The Age of Salisbury*. Ann Arbor, Michigan: University of Michigan Press, 1974.

Weber, M. *The Protestant Ethic and the Spirit of Capitalism*. Trans. T. Parson. New York: C. Sarbner and Sons, 1930.

Webster, A. *Introduction to the Sociology of Development*. London: Macmillan, 1984.

Wells, F. A. and W. A. Wermington, eds. *Studies in Industrialization: Nigeria and Cameroons*. Ibadan: Oxford University Press, 1962.

Abbreviations

A.T. & P.	African Timber and Plywood.
C.F.A.O.	Compagnie Francaise De L'Occidentale.
S.C.O.A.	Societe Commerciale De L'Ouest Africain.
U.A.C.	United African Company

Index